CREATING
FUNDABLE
GRANT
PROPOSALS

D1711618

CREATING FUNDABLE GRANT PROPOSALS

Profiles of Innovative Partnerships

BESS G. DE FARBER

ALA
Editions
CHICAGO 2021

BESS G. de FARBER is the grants manager for the George A. Smathers Libraries at the University of Florida and previously held the same position at the University of Arizona Libraries. She has provided grantsmanship instruction to hundreds of library staff members, nonprofit and academic professionals, artists, and university students over the past thirty years and has led efforts to secure millions in grant funding for individual artists and scholars, nonprofits, and academic libraries. She is the author of *Collaborative Grant-Seeking: A Practical Guide for Librarians* (2016) and the coauthor of *Collaborating with Strangers: Facilitating Workshops in Libraries, Classes, and Nonprofits* (2017).

© 2021 by Bess G. de Farber

Extensive effort has gone into ensuring the reliability of the information in this book; however, the publisher makes no warranty, express or implied, with respect to the material contained herein.

ISBN: 978-0-8389-4760-9 (paper)

Library of Congress Cataloging-in-Publication Data
Names: de Farber, Bess G., 1956- author.
Title: Creating fundable grant proposals : profiles of innovative partnerships / Bess G. de Farber.
Description: Chicago : ALA Editions, 2021. | Includes bibliographical references and index. | Summary: "Bess de Farber shares profiles of over 50 grant proposals, sponsored by several funders including federal agencies, foundations, and library organizations. A detailed ten-step workflow guides you through submitting and managing collaborative grant proposals, developing a culture of grantsmanship along the way. You'll see how ideas are shaped, how available assets are brought into the plan, and how partners are recruited"—Provided by publisher.
Identifiers: LCCN 2020015763 | ISBN 9780838947609 (paperback)
Subjects: LCSH: Proposal writing in library science—Florida—Case studies. | Library fund raising—Florida—Case studies. | Academic libraries—Florida—Finance—Case studies. | Proposal writing for grants—Handbooks, manuals, etc. | Fund raising—Teamwork—Handbooks, manuals, etc. | George A. Smathers Libraries. Grants Management Program—History.
Classification: LCC Z683.2.U62 F63 2020 | DDC 025.1/1—dc23
LC record available at https://lccn.loc.gov/2020015763

Cover design by Alejandra Diaz. Text design in the Chaparral, Gotham, and Bell Gothic typefaces.

♾ This paper meets the requirements of ANSI/NISO Z39.48-1992 (Permanence of Paper).

Printed in the United States of America

25 24 23 22 21   5 4 3 2 1

This book is dedicated to
my parents, Joseph Farber (1901–1972) and
Sara Gaíl de Farber (1917–1984);
my daughter, Casandra Tanenbaum;
my life partner, Glen Boecher;
and my small circle of cousins and friends
who give me joy . . . you know who you are.

Contents

Preface   *ix*

Acknowledgments   *xiii*

1 | Creating Collaborative Grant Partnerships   *1*

2 | Grant Partnership Proposals up to $5,000   *19*

3 | Grant Partnership Proposals from $5,001 to $25,000   *75*

4 | Grant Partnership Proposals from $25,001 to $100,000   *119*

5 | Grant Partnership Proposals over $100,000   *147*

6 | Ten Steps for Successful Grantseeking with Partners   *189*

Index   *207*

Sponsor / Program Index   *215*

Project Type Index   *217*

Preface

My landing as the grants manager at the George A. Smathers Libraries (henceforth the Libraries) of the University of Florida (UF) after decades of a full-time grants management career was serendipitous. It offered me the opportunity to mentor many librarians who wanted to become successful grantseekers. This challenge required the combined use of all my skills and tools as a former program officer, facilitator, planner, writer, financial manager, collaborator, teacher, mentor, and learner. I must note here that I am not a librarian. Since the first proposal submission by a project team at the Libraries in January 2009 up to December 2019, I have participated in the management of 187 awarded grant proposals by library workers or their partners. The gratification of co-producing and stewarding these grant-funded projects at the University of Florida is the inspiration behind this book.

Few, if any, other professionals have worked exclusively in an academic library performing this role for a period of twelve years—not to mention three years prior at the University of Arizona. When I first began working in this academic environment, most of my conversations with librarians, especially those new to the profession, focused on how to generate ideas for fundable projects that were worthy of development. Essentially, librarians want assistance discovering options for a grant proposal that would match their role in the library and their interests. They want to know everything that is involved in planning a competitive grant project, as well as all the ambiguities typical to grantseeking. Most academic library personnel, unless they have nonprofit organizational experience, have not participated in submitting fundable grant project proposals.

The large body of grant work performed at the Libraries thus offers a timely collection of awarded projects from which to illustrate how ideas are shaped, how available assets are identified and brought into a project plan, how project titles can position proposals to highlight innovativeness, how partners are selected and approached to join the project, and all of the other strategies that are normally hidden from view. Mining this collection offers a window into what happened after the award was received and how the project team handled problems (and overcame adversities) to complete projects successfully, including changes in personnel, hurricanes, an earthquake, problems with an international vendor's digitization standards, lack of partner communication, and not actually knowing how to execute projects to meet the sponsor's undisclosed standards. For those new to library organizations or grantseeking, this book provides short mental movies of how project teams have navigated the process from proposal to completing awarded projects.

Creating Fundable Grant Proposals could be considered a book of folklore, "the traditional stories and culture of a group of people."[1] The many people who have served as principal investigators (PIs, or project leaders) or on project teams at the Libraries deserve to have these hidden stories shared so that others can learn, imagine, and proceed with confidence to engage in the art of grantseeking. These PIs risked the investment of their limited time to seek funds with which to innovate new services, share primary materials online, perform research, receive or dispense specialized training, and all of the other types of projects that have been supported at the Libraries through grant-seeking activities. You, the reader, deserve access to these stories, for they are testimonies to the power of collaborative relationships and partnerships. Grit, perseverance, excellent writing, understanding of budgets, commitment to improving services, and investigative research will only take you so far when it comes to obtaining grant funding. As a grantseeker, regardless of past experience, you may benefit from reading stories about what is possible and how to achieve it.

Creating Fundable Grant Proposals emphasizes the need for and the benefits of forming partnerships with others in the library who are in different departments, as well as those outside of the library who offer the funder the opportunity to invest in more than one organization through a single grant award. Collaborations with external organizations are often a prerequisite for submitting a fundable proposal, whether this is articulated in the sponsor's guidelines or not. There is a significant competitive advantage for proposals that include partnerships.

This book is organized into six chapters. Chapter 1 provides a history of the development of the Smathers Libraries' Grants Management Program, and chapter 6 offers step-by-step guidance on how to develop viable partnership proposals. Chapters 2 through 5 contain the stories of a variety of awarded project proposals selected for their diversity, and organized by funding amounts from small awards to rather large projects. The smaller projects emphasize internal library partners, including students, since these projects are financially insufficient (and are not expected) to accommodate external partners. These four chapters contain a total of fifty-five grant proposal stories. Each story consists of (1) a prologue about how the grant project idea originated and was developed with project partners, (2) an abstract of the grant proposal submitted, and (3) an epilogue sharing the details of what happened during the grant period. Links to each awarded proposal can be found in the notes at the end of each chapter.

The competition for grant funding is increasing, and many successful grant writers are not inclined to share their how-to strategies with others. It is my belief, however, that the mechanics of grantseeking should not remain a mystery. No one is born knowing how to do this sort of work. Some may have a talent for convincingly conveying an idea in writing, but may not know how to develop a fundable project plan. This is the aspect of grantseeking that is most difficult to teach or mentor. Each grantseeking opportunity is unique. Further complicating this discipline is the length of time between the refinement of a proposal idea and the receipt of the sponsor's notification of award or declination, which can span one full year or more. In the meantime, if the practitioner stands still and waits without continuing in some way to develop their grantseeking practice, then they risk the loss of the practice itself—all of their eggs having been placed in one precarious basket.

Readers of these stories and grant proposals will see that many of the personnel in the Smathers Libraries who participated in grantseeking activities have not stood still. They developed ideas, completed awarded projects, and moved on to participate in numerous grant-funded project teams. They received promotions, changed job titles, retired, or left the Libraries to pursue other opportunities. And each of them managed to participate in a project that had an impact on an audience, a technology, a research question, a collection, or unknown strangers. Essentially, their lives and the lives of project beneficiaries were changed by these grant awards.

NOTE

1. *Cambridge English Dictionary*, s.v. "Folklore," https://dictionary.cambridge.org/us/dictionary/english/folklore.

Acknowledgments

Acknowledging the supporters and contributors to *Creating Fundable Grant Proposals*, to the Grants Management Program at the George A. Smathers Libraries, and to the narrative stories of grant projects shared in this book, is a tricky endeavor. For those listed here and those inadvertently omitted, I sincerely thank you for your faithful encouragement.

To Glen Boecher I extend my most heartfelt appreciation for his words of wisdom, compassionate ear, and his ability to synthesize complexity. Thank you for supporting the creation of this book for the past year. To Morgan Boecher, Barbara Hood, Brandon Murakami, Colleen Seale, and Danielle Sessions, your contributions to assisting me with the book's content were invaluable. And to those who worked daily to support the Grants Management Program, Danielle Sessions and Nadine Smith—you have earned my deep appreciation for your tireless commitment, collaboration, and excellent work. Over the past eleven years, I have had the privilege of working with student assistants and interns who helped make the program successful, including Kaitlin Blackburn, Rebecca Dillmeier, Kaitlyn Hof-Mahoney, Elizabeth King, Kirtana Rajan, and Suchitra Yellapantula.

Without the support of the dean, the associate and assistant deans of the Libraries, and the administrative office staff, the Grants Management Program would not exist: Misty Colson, Lela Johnson, Brian Keith, Valrie

Minson, Patrick Reakes, Melissa Rethlefsen, Judith Russell, Maggie Silva, and Benjamin Walker.

Much appreciation goes to others who support the program periodically, including staff members of the Human Resources, Fiscal Services, and Facilities departments: Jeremiah Carlson, William Hanssen, Brad Hatch, Joseph Hitzler, Anne-Marie Hollingshead, Gregory Krueger, Tina Litchfield, Peter Miller, Joseph Piazza, Bonnie Smith, Leonardo Tolentino Jr., Barbara Williamson, and Brian Word. Staff members of the Libraries' IT Department provide technical expertise to grant projects as necessary, including Thomas Bielicke, Cynthia Bowker, Will Chaney, Gus Clifton, Matthew Daley, Donald David, Debra Fetzer, Andy Hunn, Chris Nicolich, Robert Phillips, Cliff Richmond, Patricia Ruwell, John Thrasher, Mike Tyler, and Evan Wack.

To the project team members featured in this book, I thank you for your efforts to prepare proposals, execute projects, and for your participation in the Libraries' Grants Management Program. Many of you who served as principal or co-principal investigators on one or more of these projects have spent time with me in person or online to share your stories. Without your investment in helping me capture the essence of your projects, I would not have had the resources to write this book: Jessica Aberle, Sophia Acord, Gregory Allen, Gerry Altamirano, Suzan Alteri, Margaret Ansell, Shelley Arlen, Matthew Armstrong, Miguel Asencio, Joseph Aufmuth, Sharon Austin, Tiffany Baglier, Ann Baird, Claire Baralt, Christopher Barnes, James Barnett, Jessica Belcoure, Stephanie Birch, Katy Börner, Jean Bossart, Katie Boudreau, Elizabeth Bouton, Amanda Brown, Laura Browning, Amy Buhler, Gail Burton, Lisa Campbell, Will Canova, Jane Anne Carey, Kendra Carter, Thomas Caswell, Alexis Charnas, Tara Cataldo, Enrique Chmelnik, Missy Clapp, Maria Coady, Curtis Cole, Perry Collins, Michael Conlon, Robert Cook, Susana Cordova Martin, Jonathan Corson-Rikert, Cindy Craig, Charlie Cummings, David R. Curry, James Cusick, Matthew Daley, Megan Daly, Sheila de Roche, Medha Devare, Todd Digby, Ying Ding, Chelsea Dinsmore, Steve Duckworth, Fletcher Durant, Jonathan Edelmann, Mary Edwards, Bonnie Effros, Rachael Elrod, Schuyler Esprit, Tiffany Esteban, Stacey Ewing, Ixchel Faniel, Jennifer Farrington, Crystal Felima, Nita Ferree, Rebecca Fitzsimmons, Richard Freeman, John Freund, Ileana Fuentes, Sebastian Galindo-Gonzalez, Eugene Giddens, Matthew Gitzendanner, Jorge Gonzalez, Mirerza González, Jacob Gordon, Randy Graff, Margo Groenewoud, Stephanie Haas, George Hack, Susan Harnett, Terry Harpold, Haven Hawley, Kenny Herniman, Lee Herring, April Hines, Kristi Holmes, Barbara Hood, Samuel Huang, Hélène Huet, Zoe Jaques, Rebecca Jefferson, Melissa Jerome, Rae Jesano, Margeaux Johnson, Gerald Joyce, Joe Kaleita, Sriram Kalyanaaman, Brian Keith, Brittany Kester, Leslie Keys, Kenneth Kidd, Paula King, Dean Krafft, Jessica Krauth, Gretchen Kuntz, Anita Lambert, Mark Law, Michelle Leonard, Douglas Levey, Ann Lindell, Angela Lindner, David Jackson Looney, Paul Losch, Matthew Loving, Jessica Lyon, Matthew Mariner, Kevin Marshall, Carol McAuliffe, Debbie

McCollin, Robert McDonald, Leslie McIntosh, Kyla McMullen, Barbara Mennel, Ali Altaf Mian, José Millán Díaz, Valrie Minson, Sarah Moczygemba, Pia Molina, Marilyn Montalvo, Meredith Morris-Babb, Francisco Moscoso, Rakesh Nagarajan, Vasudha Narayanan, John Nemmers, Richard J. Noel Jr., Michelle Nolan, Gabriel Noriega Rodriguez, Hannah Norton, Marilyn Ochoa, Allison O'Dell, James Oliverio, María Ordóñez Mercado, Paul Ortiz, Venkitachalan Parameswaran, Jane Pen, Matthew Pendleton, Laura Perry, Ariel Pomputius, Samuel Putnam, Alan Rauch, Patrick Reakes, John Reazer, Daniel Reboussin, Randall Renner, Celia Richard, Nadjah Rios Villarini, Mary Risner, Judith Roberts, Leah Rosenberg, Melody Royster, Judith Russell, Sara Russell Gonzalez, Sadie Sanders, Lourdes Santamaría-Wheeler, Nancy Schaefer, Rachel Schipper, Colleen Seale, Danielle Sessions, Lynn Silipigni Connaway, Betsy Simpson, Bonnie Smith, Plato Smith, Jana Smith Ronan, Angelibel Soto, Laura Spears, Joseph Spillane, Patrick Stanley, Suzanne Stapleton, Nina Stoyan-Rosenzweig, Mark Sullivan, Laurie Taylor, Michele Tennant, Myra Torres Alamo, Mario Torres Ramos, Soraya Torres Villanueva, Florence Turcotte, David Van Kleeck, Margarita Vargas-Betancourt, Ben Walker, Traveler Wendell, Lois Widmer, Ernie Williams, Joe Wu, Hank Young, Naomi Young, and William Young.

1

Creating Collaborative Grant Partnerships

This chapter begins with a brief story about an unusual cross-cultural musical partnership that took place in New York City near the end of the nineteenth century and continues to have an impact on American culture. The story offers an illustrative example of the hidden potential of working with others, sometimes strangers, and especially those who have access to unique assets different from our own. After the story, the basic principles used in the successful creation of the Grants Management Program at the George A. Smathers Libraries (henceforth the Libraries) at the University of Florida (UF) will be discussed. A history of the development of the program will offer a possible model for administrators in other libraries who believe that grantseeking activities can be catalysts for supporting a creative and engaging workplace environment.

THE MUSICAL PARTNERSHIP OF ANTONIN DVORAK AND HARRY T. BURLEIGH

The Czech composer Antonin Dvorak (1841–1904) came to America in 1892 to accept the position of director of the National Conservatory of Music in New

York City. He had risen from humble beginnings to become a world-renowned composer of classical music that evoked the roots of his Bohemian (i.e., Czech) heritage. His father, a butcher by trade, played the zither, and also managed a small inn and tavern. It was in this tavern that the young Dvorak was regularly exposed to the folk music and dancing that would influence his later compositions. Encouraged by his village schoolmaster, Dvorak went on to study organ and music in Prague and began composing in his early twenties. When he was in his thirties, his compositions began to attract worldwide attention, particularly his *Slavic Dances* and major choral works, which were performed throughout Europe and in major American cities. Dvorak earned a reputation as the "first Bohemian composer to achieve worldwide recognition, noted for turning folk material into nineteenth-century Romantic music."[1]

The National Conservatory of Music had been founded in 1885 by Jeanette Thurber, a philanthropist who in the same year established the American Opera Company. The mission of the Opera Company was to perform popular European operas translated into English. The National Conservatory was designed as a complete music school for Americans, and to this end Thurber assembled a faculty that included many highly respected musicians of the day. Moreover, the Conservatory offered scholarships for women, minorities, and the disabled. Thurber perceived that classically trained contemporary composers in America had made little effort to create a distinctive American musical voice. In conjunction with the mission of the Opera Company, Thurber's vision for the National Conservatory was to incubate the creation and nurture the development of a musical identity for America that would overcome the dominance of European cultural influences. Believing that this American music would be a reflection of the shared experience of the American people, regardless of rank or status, Thurber zeroed in on Antonin Dvorak, the "Bohemian composer," as the ideal candidate to bring this vision to fruition. She began a persistent and ultimately successful campaign to lure him to New York. It would be Dvorak's charge to discover and expose the genesis of this new and elusive American symphonic music.

Soon after his arrival in America, Dvorak met Harry T. Burleigh, a black American who at the time was a scholarship student at the National Conservatory. As a child growing up in Erie, Pennsylvania, Burleigh (1866–1949) was exposed to the black spirituals sung by his parents and grandparents, and particularly his maternal grandfather, Hamilton Waters, who had been a slave until he purchased his own freedom from a Maryland plantation owner in 1832. He was also exposed to classical music in the home of the family where his mother was employed as a servant. Burleigh exhibited early musical talent and had a particularly strong singing voice. He was sponsored for voice and piano lessons by his Aunt Louise and sang in many church choirs throughout his youth. At the age of twenty-six, he was accepted to matriculate at the National Conservatory. He was given a scholarship to pay his tuition, but to pay his living expenses in New York City he found work as a handyman and secretary to the Conservatory's registrar, gave music lessons, and sang in and trained church choirs.

Dvorak and Burleigh first came to know each other through an introduction by James Gibbons Huneker, a music, art, theater, and literary critic. After hearing Burleigh sing, Dvorak began inviting the student to his home for meals and to hear his renditions of the black spirituals he had learned as a child. The two men quickly became friends and Dvorak hired Burleigh, who was a trained stenographer, to assist him, particularly with copying the musical scores composed by Dvorak for musicians to perform. Beyond their personal affinity, we can imagine the mutual benefits that each of them might have derived from this relationship with each other. Burleigh, of course, would value his access to the individual attention and tutelage of a celebrated composer. And Dvorak, a foreign visitor to this country, saw in Burleigh the key to accessing the American musical sources he was searching for. In an American culture marked by rigid racial separation, the interracial and intercultural joining of forces between an esteemed classical composer and a black American music student was unexpected, and would prove to be fortuitous.

Dvorak's best-known symphonic composition, his ninth symphony, now known as the *New World Symphony*, was responsive to Thurber's request that Dvorak compose a symphonic work reflective of his American experiences. His new composition was largely influenced by his immersion in the black spiritual songs sung to him by Burleigh. The two men were constant companions while Dvorak was composing the symphony. Just prior to its completion, the *New York Herald* (May 21, 1893) published Dvorak's now famous statement: "The future of this country must be founded upon what are called the black melodies. This must be the real foundation of any serious and original school of composition to be developed in the United States . . . In the Negro melodies of America I discover all that is needed for a great and noble school of music."

In the 1920s, nearly two decades after Antonin Dvorak's death, one of his advanced composition students, William Arms Fisher, set words to the opening melody of the *New World Symphony*'s second movement—a section of the work that is acknowledged to have incorporated musical elements inspired by the black spirituals sung to Dvorak by Burleigh. As a hymn and ballad, Fisher's "Goin' Home" eventually became ubiquitous in church hymnals throughout the country. A widely beloved hymn, "Goin' Home" was performed at the state funerals of Presidents Franklin D. Roosevelt, Gerald Ford, Ronald Reagan, and George H. W. Bush.[2]

THE BUILDING BLOCKS OF SUCCESSFUL PARTNERSHIPS

The Dvorak and Burleigh story provides a compelling example demonstrating many of the basic building blocks that lead to successful collaborative partnerships. First, there is the act of tapping into the potential creative energy that resides in one's own surroundings, as Dvorak did in America and with his friend Burleigh. This is the foundational element of the practices performed during asset-based community development (ABCD)—methods developed by Kretzmann and McKnight at Northwestern University in the 1990s. Used by nonprofit organizations, these methods identify and access hidden assets in a community, bringing them to life in their current form or in a new configuration to improve people's lives. Information about these assets can come from surveys, interviews, or focus groups that can produce an asset inventory. For libraries, examples of assets include primary and information resources, staff and volunteer time, online and in-person patrons, staff expertise, physical space, partners, equipment, supplies, funding, sponsors, programs, and projects.[3] Grant projects can be planned using this asset-based approach, which emphasizes an organization's assets rather than its needs.

Most people can easily rattle off many of the things, skills, or relationships that they lack and would like to acquire to improve their lives, organizations, or communities. This focus on "needs" supports the standard needs assessment approach to solving a problem or creating a plan. Needs assessments ask questions about what is unavailable or inaccessible to an organization or community that would be required to advance its mission or goals. The answers are often quite specific: new staff positions, new equipment, more space, and so on. These enhancements usually require funding, and if funding isn't available to those trying to make improvements, then efforts are required to access those funds which currently may be beyond their grasp. But this planning model focuses on scarcity—what an individual, organization, or community lacks. It perpetuates a sense of victimhood; it implies that the individual, organization, or community lacks control over its own destiny because it is ultimately dependent on outside or inaccessible resources. Figure 1.1 illustrates the impact on planning grant projects from both the asset-based and needs-based perspectives. Grant sponsors are more likely to invest in proposals that describe a multitude of assets that have already been committed to execute a proposed project.

Enter the facilitation method of appreciative inquiry (AI), which acts in concert with asset-based community development. Facilitators who use AI to solve a problem or improve a situation pose questions that focus on the positive history or experiences of individuals or a community. Taking this approach, with an emphasis on available assets, can completely change the nature of project-planning activities. What happens when one tries to answer these types of AI questions: What (assets) do I have to contribute to this project? What (assets) can I access now (directly or through people I already know)? What assets are available in my proximity (low-hanging fruit)? Answering these questions is much more difficult than answering the questions about need or lack. They require the inquirer to learn more about what they may already have—either by taking an inventory or brainstorming with others to answer the questions—and coming up with answers that are known, if not by the inquirer, then by a friend or a colleague. The questions themselves initiate the journey to acquire information about what already exists and what can be accessed. Then going a step further to recombine these assets into something new generates the path to innovation. Figure 1.2 illustrates the flow of assets to a project team's planning efforts. When the assets differ widely from each other, as in the case of black spirituals and a symphonic composition, combining these two distinct genres creates something unmistakably new, and in the case of the *New World Symphony*, a sound that takes the listener to a place that is distinctly American in nature.

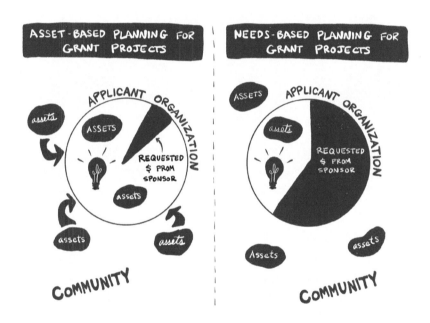

FIGURE 1.1
This infographic illustrates the different focuses of those who are planning grant projects. The image on the left shows abundant resources being contributed to the project, with the sponsor providing the funding to activate these resources to achieve the project goal. The image on the right shows that the project lacks most of the resources needed, and therefore requests a larger proportion of funds in comparison, to compensate for this lack.

Drawing by Morgan Boecher, https://ufdc.ufl.edu///IR00011057/00001

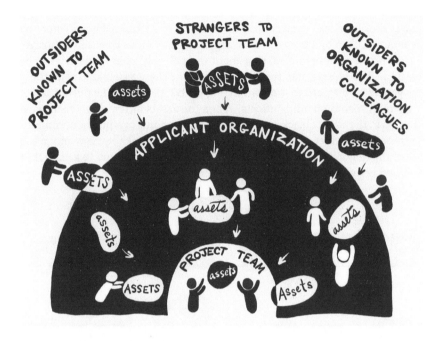

FIGURE 1.2
This infographic illustrates the abundant resources owned by those in the project team's universe that may be available through partnering to contribute to the proposed project.
Drawing by Morgan Boecher, https://ufdc.ufl.edu//IR00011057/00001

The problem here is that not everyone knows an asset when they see one, or, as in the case of Dvorak's assistant's black spirituals, when they hear one. Identifying assets is a skill that requires practice. Stephen Johnson, a historian of human innovation who created the PBS series *Where Good Ideas Come From*, says that the internal world of the brain has a lot in common with the external world in which people live. One must be in contact with others to learn about their assets such as interests, pursuits, and ideas, so that this exposure can enable the generation of new ideas.

Mutual assistance is the third important principle that is applied in successful collaborations. Burleigh and Dvorak shared a passion for music and were both engaged in individual pursuits to develop themselves musically. They were also in close proximity to each other, giving them direct access to each other's assets. Dvorak's offer to hire Burleigh as his assistant triggered the structure in which both musicians were able to provide mutual assistance.

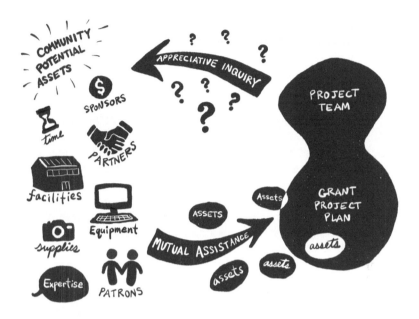

FIGURE 1.3
This infographic illustrates three concepts: (1) the use of appreciative inquiry by the project team (2) to expose community assets (3) that may be contributed to the proposed project through mutual assistance.

Drawing by Morgan Boecher, https://ufdc.ufl.edu//IR00011057/00001

All of the elements necessary for a productive partnership were now in place. This is the act of reciprocity: what I have I am willing to share because "we" will both benefit. At times, the benefit for one partner is greater than for the other. Or one partner may not be able to imagine the future benefit to be gained by contributing to a project, but they understand the importance of their contribution to achieving the end result, and this feeling of satisfaction sustains the relationship, which often reveals a mutual benefit in the end. Regardless, participants who choose to combine forces with a partner often contribute mutual assistance to each other, and this escalates their own enthusiasm for their fellow human beings and the project at hand. Figure 1.3 illustrates how the three elements of asset-based community development, appreciative inquiry, and mutual assistance together contribute to planning fundable grant projects.

HISTORY OF THE CULTURE OF GRANTSMANSHIP
IN THE GEORGE A. SMATHERS LIBRARIES

This three-legged stool of asset-based community development, appreciative inquiry, and mutual assistance eventually came to form the foundation of the Grants Management Program at the George A. Smathers Libraries of the University of Florida. In the beginning, the dean of University Libraries set aside funding to support an internal small-grants program initiated by a group of librarians who believed in the importance of training other personnel in the practice of grantseeking. Librarians and staff working at the newly created Digital Library Center at UF in the late 1990s had successfully obtained a series of grant awards to jump-start their operations. There was a sense that if more employees could learn how to navigate the processes of grant project planning, budgeting, and writing, then new external grant funds could lift more boats within the Libraries.

A Grants Management Committee was formalized in 2006 with representatives from a variety of departments within the Libraries—some of whom previously had been awarded external grant funds. Funding for small-grant projects began to be awarded through a Mini Grants Program. In 2008, the dean of University Libraries convinced the University of Florida provost of the need to hire a grants professional to lead the Libraries' grantseeking efforts. The dean's argument for the position was that the Smathers Libraries' assets were sufficiently developed to warrant a commitment to increasing the number of grant applications being submitted by the faculty and staff. And to do this well, especially because of the service nature of the organization, experienced leadership would be required. Once more applications were generated, the dean anticipated that the Libraries would garner more grant awards. This idea grounded her case for support during her successful meeting with the provost.

In the fall of 2008, the author was hired as the grants manager to serve seven libraries at the University of Florida. Her two-decade career in the nonprofit sector, along with three years at the University of Arizona Libraries, had prepared her for this challenge.[4] The author already had an excellent starting point, the Mini Grants Program (now known as the Strategic Opportunities Program), which continues to provide a maximum of $5,000 per application. An Emerging Technologies grants program was added in 2009 to incentivize pilot projects that increase the Libraries' innovative technologies offerings, products, or services, up to a maximum of $10,000 per project. The primary intent of both programs has remained the same: to professionalize the grantseeking activities, management, and skills of the Libraries' full-time employees, who number approximately 250.

To build the Grants Management Program, the new grants manager initiated multiple approaches:

- Reading past awarded and declined proposals submitted over the past ten years;

FIGURE 1.4
This infographic illustrates the process of developing a fundable proposal within the Libraries' internal grantmaking program.
Drawing by Morgan Boecher, https://ufdc.ufl.edu//IR00011057/00001

- Learning about the careers and interests of the Libraries' personnel;
- Compiling information to distribute to all staff members about funding opportunities and upcoming grant deadlines related to staff interests (not just those intended exclusively for library applicants);
- Establishing a database to capture all of the funding opportunities and grant deadlines identified;
- Understanding how UF's Division of Sponsored Programs supported campus grantseeking activities; and becoming familiar with its oversight policies and procedures related to applying for and managing awarded grant-funded projects;
- Revising the two internal grant program review processes so that Grants Management Committee members would create lists of questions to be posed to grant applicants about the gaps in information in their submitted applications. By answering the committee's questions, applicants could clarify their applications prior to the latter being evaluated by reviewers—thus offering a positive way to provide them with feedback, rather than the typically critical feedback focused on proposal weaknesses that is the common practice among most funding agencies. (See figure 1.4.)

Under the grants manager's facilitative leadership, the first two grant applications to be developed were submitted to external sponsors in January and March 2009. These were applications to the U.S. Department of Education's Technological Innovation and Cooperation for Foreign Information Access program—for the creation of a Caribbean Newspaper Digital Library in partnership with the applicant, Florida International University (see chapter 5)—and to the National Endowment for the Humanities (NEH) to host a traveling Lincoln exhibit produced by the Library of Congress.[5]

These applications (both were awarded) opened the door to developing a Grants Activities Update, a report sent to all of the Libraries' staff that shares annotated descriptions of each of the submitted applications; each description included the project title, amount awarded, amount of cost-share contribution, abstract, start and end dates, project team members, and the sponsoring agency/program, with a link to the full application hosted in the UF Institutional Repository (IR@UF). The Grants Activities Update offered employees the opportunity to see inside the Grants Management Program for the first time. This document, published monthly, continues to inform staff of recently submitted, awarded, declined, and pending grant applications, and active awarded projects. Making the Libraries' submitted grant applications broadly available online has done much to dissolve the competitive culture that is often associated with grantseeking in academic environments.[6]

Over the next few years, the grants manager added other forms of support for Libraries' grant applicants and project teams, such as delivering workshops highlighting these topics:

- information about specific funding agencies and application deadlines;
- how-to details to search for grant opportunities online;
- knowledge about which academic libraries were receiving funding and the types of projects being awarded;
- highlights of awarded internal (Strategic Opportunities Program and Emerging Technologies) and external grant projects presented by project teams, who shared what they learned while executing their grant-project activities, and the project results attained; and
- brainstorming activities for any interested staff members to share their ideas with project teams that are working on new internal or external grant ideas.

The evolving Grants Management Program began casting a broad net across the Libraries. Grant project teams composed of diverse members with varying expertise convened regularly to explore the possibility of planning new fundable projects. More employees were gradually engaging in some aspect of grant-funded project planning or were becoming involved in

FIGURE 1.5
This infographic illustrates the use of the Libraries' internal grantmaking program for small projects as a catalyst for creating larger grant projects that stimulate the organization's grantseeking culture.
Drawing by Morgan Boecher, https://ufdc.ufl.edu//IR00011057/00001

executing awarded projects. Applicants increasingly received awards for different types of projects beyond digitization, including planning, outreach, training, publishing, research, preservation, collaboration development, purchase of materials, and endowment fundraising. (See figure 1.5.)

As the Grants Management Program grew, it became necessary to add structured workflows and increase the transparency of grant-project plans in the works. Avoiding the overextension of staff effort became a priority. Ensuring that supervisors and administrators were all on board with a new project idea prior to the preparation of grant applications became essential. To accomplish this, the grants manager position moved from the Administration and Development Department to the Human Resources, Fiscal Services (and later Facilities) Department, with oversight and support provided by the assistant dean of Administrative Services and Faculty Affairs. Working side-by-side with a designated accountant, those managing hiring and personnel activities, and facilities management now partner with the grants manager to expedite grant-project planning. Using a checklist format, written workflows communicate to project teams the various step-by-step activities and associated personnel for (1) determining project feasibility,[7] (2) pre-award application preparation,[8] and (3) post-award management.[9]

It is important to note that no targeted goal requirements were imposed on the grants manager in terms of the number of grant applications applied for or the amount of grant funding received annually. Instead, the overall goal of the Grants Management Program is to make grantseeking commonplace in this academic library system—to create a culture of grantsmanship. Annual evaluations of the grants manager's performance have focused on goals related to serving as an expert resource for interested grantseeking employees, growing the number of employees that are involved on project teams, and improving the quality of the technical support and collaborative relationships that make the program successful.

In time, other units at UF became aware of the growing and successful grantseeking program at the Libraries. Faculty members, especially those in the humanities, gradually learned that working with Libraries personnel to prepare and submit their fundable proposals provided expertise and institutional support for project teams that made the process less stressful. Faculty members outside of the Libraries began to inquire about the Libraries' available assets that could contribute to enhancing the quality of any grant proposal being planned. It is unfortunately the case that too often, faculty who work in higher education fail to grasp the breadth and depth of the human and material assets that easily can be accessed to strengthen a grant proposal through partnerships with academic library and other campus personnel.

TABLE 1.1

List of Strategic Opportunities Program and Emerging Technologies grant award totals and number of awards distributed each year

Years	Total of Grant Funds Awarded	Total Number Awarded
2009	$31,586	9
2010	$46,227	12
2011	$14,192	5
2012	$52,772	10
2013	$41,271	9
2014	$17,375	4
2015	$26,436	5
2016	$9,798	2
2017	$18,343	4
2018	$24,412	4
2019	$40,763	9
Grand Total	**$323,175**	**73**

According to an internal database managed by the grants manager's assistant, the following charts share the details of proposals prepared, submitted, and awarded for internal library grants, UF competitive campus grants, and externally sponsored grants.

Table 1.1 provides information about the number and total of the Libraries' awarded internal grants (Strategic Opportunities Program and Emerging Technologies program) by year. Awards for internal library grants from 2009 through 2019 total seventy-three, with award amounts totaling $323,175. These applications require that each applicant include the contribution of at least one other Libraries' employee for effort totaling at least 10 percent of the total grant request.

TABLE 1.2

List of grant award totals and number of awards received each year from competitive internal University of Florida grant application submissions

Years	Total of Grant Funds Received	Total Number Received
2011	$12,962	1
2012	$21,947	2
2015	$222,878	4
2016	$287,979	3
2017	$181,594	4
2018	$187,809	4
2019	$49,915	3
Grand Total	**$965,084**	**21**

Table 1.2 provides information about the number and total of the Libraries' awarded competitive UF campus grants by year. Awards for grant-funded opportunities sponsored by other UF entities from 2011 through August 2019 total twenty-one, with award amounts totaling $965,084. Applications generated by Libraries project teams and partners were submitted to four campus sponsors: the Creative Campus Committee, the Technology Fee program, the Center for the Humanities and the Public Sphere, and the UF Clinical and Translational Science Institute. Although table 1.2 indicates a much smaller total number of awards in comparison to the Libraries' internal grants programs, the total amount of campus funding received has proven to be well worth the effort. The Libraries are inherently suited to be successful applicants to these campus sponsors, all of which seek collaborative projects that offer innovative activities and partnerships serving the campus broadly.

TABLE 1.3

List of grant award totals and number of awards received each year from external sponsors

Years	Total of Grant Funds Received	Total Number of Awards Received
2009	$1,891,006	6
2010	$177,686	4
2011	$70,817	10
2012	$882,602	9
2013	$550,372	7
2014	$625,148	9
2015	$896,616	7
2016	$433,586	10
2017	$489,154	9
2018	$760,240	12
2019	$878,694	10
Grand Total	**$7,655,921**	**93**

Table 1.3 provides information about the number and total of awarded externally sponsored grants by year. Awards for grant-funded opportunities offered by sponsors external to UF from 2009 to 2019 total ninety-three, with award amounts totaling $7,655,921.

Applications prepared by Libraries project teams and partners were submitted to and awarded by the following external sponsors:

- American Library Association
- Andrew W. Mellon Foundation
- Arts and Humanities Research Council, United Kingdom
- Association of Research Libraries
- Bowden Massey Foundation
- Center for Research Libraries
- Council on Library & Information Resources
- Digital Library of the Caribbean
- Fanny Landwirth Foundation
- Florida Department of State, Division of Library and Information Services
- Florida Fish & Wildlife Service
- Florida International University
- Florida State University Research Foundation
- Futernick Family Foundation

- Institute of Museum and Library Services
- Jack Chester Foundation
- National Endowment for the Humanities
- National Historical Publications and Records Commission
- National Institutes of Health
- National Library of Medicine
- National Network of Libraries of Medicine
- National Park Service
- National Science Foundation
- Northeast Florida Library Information Network
- Procter & Gamble
- Shorstein Foundation
- U.S. Agricultural Information Network
- U.S. Department of Agriculture
- U.S. Department of Education
- U.S. Department of Health and Human Services
- U.S. Fish and Wildlife Service

With each new application submission, so grew the Libraries' partnerships. Whether internally focused with personnel new to the grantseeking process in the Libraries—most of whom had never prepared grant applications or executed awarded projects—or in partnership with other professionals at UF, in Florida, nationally, or internationally, the Libraries have become a hub for grantseeking activities.

In cooperation with the grants manager, those working in the centralized Grants Management Program housed in the Human Resources, Fiscal Services, Grants, and Facilities Department gained a reputation for nurturing and supporting all grant projects, from the birth of a grant-project idea to the completion of the awarded project. UF is like other large public universities in constructing a multilayered authorization and accountability system to manage its funded research programs. In 2015, UF initiated a mandatory, campus-wide electronic system which replaced the paper process for tracking the approval and subsequent submission of all UF grant applications. The new system, UFIRST, required a new knowledge and understanding of workflows that would permanently change the way grant applications were pre-submitted for UF review, approval, and tracking, as well as the post-award management of the award until its completion. Because of the Libraries' centralized grants management workflow process, only three employees were significantly impacted by the system-wide changes: the grants manager, the grants assistant, and the grants accountant. Together, these three employees collaborated to reduce any negative repercussions created by the implementation of UFIRST. Their mutual goal was to protect the Libraries' employees involved in producing grant applications from feeling any additional stress that might discourage them from wanting to engage in the grantseeking program.

In spring 2020, the COVID-19 virus pandemic created unanticipated changes in aspects of grantseeking and grants management activities. Sponsors of the Libraries grant awards offered the options for requesting no cost extensions to support those project teams who required more time to complete their projects. Some project teams with grant periods ending in spring, summer, and fall 2020 took advantage of these extension opportunities. Other project leaders continue to convene by video conferencing to plan their upcoming grant proposals with their partners.

MOTIVATIONS TO PARTICIPATE IN THE LIBRARIES' GRANTSEEKING PROGRAM

At UF, the librarians are considered to be tenure-accruing faculty members in the advancement and promotion categories of assistant, associate, and university librarian. Prior to 2015, the librarians' activities which were assessed for academic distinction that contributed to the eligibility of achieving tenure and subsequent promotions included (1) performing service, including serving on local, regional, national or international committees, and (2) scholarship, including authoring publications, especially in peer-reviewed journals, but also in open-access publications; and the planning, preparation, submission, and execution (if awarded) of grant applications, especially as a principal investigator (PI, also known as the project leader) or as a co-principal investigator (co-PI, also known as the co-project leader). (Other relevant categories of grant participation include director, investigator, and consultant.) Beginning in 2015, and culminating with the adoption of a new tenure and promotion process in 2017 that impacted many UF librarians, changes specified in the new tenure and promotion criteria emphasize evidence of distinction in scholarship (which includes grantsmanship). Previously, evidence of distinction in either service or scholarship had been emphasized. The changes in tenure and promotion emphasis coincided with the UF president's goal to raise the ranking of UF to be among the top ten public universities in the country as assessed by *U.S. News & World Report*. Not surprisingly, from 2015 to the date of this writing, interest in planning, preparing, and submitting grant proposals by Libraries' personnel has escalated to new levels. The increase in participation was especially fueled by the thirty-seven new librarians hired since 2015.

Without a doubt, acquiring grant money is the primary motivator behind grantseeking. But it's not all about the money. Beyond supporting tenure and promotion eligibility, participation in grantseeking offers many other intrinsic benefits. Pursuing grant opportunities provides employees with a creative outlet for designing and planning projects that meet the interests of sponsors as articulated in their guidelines, while offering a certain amount of independence and leadership opportunities to fulfill their own professional missions—as long as these align with their employment roles and perfor-mance goals in the organization.

Most librarians receive only limited grantseeking training, if any, during their enrollment in MLIS degree programs. Project planning and manage-ment is another topic that may elude those preparing to enter the library field. Coincidentally, engaging in on-the-job grantseeking activities can both provide desired grantsmanship training while simultaneously supporting a worthwhile means for developing skills in project planning and execution. Using grant applications as project-planning tools offers structure and the constraints—in the form of page or character limits, deadlines, and grant review criteria—that often stimulate creativity. Working with a team of peo-ple toward a common goal of submitting a fundable proposal may be enticing for those who don't have other opportunities for this type of creative pursuit in their day-to-day library jobs. And the possibility of being part of an effort that leads to an award can serve as a compelling motivator to gain commit-ments from possible team members.

Most people in workplaces care about the prospect of receiving an award that signifies their extraordinary contribution to an organization. It doesn't even matter how much the award is worth; it is sufficient that others deem the work of the individuals or group as being exceptional, and worthy of dis-tinction. Consequently, working on grant-project teams is an opportunity to demonstrate one's commitment and loyalty to a cause greater than one's indi-vidual efforts. When employees receive awards, including grants, these often enhance the quality of loyalty and bonds within the team. And if it happens that the team accomplishes results beyond its expectations, then these feel-ings of achievement can greatly enhance workplace satisfaction.

Going a bit further, it is widely known that learning something new can contribute to one's happiness. For readers who have not engaged in grant-seeking activities, or for those who have been frustrated by the experience, consider this thought experiment. Imagine working in a team of people—some that you know well, others that you somewhat know, and still others that you don't know at all. Together you brainstorm and refine a grant appli-cation for a project that comes together perfectly—in terms of timing, con-tent, expertise, the right sponsor, and so on—and have the opportunity to participate in proposing a project that combines assets in a way that has never been conceived previously. After submission, the team then waits for eight months—hoping that the project will be awarded or forgetting that it was ever submitted. Either way, if the project is awarded, then this extraordinary event is celebrated at all levels of the organization while the team considers its next steps. If, on the other hand, the project is declined, the team members might experience disappointment, but they also might reflect on what they learned while they were planning and writing the proposal, and on the advan-tages of getting to know colleagues in new ways while they were contributing to a newly conceived idea.

NOTES

1. David Mathias Lloyd-Jones, "Antonín Dvorak," *Encyclopaedia Britannica*, www.britannica.com/biography/Antonin-Dvorak.

2. All of the content for this opening story was referenced from the following sources: David Mathias Lloyd-Jones, "Antonín Dvorak," *Encyclopaedia Britannica*, www.britannica.com/biography/Antonin-Dvorak; John C. Tibbetts, ed., *Dvorak in America, 1892–1895* (Portland, OR: Amadeus, 1993); Michael Beckerman, ed., *Dvorak and His World* (Princeton, NJ: Princeton University Press, 1993); and Anne Key Simpson, *Hard Trials: The Life and Music of Harry T. Burleigh* (Metuchen, NJ: Scarecrow, 1990).

3. John P. Kretzmann and John L. McKnight, *Building Communities from the Inside Out: A Path Toward Finding and Mobilizing a Community's Assets* (Evanston, IL: Institute for Policy Research, 1993).

4. Bess de Farber, "Smathers Libraries Grants Manager Position Description," George A. Smathers Libraries, University of Florida Digital Collections, https://ufdc.ufl.edu/IR00011086/00001.

5. Brooke Wooldridge, Laurie Taylor, and Bess de Farber, "Caribbean Newspaper Digital Library: Disseminating and Preserving Records of Daily Life," George A. Smathers Libraries, University of Florida Digital Collections, https://ufdc.ufl .edu/UF00091464/00001; Chelsea Dinsmore, Colleen Seale, and Shelley Arlen, "NEH Small Grants to Libraries: Lincoln: The Constitution and the Civil War," George A. Smathers Libraries, University of Florida Digital Collections, http:// ufdc.ufl.edu/UF00091755/00001.

6. Bess de Farber and Danielle Sessions, "Grants Activities Update as of January 15, 2020," George A. Smathers Libraries, University of Florida Digital Collections, https://ufdc.ufl.edu/IR00011087/00001.

7. Bess de Farber and Brian Keith, "Checklist of Activities and Responsible Parties: Determining Grant Project Feasibility (Part I)," George A. Smathers Libraries, University of Florida Digital Collections, https://ufdc.ufl.edu/ IR00011088/00001.

8. Bess de Farber and Brian Keith, "Checklist of Activities and Responsible Parties: Grants Preparation for Completing Project Proposals (Part II)," George A. Smathers Libraries, University of Florida Digital Collections, https://ufdc.ufl .edu//IR00011089/00001.

9. Bess de Farber and Brian Keith, "Checklist of Activities and Responsible Parties: External Grants Award Setup and Post Award to Manage the Awarded Project (Part III)," George A. Smathers Libraries, University of Florida Digital Collections, https://ufdc.ufl.edu//IR00011090/00001.

2
Grant Partnership Proposals up to $5,000

This chapter contains eighteen stories about funded grant projects with budgets ranging up to $5,000 awarded to the George A. Smathers Libraries and its partners from 2010 through 2020. The most frequent sponsor of projects in this funding range was the Smathers Libraries itself, with grant awards generated by an internal grant review and mentoring program known as the Strategic Opportunities Program (SOP); these grants were formerly known as Mini Grants. SOP proposals can be submitted by any full-time employee, biannually in the spring and fall semesters.

The types of projects featured in this chapter include collection acquisitions, planning digital collaborations, professional development, digital oral histories, bibliography development, accessibility, marketing, research, health information dissemination, digitization, collection development, collection planning, metadata, outreach, database development, course development, and documentary film development. The stories are organized in reverse chronological order, from those most recently submitted to those submitted earlier.

Included in this chapter are awarded proposals submitted to the following sponsors and respective programs:

- American Library Association / Carnegie-Whitney Grant

- American Library Association / Carroll Preston Baber Research Grant
- Arts and Humanities Research Council (UK) / Research Networking in UK–US in Digital Scholarship in Cultural Institutions
- University of Florida, Center for the Humanities and the Public Sphere / Library Enhancement Grant
- University of Florida, Center for the Humanities and the Public Sphere / Programs in the Public Humanities
- University of Florida, George A. Smathers Libraries / Strategic Opportunities Program

COLLECTION DEVELOPMENT

UF Center for the Humanities and the Public Sphere / Library Enhancement Grant

Prologue

The librarian for classics, philosophy, and religion joined the Libraries in 2017. While perusing the Center for the Humanities and the Public Sphere website, she noticed its call for Library Enhancement Grant applications.[1] She was confident that finding a need within one of her departments would be easy. First, the librarian sought gaps in the collections related to both ancient philosophy and ancient Greek studies in the classics. Professors in these two departments verified that they work heavily with these categories of texts, so the librarian proceeded to analyze UF's holdings against those in the Oxford Classical Texts to find gaps. But she noticed that these gaps could easily be filled using existing Libraries acquisitions funds.

The librarian tried another approach to determine what additional library materials would be a significant addition to better serve students and faculty. After several chats with various professors during their office hours, she met up with a new faculty member in Hindu Studies who had big ideas about the books he needed for his students, and together with another faculty member in the same area, the two built a list of desired books. Graduate students and other professors in Religion who responded to an e-mail list for their feedback about the proposed acquisitions then added to the list of desired books. The Hindu art curator working at UF's Harn Museum of Art had met the librarian while working on a committee together. The curator was planning a Hindu art exhibit, and she responded to the e-mail query with a list of art books to complement the upcoming planned exhibit.

The growing list of books posed issues related to acquisitions. The librarian had to identify the publisher and ISBN, as well as determine whether each book needed to be a print or an e-book version. At this point, the librarian contacted the grants manager for assistance in the development of the application's narrative and discovered that applicants for this particular grant award must be faculty members at UF, not library personnel. With edits from the grants manager, the librarian then worked with Religion faculty to finalize and submit the proposal. The two Religion Department faculty members were more than willing to be the applicants alongside the librarian on the project team.

Project Summary

Library Enhancement Grant for Hindu Studies (cash request for the Religion Department: $5,000)

The team seeks to fund the expansion of the Libraries' Hindu Studies Collection to purchase seventy-nine works. There are approximately fifteen faculty members in the Religion Department, twenty-four graduate students, and about forty undergraduate students. A stronger collection is fundamental

FIGURE 2.1
Vasudha Narayanan, PhD; Megan M. Daly, PhD; and Jonathan Edelmann, PhD (pictured from right to left) with an exhibit showcasing a sample of the books purchased with the Library Enhancement Grant award for Hindu Studies.
Photo by Barbara Hood, https://ufdc.ufl.edu/IR00011033/00001

for the Hindu Traditions track, but it will also benefit the Buddhism, Global Islam, Religion and Nature, and Religion in the Americas tracks. The Libraries currently house a modest collection of Hindu-topic works with some significant gaps, especially in core serials from Routledge, Oxford, and Columbia. Project team includes the distinguished professor of Religion (PI); assistant professor of Religion; and librarian of Classics, Philosophy, and Religion (one year: 2019 to 2020).[2]

Epilogue

The proposal was fully funded. The librarian proceeded to order the books through Gobi, which was made easier by her list preparation and budgeting for the grant application. The books arrived and due to the vendor's discounts, the project unexpectedly had a remaining balance. The team determined that the sponsor would allow the purchase of additional books, and was able to purchase a new list of selected titles approved by the sponsor.

To promote the new collection, an exhibit was installed in the Humanities and Social Science Library for the fall semester with coordination provided by the exhibit director. The exhibit was promoted widely through the Libraries' social media program posts, and e-mail messages were blasted to announce the list of new titles being added to the Libraries' collections.

It turns out that seeking faculty input was a much more effective means for identifying needs in these humanities departments. Hindu Studies, one of the five major branches of the Religion Department, also presents an ideal discipline in which to invest new resources due to the steady stream of South Asian graduate students landing at UF. The librarian's next step will be to determine how adding these selected books impacted UF faculty and students, by analyzing circulation statistics.

In fall 2019, a new faculty member who specializes in Islamic Studies approached the librarian to discuss the possibility of supporting his areas of scholarship not yet represented in the Libraries' collections (Islam in South Asia; history of Muslim theology, mysticism, and legalism; and gender sexuality, race, and migration). This idea offered a new opportunity to apply for a second Library Enhancement Grant. With knowledge and confidence gained during the first awarded proposal process, the two worked together quickly to create the application abstract, narrative, and list of materials to be purchased by the Libraries for submission to the Center for the Humanities and the Public Sphere.[3] Recently, the team received notification that the proposal was fully funded at $5,000.

PLANNING

Arts and Humanities Research Council UK / Research Networking in UK–US in Digital Scholarship in Cultural Institutions

Prologue

In 2018, the curator of the UF Baldwin Library of Historical Children's Literature received an inquiry from two United Kingdom (UK) scholars to join a partnership to plan future collaborative digital projects related to digital children's literature collections. The UK scholars had been visiting UF's Baldwin Library for years. They first met the current curator in 2012 when they were engaged in research concerning *Alice in Wonderland*. One of the scholars is a well-known children's literature scholar. The three built a close relationship over the years through annual repeat visits to the Baldwin Library and through their friendship with a UF professor of English who works in Anglophone children's literature studies.

The invitation contained a call for proposals from the Arts and Humanities Research Council, in the United Kingdom, to create a research network. It proposed that UF and other university partners might explore future digital collaboration opportunities. The Brits viewed the Baldwin Library as having a superb digital children's literature collection, and they aspired to create their own physical and digital children's literature collection. The Homerton Library at the University of Cambridge is a small library in comparison to UF's Special Collections. Creating a digital collection at the Homerton Library was an entirely new concept for the library's staff. Homerton Library staff sought to increase their knowledge of how to do this digital work with the help of experienced UF partners and others. They were at the very beginning stages of this digital collection work.

After some discussions at UF, the curator of the Baldwin Library received commitments from three additional faculty members to join the project: two English professors (one of whom was the associate director of UF's Center for the Study of Children's Literature and Culture), and the Smathers Libraries' director of digital partnerships and strategies. Two digital humanities scholars from Georgia Tech and a scholar from the University of Antwerp also joined the project.

The key to submitting a fundable proposal, according to the guidelines, was the contribution of funds by U.S. partnering organizations. To this end, the two Smathers Libraries' faculty members determined the amount of time they planned to contribute to the project should it be awarded, and contributed funds from the Baldwin Library's endowment income to support travel to the Baldwin Library for those traveling from Europe, as well as funds to host the visiting partners during their weeklong site visit to UF. If awarded, travel funds would cover the cost of the four UF faculty members to travel twice to the University of Cambridge during the grant period.

The Baldwin Library curator was motivated to join the project as a partner for a variety of reasons. It offered opportunities to learn how international users benefit from using the Baldwin Library, since it is much better known in the United Kingdom than in the United States. Moreover, the curator wanted to enhance and expand her library's connections with European partners. The proposed partnership offered a good way to plan for future collaborative ideas.

It is important to note that the grant proposal was submitted with the anticipation that no funds would be directly awarded to the University of Florida. The benefits of the budgeted travel funding for the four UF faculty members (included in the applicant's budget request) to allow for face-to-face collaborative conversations and site visits far exceeded the need for UF to receive any portion of the funds. Being able to contribute faculty effort and funding from the Baldwin Library's endowment interest income allowed the University of Cambridge and all of its partners to submit a strong collaborative proposal.

Project Summary

Digital Collections in Children's Literature: Distance Reading, Scholarship, Community ($0 subaward cash to Libraries; $24,912 cost share contribution)

The project team plans to create a research network to investigate digital children's books while uniting experts from one of the largest collections in the world, the Baldwin Library of Historical Children's Literature (UF), with a growing collection in the UK, at Homerton College. Cambridge scholars and archivists will examine gaps in provision, trends in digital archival scholarship, and future directions in the field. During four meetings (two in Cambridge and two in Florida), participants will consider how recent developments in "distant reading" and digital humanities—using computers to access large bodies of texts—can influence digitization policies. The team is especially mindful of issues of visual media and interactive books, important elements of the reading experience for young children, and how these can be captured digitally not only through library platforms, but also through social media. This work will enhance the scholarly uses of such collections and further enable digital access by the general public. Project team includes the senior lecturer in children's literature (PI- University of Cambridge, UK); Kinner-Young professor of Shakespeare and Renaissance literature (Co-PI-Angela Ruskin University, UK); from the Libraries, the project team includes the curator of the Baldwin Library of Historical Children's Literature (subaward PI) and director of digital strategies and partnerships (subaward Co-PI), with the UF associate director of the Center for the Study of Children's Literature and Culture (one year: 2019 to 2020).[4]

FIGURE 2.2
An ABC for Baby Patriots, the third most requested item in the University of Florida Digital Collections.

Source: https://ufdc.ufl.edu/UF00086056/00001

Epilogue

The proposal was fully awarded. It truly is a rare event to celebrate the success of a grant award that doesn't yield any funding for the partnering institution. But that was exactly the result. The UF project team enthusiastically completed two site visits to the Homerton Library, and the European team plus partners from Georgia Tech traveled to UF for extensive meetings and tours. Much information was exchanged about the behind-the-scenes work at each of the two libraries, and the meetings produced new knowledge about the assets available for future collaborative endeavors. Of course, there was endless discussion about metadata creation processes and the various challenges involved in cataloging digital children's books.

The project team's tangible results include the creation of more than twenty YouTube videos on the topic of movable books, and a Twitter feed about the project.[5] A survey of scholars yielded eighty respondents who described how they use children's literature digital collections, and the specific collections they use. The partners learned about different collections of children's books, and about the strong demand for access to digital collections because of the rising costs of travel and the reductions in available travel funds for faculty. The partners also learned that scholars seek to have access to more diverse children's books that highlight different cultures and races within digital collections.

The challenge here is that books published up to 1923 are free of copyright restrictions and can be digitized without rights concerns; however, culturally diverse children's books published prior to 1923 frequently include racial intolerance and degradation of non-white characters. In consultation with the Libraries' scholarly communications librarian, the partners learned that for books published from 1923 to 1963 the copyright is in question, thus increasing the likelihood that some children's books published during these forty years featuring the appreciation of diverse characters and cultures could be selected for future digitization and inclusion in digital collections if funding was available. Training to determine the copyright status of these books provided by the scholarly communications librarian encouraged the partners to explore a future grant-funded project focused on increasing digital access to culturally diverse children's books. Everyone participating in the project came away motivated to expand the reach of children's literature collections and research topics as a means of inspiring more involvement in the field.

A new grant proposal, *Decolonising Digital Childhoods: Enabling Participation to Diversify Children's Literature*, was submitted in fall 2019 by the University of Cambridge to the same sponsor to implement plans made during the initial partnership planning project. The partnership was awarded $98,901 in early 2020 to digitize 100 books with culturally diverse themes, enhance metadata by offering a rich set of keywords, develop automated trigger warnings for derogatory content, enhance the digital curation of content by adding commentary, and present a professional development workshop on decolonizing the digital archive for doctoral students, librarians, and archivists. In this implementation award, the UF project team will not receive funding directly, but will receive reimbursements for their travel expenses as they did in the planning grant project.

PROFESSIONAL DEVELOPMENT

George A. Smathers Libraries / Strategic Opportunities Program and Center for the Humanities and the Public Sphere / Programs in the Public Humanities

Prologue

The catalyst that inspired the relatively new African American studies librarian to begin planning a grant-funded project was an invitation to attend an AFRO Publishing Without Walls "Incubation" train-the-trainer workshop in

Savannah, Georgia, in 2018.[6] The workshop was attended by other teaching faculty, a couple of librarians, and a few community folks from around the country. The training emphasized the use of open-source digital tools like Scalar, open-source journals, and other forms of digital publishing. Participants learned how to use these tools, and about the example projects shared by trainers and participants alike during the workshop. There were only two participants from Florida. The ultimate workshop goal was that new trainees would return to their regions to share their new digital publishing skills with other colleagues.

For her grant-funded project, the African American studies librarian envisioned an incubation-like workshop that would incorporate librarianship concepts of community and capacity-building in North Florida, where UF is located. The workshop could serve as a bridge to other stakeholders and stewards of Florida's black history, including scholars, students, community historians, museum professionals, and public librarians. She was aware of the many professionals and volunteers already doing this type of digital humanities work in different locations and in multiple disciplines in Florida. She aspired to share the free, open-source methods of broadening the electronic access and analysis of black historical materials of Florida, but more importantly, she wanted to explore new collaborative practices that would increase the likelihood that collaborative digitization would emerge while participants were learning about each other's interests and skills. Technology normally follows closely behind the conception of a collaborative project, and the latter is the more difficult step in most digital partnership planning. Because of this, the librarian's emphasis shifted from the transfer of technical knowledge to recruiting qualified and interested participants who could suggest potential digital partnerships.

The librarian was already aware of existing partnership prospects, and she compiled a list of prospective organization participants, including members of the Florida African American Heritage Preservation Network, which provides organizational technical and informational assistance to its more than sixty museum and affiliate members.[7] Selected public libraries were added, since they often take on the role of hosting materials from local groups in efforts to preserve African American historical documents and photographs, but lack the expertise to fully carry out the digital processes requiring experienced staff. Finally, academic libraries increasingly maintain digital technologists who can support the digital preservation of historical materials, thus making academic libraries ideal partners for carrying out community digitization and digital humanities projects.

A team was formed by the African American studies librarian to determine how to convene those in North Florida working in this genre to go beyond the workshop experience modeled by AFRO Publishing Without Walls. How should the team approach black history in Florida? And who should be at the table? It was obvious to the team that the success of a Gainesville-UF-statewide workshop would depend on convening diverse participants, expertise, skills, and exhibit professionals, and on the inclusion of a local black history curator's genuine participation. Her commitment to partner with the team would provide the project with the community credibility it needed.

With mentoring from the grants manager, the African American studies librarian prepared a proposal to ensure the inclusion of those participants who could not afford the necessary funds to travel to Gainesville (where UF is located). Participation in the workshop would be free to all. To demonstrate broad support for this pilot project, the librarian actively solicited commitments from various partners, including the director of AFRO Publishing Without Walls, and local and statewide organizations that are involved in preserving and disseminating Florida's black history.

Proposal Summary

Digital Publishing on Black Life and History Collaborative Workshop ($4,940 cash request; cost share contribution $5,459)

The project team, in partnership with AFRO Publishing Without Walls, seeks to leverage relationships in the Libraries and among multidisciplinary faculty in the humanities and social sciences to: (1) establish a cohort of Black Studies scholars, heritage professionals, and culture keepers from academic institutions and community organizations in North Florida; (2) introduce cohort members to the AFRO Publishing Without Walls (AFRO PWW) initiative, which provides training and support in Black Studies digital publishing throughout the United States; (3) increase collaborative partnerships in Black-centered research and digital scholarship; (4) identify and connect cohort members with resources (human, informational, and technological) from other participant institutions to support the creation of digital projects; and (5) create an asset map of Black studies and history resources, projects, and professionals in the state of Florida. Project team includes the African American Studies librarian (PI), with the history librarian, literary collections archivist, director of digital partnerships and strategies, and grants manager (one year: 2019).[8]

Epilogue

Sixty-six participants attended the two-day workshop hosted at the Libraries. The participants included representatives from twelve colleges and universities, three K–12 schools, twelve museums and historical organizations, three community organizations, six public libraries, and four independent individuals. Thirty participants from nineteen cities in Florida, from Miami north to Pensacola, identified themselves: all thirty work as librarians and archivists, sixteen are pursuing graduate degrees, sixteen self-identified as culture keepers, thirteen serve as professors and scholars, and five participants teach K–12. The agenda for the two-day workshop included a Collaborating with Strangers Workshop for generating new collaborations, and a series of short sessions for learning about tools for creating digital collections and exhibits, social media promotional strategies, the AFRO Publishing Without Walls initiative to increase publishing by black scholars; and a panel discussion on community and university collaboration.[9]

FIGURE 2.3

The 1947 Lincoln High School (LHS) homecoming parade in Gainesville, Florida. Lincoln High was the second accredited black high school in Florida to offer education through the twelfth grade. The home of the LHS principal, A. Quinn Jones Sr., can be seen in the background, which stands today as the A. Quinn Jones Museum & Cultural Center. The AQJ museum coordinator, Desmon Walker, presented at the *Digital Collaborations* workshop on a panel discussing critical approaches to community-university collaboration.

Source: https://ufdc.ufl.edu/AA00063526/00006

During the feedback and reflection activity, participants representing Broward College, the University of South Florida, Florida State University, and the University of Central Florida requested that the workshop be replicated on their own campuses, using the community partnership format and agenda employed by the project team. Moreover, Florida African American Heritage Preservation Network staff expressed interest in doing more work with the Libraries team around the issue of developing community archives. The Florida Humanities Council representative announced his interest in supporting small black community organizations through seed grants to get pilot projects off the ground. The UF workshop provided him with a space to share this prospective funding opportunity. The Samuel Proctor Oral History Program at UF plans to contact folks in South Florida to follow up on opportunities to collect oral histories from members of the Black Elks Lodge (who were represented at the workshop) near Broward County.

A highlight of the workshop was the placement of the Collaborating with Strangers (CoLAB) Workshop at the very start of the workshop on day one. As participants started arriving, few knew each other and the large conference room was relatively quiet. Once the one-on-one speed meetings began, the room erupted in conversation as participants learned about each other's assets, interests, passions, and aspirations. The facilitated CoLAB process cut through the discomfort of being alone in a space where participants were surrounded by strangers. During this three-hour workshop, participants explored their relationships during an Idea Table discussion focused on how they could leverage the untapped assets in the room. By the time lunch arrived, everyone had found folks with whom to continue their conversations and collaborative planning. And throughout the two-day workshop, during the breaks between presenters and activities, there was never again a quiet moment. They wouldn't (or couldn't) stop talking!

COLLECTION DEVELOPMENT

George A. Smathers Libraries / Strategic Opportunities Program and Center for the Humanities and the Public Sphere / Programs in the Public Humanities

Prologue

In 2018, the grants manager made the acquaintance of a University of Florida professor of ESOL at a meeting of a small group of faculty members interested in the topic of multilingualism. After the meeting, the two of them chatted about a digital collection of oral histories and historical documents related to the first bilingual public school in the United States, the Coral Way Elementary School (Miami, Florida). The grants manager had developed this collection in 2008 under the leadership of Richard Ruiz, an internationally acclaimed professor of bilingual education at the University of Arizona (UA) Libraries. Coral Way Elementary's bilingual and bicultural education program had been created in 1963 in response to the many Cuban immigrant children arriving in this particular Miami neighborhood after Cuba's revolution. The ESOL professor was unaware of the UA collection but knew Richard Ruiz, who had passed away in 2015, and she wanted to know more. Her enthusiasm for learning about the details of Coral Way's hidden history led to a follow-up feasibility meeting with the grants manager and a new UF education librarian who was looking for a grant project in which to participate.

An inquiry to the UA Libraries' director of campus repository services about whether it would be possible to create a mirror digital collection of UA's Coral Way materials at the University of Florida was positively received, and the Coral Way files arrived along with all of the accompanying metadata. With this in hand, the team decided to apply for a Libraries Strategic Opportunities Program grant to expand the digital collection with new oral histories to be acquired through the grants manager's connections with Coral Way Elementary alumni of the first six years of the bilingual program, given that she herself had attended the school during those years. With museum studies expertise provided by the education librarian, the project included the creation of an online exhibit in the proposal to augment promotion of the expanded new collection. A serendipitous conversation with the Caribbean Special Collections librarian revealed that she would soon be hiring a graduate student to scan relevant materials for uploading to the UF Digital Collections, and the Coral Way project would line up with the prospective student's interests in bilingual education. Latin American and Caribbean Special Collections librarian welcomed the idea of joining the project team to lead the scanning of newly acquired collection materials (provided by the grants manager that were excluded from the UA digital collection) and the development of accompanying metadata to be added to the digital collection received from UA.

Proposal Summary

The Coral Way Bilingual Experiment Digital Collection (1961 to 1968) ($4,229 cash request; $5,598 cost share contribution)

The project team, in partnership with the UF College of Education (COE) and the University of Arizona (UA) Libraries, will expand the "Coral Way Bilingual Elementary School" digital collection that was previously housed at the UA. The project team plans to (1) add newly donated materials and oral histories, and (2) promote the collection through social media and an online exhibit. The enhanced digital collection will allow students, faculty, educators, researchers, and the general public direct access to primary source material and previously unavailable information about the first publicly funded dual-language immersion program in the United States, located in Miami, FL. Project team includes

FIGURE 2.4
Second-grade children in the bilingual program at Coral Way Elementary, 1963, Miami, Florida; the author is seated in the first row, second from the right

Source: https://ufdc.ufl.edu/AA00065932/00001

FIGURE 2.5
Book cover of *The Coral Way Bilingual Program*, published in November 2019

Image by Multilingual Matters, https://ufdc.ufl.edu/IR00011033/00001

the education librarian (PI), with the grants manager, Latin American and Caribbean Special Collections librarian, and with the College of Education professor in ESOL and bilingual education (one year: 2019).[10]

Epilogue

The proposal was fully awarded. The team quickly realized that the new historical materials to be digitized, new oral histories to be recorded and transcribed, and previously digitized materials being contributed by UA required expertise in copyright-related issues, and so they invited the scholarly communications librarian to join the team as a consultant. As the project began, the ESOL professor's discovery of the mountain of evidence revealed in all of the materials inspired her to read, listen to, and analyze all of the available materials. She created a codebook to qualitatively analyze the content of the original fifteen oral history interviews with alumni, retired teachers, and a former Cuban aide from the school. The discovery of the existence of a Ford Foundation grant awarded in the 1960s to the Miami-Dade County Schools prompted its acquisition from Ford's microfilm archive in Sleepy Hollow, New York.

But the team could not find evidence of the program's historical student assessment data until it learned of a 1968 dissertation written by the grants manager's first-grade Coral Way teacher while she was at Coral Way and seeking her doctorate at the University of Miami. The dissertation became the only source of Coral Way student test scores, along with comparisons with other student test scores from a nearby English-only elementary school.

Access to Coral Way's previously unknown history led the ESOL professor to spend her 2018 winter break writing chapters that became a book proposal submitted to the British publishers Multilingual Matters. The book, *The Coral Way Bilingual Program*, was published in November 2019.

This achievement led the team to seek public program funding from UF's Center for the Humanities and the Public Sphere. The funding would cover travel costs and the distribution of books to support two presentations during which the newly analyzed history of Coral Way and the expanded UF digital collection would be shared with teachers and staff members working at the school, and families living near the school in Miami.

Proposal Summary

Revealing a Hidden History: The Coral Way Elementary School Bilingual Experiment (1962–1968) ($3,000 cash request)

This project will support the dissemination of information to tell the unknown story of the origins of the country's first public bilingual school, Coral Way Elementary. During a site visit to Coral Way Elementary in December 2018, the applicant was invited to partner with administrators at the school to present a program about research and findings related to what happened in Miami in the early 1960s as a result of Cuban immigration. The applicant also visited the American Museum of the Cuban Diaspora located near Coral Way Elementary. Its founder was enthusiastic about the project and invited the team to share their findings with the local community. Project team includes the COE professor of ESOL and bilingual education with the grants manager, education librarian, scholarly communications librarian, and the Latin American and Caribbean Special Collections librarian (seven months: 2019).[11]

Epilogue

The proposal was fully funded. The book, *The Coral Way Bilingual Program*, was published in November 2019.[12] The team coordinated and completed the two presentations—one to eighty Coral Way Elementary teachers and staff, and another to the general public, including thirty former and current teachers, parents, students, alumni, and a former school board member at a program hosted by the Shenandoah Public Library, which serves the Coral Way Elementary neighborhood. Unfortunately, the team was unable to coordinate with the American Museum of the Cuban Diaspora to host a presentation. In-person and online exhibits to promote the new digital collection and the release of the new book were completed.[13]

At the time of this writing eight new oral history recordings, transcripts, and other primary materials about the bilingual program have been added to the original digital collection. To the team's surprise, the UA Libraries' digital librarian decided to transfer all of the collection materials to UF during a restructuring of its digital collections platform. A public presentation at the Smathers Library, which houses UF's special collections, to share the online exhibit, oral history and document collection, book, and the team's research results took place on February 19, 2020 for forty-seven participants with sponsorship from the Center for the Humanities and the Public Sphere, the Libraries, and the College of Education. The team recently received a no-cost extension approval from the Libraries' Grants Management Committee with a new grant period end date in June 2020 to complete and promote the project oral histories, collection, and add the video-recorded presentation, "Revealing a Hidden History: Coral Way, The First Publicly Funded Bilingual Program in the U.S.," to the UF digital collection.

COLLECTION DEVELOPMENT

American Library Association / Carnegie–Whitney Grant

Prologue

The librarian for physical sciences, mathematics, and visualization in the UF Marston Science Library became aware of the ALA/Carnegie-Whitney Grant award made to the curator of the UF Baldwin Library of Historical Children's Literature to develop a bibliography for British children's books about science written by female authors. (See later in this chapter.) This particular ALA award appealed to her desire to engage in a grant-funded project that did not involve a research study, but rather created a new product. She knew that library and school personnel who were interested in makerspaces were unaware of the wealth of information on this subject that has become available over the past five years, despite the popularity of these new types of programs. And she had a deep knowledge of makerspaces through her work co-creating the Made@UF space in the Marston Science Library, as well as her work co-authoring the book *3D Printing*, which was published in 2016. During ALA conferences, the librarian frequented the exhibit hall, where publishers were exhibiting new books about the topic. She was surprised at the large variety of publishers featuring makerspace books, and the broad range of topics being covered. Many of the books were written for middle and high school-aged students, not necessarily for higher academic libraries. Her awareness of different titles sparked her interest in applying for an ALA Carnegie-Whitney grant award that would fund the creation of a digital annotated bibliography of books and web resources on maker activities and makerspaces. Using the previously awarded application prepared by the curator of the Baldwin Library as a model facilitated the grant content preparation.

Prior to committing to preparing the proposal narrative, the librarian wanted to ensure its fundability and feasibility. One important step was to verify, through web searching and reviewing all of the previously awarded bibliography development projects, that no other applicant had authored a bibliography of the extant makerspace literature. In determining the budget, which relied on hiring a student assistant to help carry out the project, the librarian determined an excellent prospect for this position. A previously funded Libraries graduate intern in the English Department who had worked on an augmented reality crafting project for a Girls Tech Camp would probably be available to join the project. By addressing these two factors in advance, the proposal basically wrote itself once all of the vetting and rationale had been justified—mainly by the fact that makerspaces were a popular topic to many different types of library employees.

Proposal Summary

Building Makers: An Annotated Bibliography of Maker Resources for Libraries, Schools and Museums ($4,995 cash request; $8,604 cost share contribution)

The project team seeks to create a digital annotated bibliography of approximately 200 books and web resources describing the technology, software, and best practices for maker activities and makerspaces. This proposed digital annotated bibliography will serve as a pathfinder for existing makerspaces and readers who are seeking to identify useful titles and websites to further their making skills and learn new technology. Depending on the user activity and type of space, librarians will be able to search this bibliography to identify the book or website that best meets their need. Project team includes the physical sciences, mathematics, and visualization librarian (PI) and a graduate student (two-year project: 2018 to 2020).[14]

Epilogue

The project was fully awarded. The graduate student in English whose dissertation focuses on critical making was hired to assist with identifying and annotating books for the bibliography because she was, at this point, very familiar with all the relevant topics. The librarian's tasks included identifying the relevant topics within the makerspace universe, which she assessed to include fifteen unique categories identified through an extensive survey of relevant books published within the past five years. Using her survey results, she mapped out other criteria for evaluating which titles to include, essentially creating a database of topics to include in the bibliography.

According to the sponsor, there were no requirements for completing the awarded project beyond sharing the bibliographic list online. Striving for a more impactful result, the librarian embarked on a quest to develop a searchable database for the new bibliography. Her goal is to create a product that allows users maximum searching ability; however, she has had no previous experience developing such a database and is exploring options in partnership with the UF Libraries Information Technology department. From December 2018 to December 2019, the project team, which now includes two trained students (the original student graduated), expanded the title list to include nearly 166 books covering twenty-two subject areas. These were methodically retrieved through interlibrary loan to examine and create annotations. The team used Airtable to store annotations although Zotero was used as a staging area to manage the bibliographic information

As of April 2020, the grant project received a three-month no-cost extension to continue the bibliography and website development. The librarian planned on finishing the website by the end of May 2020 with 218 annotated records.[15] Another extension due to COVID-19 was received to complete the project by August 2020. The librarian was able to hire a graduate computer science student programmer to design and build the fully searchable website by that date.

OUTREACH

George A. Smathers Libraries / Strategic Opportunities Program

Prologue

Since 2016, the Libraries' human resources assistant was charged with organizing and executing new employee tours of the six campus libraries at the University of Florida. Over time she realized that these tours, which averaged four per year, were not serving all of the Libraries' new employees, whether because they were unavailable to attend or had mobility issues that prevented their participation. After completing a course on "Digital Tools for the Arts and Humanities," she became inspired to create a project using 360-degree photography. The HR assistant's goal to create a virtual tour of all the campus libraries featured in the tours arose out of the disappointment many new employees felt about not being present for the actual tours.

Her first step was to learn about the extant virtual tours created by other academic libraries: Which libraries were offering 360-degree virtual tours? What specific software did those libraries use? What were the pros and cons of each type of software, including its costs and capabilities? What library features and spaces were highlighted by the virtual library tours that were most effective in orienting new visitors to those libraries? What were the best practices that could be identified by the most outstanding virtual tour examples? What would it take and what would the schedule look like to complete a 360-degree virtual tour for each of the six libraries?

The assistant determined that to create an effective project team, she would need to recruit those who were passionately interested in planning and executing the project if funding was granted through the Libraries' internal funding program. She recruited the social sciences outreach librarian, the librarian in charge of virtual reality at the science library, and the social media specialist to serve on the project team. Each of these team members offered unique skills and resources to propel the project forward.

After viewing and assessing twelve virtual tours, the team selected the Vassar College one as its virtual tour model because it presented a static menu at the top of the screen to allow users the option to navigate to other physical areas.[16] Beyond simply determining the steps to actualize the virtual tours, through their conversations the team became aware of all the different types of users who would benefit from having access to these virtual tours: the parents of prospective UF students and the prospective students themselves, applicants for job positions in the Libraries, visiting professors and guest lecturers planning their UF visits, and new and current students who are unfamiliar with the Libraries' facilities, collections, and technological offerings.

Proposal Summary

Advancing Accessibility: Smathers Libraries 360-Degree Virtual Tours
($4,998 cash request; $5,826 cost share contribution)

The project team plans to design and execute the first 360-degree virtual tour of the Smathers Libraries. Multiple spots in six campus libraries (Library West, Smathers, Architecture & Fine Arts, Marston, Health Science Center Library, and Education) will be photographed to create an interactive web page. At each of these spots to be featured on the web page, virtual windows will allow the user to access additional information about the displayed area. The virtual tour will (1) be promoted to new students to introduce library

FIGURE 2.6
UF student photographer testing 360-degree image of the Architecture and Fine Arts Library

Photo by Matthew Abramson, https://ufdc.ufl.edu/IR00011033/00001

services, (2) be made available to existing students to encourage library usage, and (3) serve some of the accessibility needs of students. When creating 360-degree videos, a camera with multiple lenses films overlapping images simultaneously. The images are then stitched together electronically with video-editing software. The proposed Panotour software requested to execute this project has the ability to use an iFrame to embed the videos into sites (such as LibGuides and the Libraries home page) and also has a Word-Press plug-in for easy adaptation for multiple platforms. In addition to producing the video tours, the team plans to write a how-to guide for publishing in the institutional repository (IR@UF), and to create a webinar/conference session for presentation during a regional meeting of the library employees at UF and beyond. Funds will be used to hire three temporary student employees to shoot the panoramic photos, stitch them together, and code the text information; purchase one license of Panotour editing software; and advertise on Twitter and Facebook. Project team includes the HR assistant (PI), with the social sciences outreach librarian, social media specialist, and science outreach librarian (one year: 2018 to 2019).[17]

Epilogue

The proposal was awarded full funding. The project team hired three graduate students in computer science who were well-versed in 3D photography and creating virtual tours. The team completed all of the photographic work—selecting seventy 3D photographs of all the specific locations mapped out by the project team, in consultation with the chairs from each library. Because of the nature of 360-degree photographs, the team learned the mantra: if you can see the camera, the camera can see you—meaning the strategy for each photograph had to be meticulously planned. Provisions were made to include photographs of the libraries' available technology, including high-speed scanners, reference services, computers, printers, and book checkout stations. In partnering with the campus Disability Resource Center (DRC), the team learned about "invisible disabilities" and the barriers that many students face. This knowledge inspired the team to highlight areas such as quiet study floors for those students who require minimal stimulation.

The student photographers have added the audio clips for the information boxes and the project team will review for edits and present it to the DRC so that its student ambassadors can review it for accessibility. Their feedback will most likely result in further edits before launching the project. The completed tour will be made available on the George A. Smathers Libraries home page.[18] While the tour was being developed, the HR assistant (who holds an MLIS degree) began submitting applications to present at library conferences. In fall 2019 she presented a poster at the Annual Conference of the Florida Association of College and Research Libraries. Due to the COVID-19 quarantine, the project was extended until December 2020.

HEALTH INFORMATION DISSEMINATION

George A. Smathers Libraries / Strategic Opportunities Program

Prologue

The idea for this Strategic Opportunities Program (SOP) project derived from a declined National Library of Medicine (NLM) proposal submitted by a project team the previous year. The NLM proposal emerged from the hiring of a new medical librarian at UF's Health Science Center Library (HSCL) who was particularly interested in communicating trustworthy health information to consumers via comics illustration. She was looking for partners in Gainesville and, through a conversation with the HSCL webmaster (who is an artist), she learned about the Sequential Artists Workshop (SAW), a nonprofit organization in downtown Gainesville. SAW's executive director was interested in exploring the partnership project to develop a social media campaign to promote HIV/AIDS prevention and health information using comics illustrations, text, and links to trustworthy medical information. The team developed and submitted a proposal to create a collaborative outreach initiative led by HSCL, in partnership with the UF Student Health Care Center, UF Counseling & Wellness Center, GatorWell, UF Department of Health Education and Behavior, UF Center for Precollegiate Education and Teaching, and the Sequential Artists Workshop. The goal of the project was to increase and enhance access to HIV/AIDS information resources to local adolescents and young adults, since these have both a high and rapidly growing number of HIV-infected individuals. The project team sought to improve the information-seeking behaviors of the adolescent and young adult populations in North Florida regarding HIV/AIDS risks, prevention, and treatment through trainings targeted at them, health care providers, and educators; to develop a social marketing campaign and short graphic novels targeted at younger populations; and to generate awareness of HIV/AIDS's history and societal impact through the proposal of a one-credit course focused on the book *And the Band Played On: Politics, People, and the AIDS Epidemic* by Randy Shilts.

The project was declined by NLM, but this did not deter the project team. They regrouped and decided to apply for the next SOP deadline. The SOP proposal concept scaled down the NLM project, eliminating the staff salaries and fringe benefits costs which are disallowed in SOP budgets, along with expenses related to producing training videos, and a planned external evaluator which made up most of original budget. Instead, they honed in on only the essential expenses to complete a pilot project to prove that the concept would serve local audiences with health information through a new communications medium. For the team, the SOP provided their first concrete opportunity to formalize a deliberate plan to use social media as a promotional outlet for disseminating trustworthy health information on a specific topic. But they needed access to professionals experienced in launching and managing social media campaigns related to health information dissemination.

The HSCL team began talking with the UF GatorWell health promotion specialist on campus, who is an expert in HIV/AIDS and sexual health in general, serving students at UF. The specialist walked the team through the process of creating a health information campaign. They also met with the UF-affiliated HealthStreet social media coordinator, who trained the team in how to create a message, test the efficacy of a message with a target audience, and the process of how health information promotion works. HealthStreet is an innovative community engagement program that bridges gaps between health care and health research for over 8,000 low-income and homeless residents in Gainesville who are interested in participating in research studies.

The project budget relied on the cost-sharing of staff effort to execute most of the activities outlined in the timeline. SAW personnel were satisfied with receiving a $500 honorarium for presenting a workshop on how to create comics for specific messaging and for pacing the story—offering their downtown production space as the workshop venue—judging illustrated submissions and providing project consultant expertise. The lean budget included funding for Facebook advertising, and comic graphic contest award prizes.

Proposal Summary

Creative Campaigns to Promote HIV/AIDS Awareness among UF Students ($1,350 cash request; $8,373 cost share contribution)

This project is a collaborative outreach initiative led by the HSCL in partnership with campus health care organizations including the UF Student Health Care Center and UF Counseling and Wellness Center, and also the Sequential Artists Workshop. The project goal is to increase and enhance UF students' access to reputable information on HIV/AIDS risks, prevention, and treatment. Project objectives and activities include (1) improving the information-seeking behaviors of UF students regarding HIV/AIDS through trainings targeted at their health care providers; and (2) enhancing the access of UF students to effective materials on HIV/AIDS through development of a social marketing campaign and short graphic novels targeted toward this population. A graphic novel contest, open to UF students and the Gainesville community, will result in the production of at least three comics/brief graphic novels focusing on HIV/AIDS. A social marketing campaign will provide high-quality information in an appealing format, with a minimum of fifty messages developed across social media platforms (twelve of these being Facebook-promoted posts).

SOP funds will cover costs related to Sequential Artists Workshop services, awards for outstanding graphic novels, and Facebook post promotion. Project team includes the HSCL reference and liaison librarian (PI), a second reference and liaison librarian (Co-PI), with nursing and consumer health librarian, webmaster and graphic designer,

FIGURE 2.7
Excerpt from the publication featuring winning HIV/AIDS graphic novel contest entries

Drawing by Lisa Klug; see page 6,
https://ufdc.ufl.edu/IR00010220/00001

health literacy and liaison librarian, and the health sciences liaison librarian (one year: 2017 to 2018).[19]

Epilogue

The proposal was fully awarded. First the team and other interested graphic novel contest participants attended the training workshop presented by SAW artists at their downtown studio. The artists gave a tour of the workshop space and laid out all the steps needed to create an effective graphic novel storyline and messaging. The participants practiced brainstorming ideas for possible ways to disseminate, through the medium of a graphic novel, trustworthy health information about HIV/AIDS to campus students and others of this age group living in Alachua County, where the University of Florida is located.

Next, to advertise the contest and call for submissions, the team worked with SAW artists to create contest eligibility, rules, and criteria for judging. An online LibGuide featured information about the call for submissions, contest rules, how entries would be displayed and used for health information dissemination, and other related information. A "UF Health Science Center Library Graphic Novel Contest" page was posted on the HSCL website and was linked to the LibGuide, and a Facebook page was created for the project.[20] Bookmarks promoting the contest were distributed at various events.

Four high-quality entries were received. The contest judges included the chair of the Architecture and Fine Arts Library, the executive director of SAW, a UF Center for Arts in Medicine program faculty member, and the GatorWell health promotion specialist. Entries were evaluated on the quality of the story being told, the visual appeal, and the quality of the medium to communicate health/HIV/AIDs messages.

The three winning graphic novels were tested by randomly selected students in the outdoor campus plaza, where daily tabling is sponsored by a variety of student organizations and groups. Posters reflecting different messages were tested to access student feedback, eliciting responses to questions such as: "What is this about?" and "Does it make you feel: offended, interested, engaged, or empowered?" All of the responses were captured and were then used to inform the social media campaign's content.

The graphic novel images were used in twenty-eight social media posts on Facebook leading up to World AIDS Day. Each post emphasized different types of health information such as treatment options, how to live with HIV/AIDS, dealing with the stigma associated with AIDS, how the HIV virus is transmitted, and other topics, along with links to trustworthy local and national resources, and information about the work of UF researchers in these fields. The campaign's messages were viewed 52,000 times—5,000 resulted from the HSCL's organic reach in Facebook, and the remaining 47,000 were generated by the inexpensive paid promotional Facebook posts directed to those audiences defined by the project team, including young people in Alachua County and UF-affiliated people regardless of age.

COLLECTION DISCOVERY

George A. Smathers Libraries / Strategic Opportunities Program

Prologue

The map and imagery librarian was posed a question by the dean of the Libraries: How many maps of Cuba do the Libraries have in its collections? The number of individual maps of Cuba was easy to ascertain, but then she thought about all the maps hidden in other locations. Her question became: What would it take to find all of these maps that are not cataloged? The maps included in rare books have become a preservation issue for many libraries due to map thieves who prey on library collections, as chronicled in *The Map Thief: The Gripping Story of an Esteemed Rare-Map Dealer Who Made Millions Stealing Priceless Maps* (2014), by Michael Blanding. The maps in books have not been tracked, and this poses an international preservation problem that, according to the map librarian, remains unresolved. Her team decided to tackle the issue of finding the hidden maps of Cuba because of the Libraries' ongoing "Celebrating Cuba! Collaborative Digital Collections of Cuban Patrimony" project.[21] Eventually, the dean was interested in digitizing all of UF's maps of Cuba for inclusion in the collection. With only two weeks until the SOP deadline, the team tested a procedure to locate the maps that was sufficient to design a feasible project plan worthy of a proposal submission.

Proposal Summary

Buried Treasure: Hidden Collections of Cuba Maps ($4,834 cash request; $7,460 cost share contribution):

The primary goal is to position the Libraries for external funding to discover, inventory, preserve, and digitize maps in the books of the Department of Special and Area Studies Collections (SASC). The team will test a new methodology for identifying, describing, and providing access to these hidden collections of maps with the express purpose of prioritizing their future preservation and digitization. The team will also support current library initiatives with the Biblioteca Nacional de Cuba Jose Marti by focusing the scope of the pilot project on uncovering maps of Cuba (1500–1923) hidden within books. Specific objectives include (1) identifying 300 to 400 books containing maps of Cuba from across the SASC collections, and specifically within the P.K. Yonge Library of Florida History, the Rare Book Collections, the Latin American

FIGURE 2.8
Map of a railroad in Cuba. The book where the map was found, *The Cuba Railroad: Through the Land of Promise*, published in 1909–10, had to be sent to the Preservation Department for conservation, and was then digitized.

Source: https://ufdc.ufl.edu/AA00062518/00002/1x, page 7

and Caribbean Collection, and the Map and Imagery Library; (2) describing all maps found and updating book records in the UF Library Catalog with information about the uncovered maps; (3) evaluating the efficiency and accuracy of the methodology used to (a) identify books relevant to the project, (b) describe the maps, and (c) update the Library Catalog; (4) developing a preservation and digitization plan of selected Cuba materials based on the information collected; and (5) creating a plan to apply for external funding. SOP funds will cover the costs for OPS graduate student labor, and travel to the University of Minnesota, which will provide a prototype for this project. Project team includes the head of Map and Imagery Library (PI), with interim head of the Latin America and Caribbean Collection, the Caribbean Basin librarian, rare books librarian, map cataloger, and cataloger of materials in Area Studies (one year: 2017 to 2018).[22]

Epilogue

The proposal was fully funded. One of the most important steps in the project was to travel to the University of Minnesota's Bell Library to learn about a completed NEH Preservation and Access grant-funded project[23] on which the concept for the *Buried Treasure* project was based. The Bell Library project team had completed their library's inventory, description, and digitization of the bound maps found within 22,000 volumes—a massive undertaking! The site visit provided a hands-on experience detailing the process and its ratio-nale, thus helping the map librarian to fully understand the project's chal-lenges and solutions.

At UF, the project team viewed the funded activities more as a large track-ing project. Rather than creating narratives describing each of the discovered bound maps for a traditional inventory, instead, a photograph of each map was captured, which was an innovative approach to reduce the team's effort. This simple solution provided more time to search through more books. In the end, the team produced an inventory of books that included maps of Cuba, accom-panied by photographs of each discovered map to generate a photographic index. Using this method, the team searched through 105 books in three dif-ferent locations: the Latin American Center Collections, the Rare Books Col-lection, and the Map Library. Within these books the team inventoried 422 maps; and of those, 298 maps, or 71 percent, were related to Cuba. The indi-vidual maps listed in the original Cuba map inventory developed prior to the SOP grant period contained fewer than 200 maps. Notes to catalog records indicating the map's location in the book, and the cartographer or engraver of each discovered map, were added, generating another valuable output of the project. In the future, newly discovered bound maps can easily be added to the photographic index, providing a sustainable long-term method for capturing these maps. This innovative methodology was shared during a presentation at a conference of the Society of the History of Discoveries in 2019.

COLLECTION DISCOVERY

American Library Association / Carnegie–Whitney Grant

Prologue

The Baldwin Library of Historical Children's Literature is the largest Anglo-phone collection of children's literature in the world, with just over 120,000 texts and other materials dating from 1667 to the present day. The curator of the Baldwin Library received a suggestion from the chair of Special Collections to consider the funding opportunity promoted in one of the Libraries' Fund-ing Alerts for an ALA/Carnegie-Whitney grant. It seemed like an excellent prospect for acquiring funds to more broadly promote the contents of this large, unique collection. The deadline provided only two months to prepare a fundable proposal, which seemed insufficient due to the curator's daily work-load. But her chair's interest in the history of science as a possible theme for a new annotated bibliography captured the curator's imagination and would not let go. She first considered the resources that were already available to her.

A visiting scholar to the collection six months earlier had presented on the topic of his book *Useful Knowledge: The Victorians, Morality, and the March of Intellect* (2001) and had discussed nineteenth-century science in children's literature. To prepare for any scholar's visit to the Baldwin Library, the curator pulls collection items from the Special Collections stacks related to the scholar's research topic. This practice encourages scholars to return to use the collection time and time again, thus strengthening these valuable relationships. To prepare for this scholar's visit, the curator began pulling science books, having no idea how many she would find using the catalog to search for a variety of science topics. As it turned out, the collection contains thousands of these books, and many of the older books were authored by women.

In the curator's estimation, she had struck gold in terms of identifying the types of books that would generate benefits from greater exposure through inclusion in an annotated online bibliography. A follow-up conversation with the visiting scholar, who by now was serving on the Baldwin Library's Advisory Council (see the planning grant that established the Advisory Council later in this chapter), led to his agreement to join the project as an expert advisor. With assistance from the grants manager, a proposal was developed to fund an honorarium for the scholar's travel expenses, and to cover the costs for a student assistant to work side-by-side with the curator to create a new online bibliography.

Project Summary

Women-Authored Science Books for Children 1790–1890: An Annotated Bibliography ($5,000 cash request; $6,736 cost share contribution)

This project seeks to research and design a digital annotated bibliography of 200 primarily nonfiction science books written by women for children between 1790 and 1890. This will be the first project to create an annotated bibliography of an important topic within the collection. The project plan is to (1) select 200 titles from the Baldwin Library based on date, authorship, reputation of author, scarcity, cultural impact (if known), and condition; (2) conduct research focusing on specific titles, themes, authors, and cultural significance through a contract with the literature expert Alan Rauch, PhD, a professor of English at the University of North Carolina–Charlotte; (3) design the format of the annotated bibliography to meet online user requirements; (4) using the research results, write annotations with notes for multiple editions where appropriate; (5) promote the completed bibliography; and (6) evaluate usage and benefits once the project is complete. Project team includes the curator of the Baldwin Library of Historic Children's Literature (PI) and cataloger for children's literature (two years: 2015 to 2017).[24]

Epilogue

The proposal was fully awarded. A student from UF's Children's Literature program was hired to assist in gathering information for the bibliography

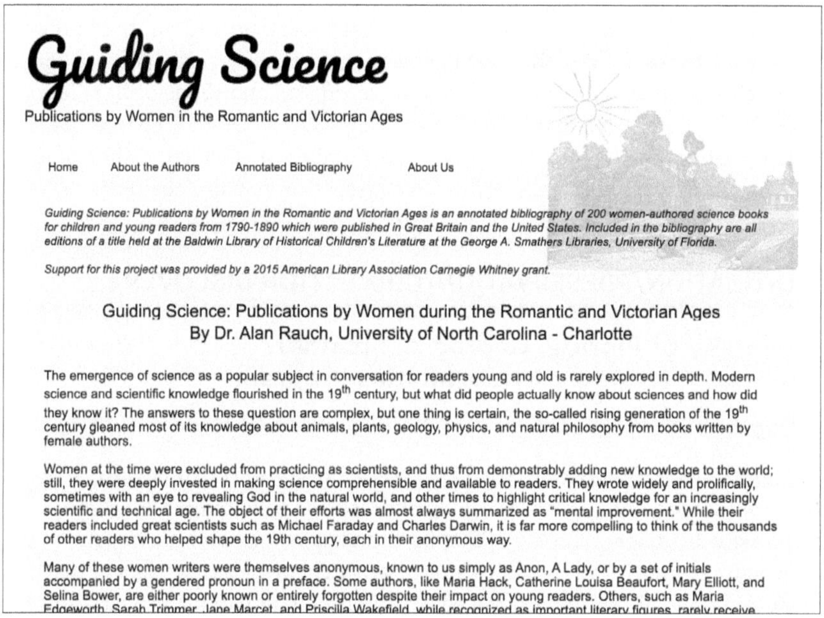

Guiding Science
Publications by Women in the Romantic and Victorian Ages

Home   About the Authors   Annotated Bibliography   About Us

Guiding Science: Publications by Women in the Romantic and Victorian Ages is an annotated bibliography of 200 women-authored science books for children and young readers from 1790-1890 which were published in Great Britain and the United States. Included in the bibliography are all editions of a title held at the Baldwin Library of Historical Children's Literature at the George A. Smathers Libraries, University of Florida.

Support for this project was provided by a 2015 American Library Association Carnegie Whitney grant.

Guiding Science: Publications by Women during the Romantic and Victorian Ages
By Dr. Alan Rauch, University of North Carolina - Charlotte

The emergence of science as a popular subject in conversation for readers young and old is rarely explored in depth. Modern science and scientific knowledge flourished in the 19th century, but what did people actually know about sciences and how did they know it? The answers to these question are complex, but one thing is certain, the so-called rising generation of the 19th century gleaned most of its knowledge about animals, plants, geology, physics, and natural philosophy from books written by female authors.

Women at the time were excluded from practicing as scientists, and thus from demonstrably adding new knowledge to the world; still, they were deeply invested in making science comprehensible and available to readers. They wrote widely and prolifically, sometimes with an eye to revealing God in the natural world, and other times to highlight critical knowledge for an increasingly scientific and technical age. The object of their efforts was almost always summarized as "mental improvement." While their readers included great scientists such as Michael Faraday and Charles Darwin, it is far more compelling to think of the thousands of other readers who helped shape the 19th century, each in their anonymous way.

Many of these women writers were themselves anonymous, known to us simply as Anon, A Lady, or by a set of initials accompanied by a gendered pronoun in a preface. Some authors, like Maria Hack, Catherine Louisa Beaufort, Mary Elliott, and Selina Bower, are either poorly known or entirely forgotten despite their impact on young readers. Others, such as Maria Edgeworth, Sarah Trimmer, Jane Marcet, and Priscilla Wakefield, while recognized as important literary figures, rarely receive

FIGURE 2.9
Bibliography of science publications authored by women

Source: https://cms.uflib.ufl.edu/guidingscience

and in identifying all of the possible appropriate nineteenth-century woman-authored books on science in the collection, using multiple Excel spreadsheets to capture and search for this information. (For instance, one title appeared with fifty different editions.) The team split the alphabet, writing annotations about each book's topics and its author. Most of the books were well-cataloged, although 5–10 percent were not. With metadata enhancements provided by the team's cataloger, the team forged ahead to improve provisional records.

Although the proposal described the team's goal of including 200 titles, in reality the resulting bibliography features 500 titles because of the many multiple editions. This, of course, was not anticipated. Every title discovered within the boundaries of women authors, published between 1790 and 1890, and related to science topics added to the workload, and expanded the bibliography. The visiting scholar provided ideas for short essays to describe each book and proofread all of the essays. The project team decided that it would be beneficial for users to have access to information about each author, in addition to the bibliography, thus expanding the project's scope well beyond the proposal's original goals. The project remains active at the time of this writing, especially as more biographical descriptions of the authors are discovered and this new information is added to the website. (For example, some authors were simply described in relation to their male relatives.)

One of the graduate students who had participated in the Baldwin Library's Advisory Council meetings secured a faculty position at Georgia Tech after graduating from UF. Through her efforts and those of her Georgia Tech students, there is now a technology project to design a new annotated bibliography website, and to increase the number of selected author biographies for the selected science books for aggregation to the website.[25]

DIGITIZATION/PRESERVATION/COLLECTION DISCOVERY

University of Florida, George A. Smathers Libraries / Strategic Opportunities Program

Prologue

William Stetson Kennedy (1916–2011) was a Florida author, folklorist, activist, freelance writer, and journalist. In his nineties he spoke to his wife about what to do with his papers. In the 1990s he contributed parts of his papers to the University of South Florida (USF), but he still held on to a great deal of his life's work. He decided that he wanted to contribute his remaining collection items to the University of Florida, in hopes that USF library administrators would agree to move all of USF's collection items to UF, creating one more complete collection. This unification was eventually achieved through USF's generosity in transferring forty-five boxes of papers from its own collection to UF, and adding another forty-five to fifty boxes of new materials. Some of Kennedy's materials previously had been given to the Library of Congress, George State University, and the Schomburg Center. His best-known work reflects his activities as a folklorist with the Federal Writers Program, and his book *Palmetto Country*. His undercover infiltration into the KKK led to his book *The Klan Unmasked*.

The problem with the collection was that it contained many audio and video recordings, on cassettes and microcassettes. Kennedy was always recording himself and others, especially during his journalistic interviews, because of his penchant for checking the accuracy of his quotes. Further complicating the processing of the collection was the fact that the labels for these recordings were either nonexistent or in handwriting that made no sense.

The curator of UF's P.K. Yonge Library of Florida History needed to determine what was recorded on these tapes—who was being interviewed and was the content confidential or not. He had the tapes converted to digital files and determined that the only way to know what was there was to listen to each of them. Transcribing all of the tapes was unreasonable due to the cost at the time. In a consultation with staff at UF's Samuel Proctor Oral History Program (SPOHP), he learned that creating an index or table of contents of the topics discussed by interviewees in the recordings, along with the digital time these topics appeared on the recordings, would be a viable option to learn about the many recordings' content.

Project Summary

The Legacy of Stetson Kennedy: A Digital Archive for Social Justice ($4,987 cash request; $9,914 cost share contribution)

This project will create a pilot digital archive for the Stetson Kennedy Papers, the Libraries' most significant collection related to activism and social justice. The archive will host a photo gallery, selected print works, and audiovisual interviews in which Kennedy speaks out on civil rights, environmentalism, fair labor practices, and other topics. Funds will be used to hire a processing archivist for two months to index the AV content and establish online content. The main goals of this project will be to digitize approximately 100 photos with appropriate metadata and identification; to create online digital versions of 300 pages of unpublished essays and short articles; and to create audio-logs for fifty online digital audio and audiovisual files previously made from selected AV materials (100 hours of recorded data). This table of

---

FIGURE 2.10
Author Stetson Kennedy signing copies of his book *The Klan Unmasked* in its 1990 re-release by the University Press of Florida
Source: https://ufdc.ufl.edu/IR00011033/00001

contents for AV recordings will serve as indexes to digital files and will ensure that users can easily find and listen to segments of Kennedy speaking on a variety of topics. Project team includes the curator of the P.K. Yonge Library of Florida History (PI) with head of collections services, digital production manager, bibliographic control coordinator, and director of communications (one year: 2014 to 2015).[26]

Epilogue

The proposal was fully awarded. First, the curator set out to hire a student to execute the project. An undergraduate interested in going to law school had recently completed an oral history internship at SPOHP where she practiced listening and transcribing oral histories. She was aware of Stetson Kennedy's history and was hired to create the time-based recording summaries. Her challenge was to determine whether interviewees had consented to the interviews, and Kennedy's intentions for the recordings' use—some would need to be kept "dark" from researchers, depending on the situation and information found in the recordings. Other tapes were formal interviews that contained Kennedy's recollections of events, history, protests, and people like Zora Neale Hurston and Woody Guthrie, as well as narratives of his time in Europe and the People's Republic of China. These recordings held the potential to enhance the research experiences of those reviewing Kennedy's documents and photographs. The project was completed by the original student within the grant period. Eventually, the student completed her degree at the UF College of Law, passed the bar exam, and successfully applied to the bar to practice law in Florida.

DIGITIZATION/PRESERVATION

George A. Smathers Libraries / Strategic Opportunities Program

Prologue

In 2013, when the Libraries staff began working with newly accessioned materials from UF's Panama Canal Museum Collection, the stereographs in the collection became more than just a curiosity. These commercially produced photographs historically had been used to chronicle natural disasters, triumphs, and expeditions for viewing in living rooms and classrooms. Narrative texts and captions add to the context of how events and diverse people were characterized for popular consumption in the late nineteenth and early twentieth centuries when this technology was popular.

The stereographs in this collection were contributed by a single donor and told the story of expeditions to determine a feasible passage for the canal through Panama's tough terrain. Whether through racially biased overtones or exaggerations in the narratives, the stereographs portray hidden information about this time in history. They were used to promote these types of projects to the American general public. After the expeditions, the stereographs documented the United States coming in with its technology, slicing up the land, and overcoming the landscape to create a marvel of engineering. The stereographs document the entirety of the journey, culminating in the opening of the Panama Canal.

A project team was formed by new Libraries' employees supported by Institute of Museum and Library Services funding (see chapter 5) to prepare an internal SOP grant application to digitize the stereograph collection. The team viewed the grant proposal as a way to support the goals of that project, one of which was to integrate UF student and Zonian—those who had formerly resided in the U.S. Canal Zone—volunteers to contribute to the metadata creation work that would expose the collection to all types of audiences, including educators. One of the project's goals was to animate the stereographs by converting them into GIFs.

Proposal Summary

Panama Canal Museum Collection: Digitization, Metadata Capture, Outreach and Educational Tool Creation for a Set of Panama and Canal-Focused Stereographs ($2,350 cash request; $5,786 cost share contribution)

This pilot project will create an ongoing model for digitizing resources from the Panama Canal Museum (PCM) Collection while leveraging the talents of former PCM volunteers and members as volunteers for record creation. The project will mirror the goals of the current IMLS grant by focusing on the digitization of materials that are the subject of scheduled Canal Centennial physical and virtual exhibitions, using PCM volunteers for collection identification, and creating educational modules to promote outreach and wider use of the collection. The selected 200 stereographs meet the teaching and research needs and interests of various UF faculty and 2014 exhibit requirements. The project fills an important gap in existing resources related to stereographs of Panama and the Panama Canal by making many of these resources available online for the first time and by showcasing the equally significant accompanying text, which has, until recently, been largely ignored in photographic digitization projects. Lastly, the New York Public Library has a website showcasing GIF animations of views in its stereograph collection, which is a technology that makes stereograph cards appear 3D. The project proposes to build on this idea to offer viewers the chance to experience the original intent of stereographic technology. Project team includes the Panama Canal Museum volunteer coordinator (PI), Panama Canal Museum Collection coordinator (Co-PI), Area Studies cataloger, Panama Canal Museum marketing coordinator, education

FIGURE 2.11
Old dredge, abandoned by the French on the Chagres River, Bohio,
Panama Canal Zone

Source: https://ufdc.ufl.edu/AA00015213/00001, Keystone View Company

librarian, exhibit coordinator, digital imaging specialist, and the Caribbean
Basin librarian (one year: 2013 to 2014).[27]

Epilogue

The project was fully funded. The primary challenge with the project was to
create trained volunteers who would be able to work with the digitized materials to add substantive metadata to each stereograph image. Commonly, digital
projects begin with the creation of metadata for each physical item and move
to digitization once this step is complete. However, in this case, volunteers
from the Panama Canal Museum who had formerly lived in the U.S. Canal
Zone did not reside near the University of Florida. Contributing to the project was impossible unless the stereograph images, front and back, could be
viewed online.

A volunteer training curriculum and student recruitment program was
created to support the creation of stereograph metadata. This kept a steady
stream of trained students prepared to tackle the many hours (twelve to fifteen hours per week for most of the grant period) it took to complete the
metadata. Support for the Zonian volunteers was more hands-on for those
who felt technologically comfortable working in a digital environment that
used Dublin Core metadata fields to create item-level records. The project
essentially became a crowd-sourcing project. Volunteers directly interacted
with the digitized collections in a private mode while they were entering the
detailed metadata. The project successfully demonstrated that with sufficient

oversight, volunteers could adequately contribute in a meaningful way without disrupting the digital collections that contained only barebones metadata records. Volunteers were trained to understand the exact specifications for what needed to be entered into each field, in order to standardize the content in the fields. To add educational value to the project, the education librarian and the collections coordinator interviewed teachers who created educational materials to put online for K–12 education, increasing the collection's accessibility for those audiences in particular by using animated GIFs.

The success of the project was only made possible by many collaborators, including a software engineer who was willing to allow volunteers who were working remotely to have limited access to records in the digital collections. Programmers added features to the platform to allow this to happen. Without their commitment to experimentation and their enthusiasm for the project, the team would not have benefited from the knowledgeable volunteers who did not have access to the collection. Interestingly, the original donor of the stereograph collection contributed other photographs related to the Panama Canal, thus increasing engagement in the overall Panama Canal Museum Collection initiative.[28]

COLLECTION DISCOVERY

George A. Smathers Libraries / Strategic Opportunities Program

Prologue

This project began with a gift of manuscript records that became part of the UF Ian Parker Collections of East African Wildlife Conservation, and which were produced during the culling of elephant families because of overpopulation in the 1970s. These manuscripts recorded the bodies of elephants postmortem by professionals in the field the day of the culling, including measurements of every part of the elephant along with its sex, approximate age, and other defining characteristics, creating a unique and large dataset. Unlike printed materials, which can easily be digitized and coded for optical character recognition, these more than 3,000 records, because they were handwritten, were virtually unusable to researchers and students.

The African studies librarian consulted with the grants manager about how to design a project to transcribe all of the data sheets for input into a searchable database. He learned that a previously awarded Libraries SOP project had successfully supported the completion of a database of transcribed information related to reference requests made by Health Science Center medical faculty to librarians working in the Health Science Center Library (HSCL). These requests had been recorded by hand on more than 100 individual slips of paper—one per request. The REDCap database management system was

FIGURE 2.12
Data sheet from the Ian Parker Collection of East African Wildlife Conservation: Elephant Data Sheets

Source: https://ufdc.ufl.edu/AA00013409/00001/25

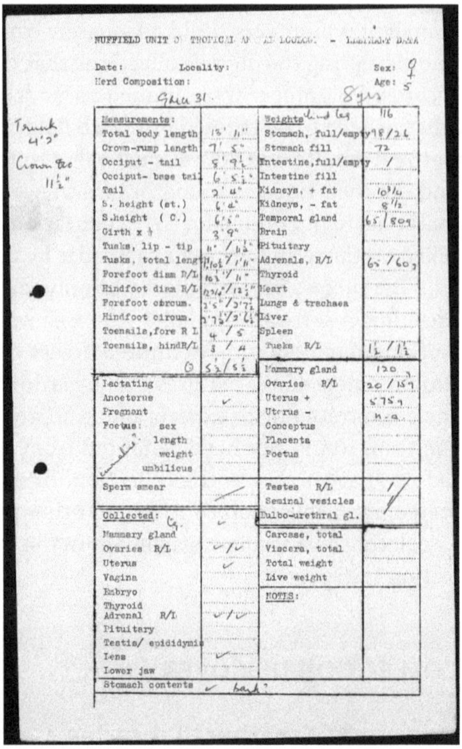
NUFFIELD UNIT OF TROPICAL ANIMAL ECOLOGY - ELEPHANT DATA

Date: Locality: Sex: ♀
Herd Composition: Age: 5

Trunk 4'2"
Crown tec 11½"

Measurements:		Weights	
Total body length	13' 11"	Stomach, full/empty	98/26
Crown-rump length	7' 5"	Stomach fill	72
Occiput - tail	8' 9½"	Intestine, full/empty	/
Occiput- base tail	6' 5½"	Intestine fill	
Tail	2' 4"	Kidneys, + fat	10¾
S. height (st.)	6' 4"	Kidneys, - fat	8½
S.height (C.)	6' 5"	Temporal gland	65/80g
Girth x ½	3' 9"	Brain	
Tusks, lip - tip	11" / 11½"	Pituitary	
Tusks, total length		Adrenals, R/L	65/60g
Forefoot diam R/L		Thyroid	
Hindfoot diam R/L		Heart	
Forefoot circum.		Lungs & trachaea	
Hindfoot circum.		Liver	
Toenails, fore R L	4 / 5	Spleen	
Toenails, hindR/L	3 / 4	Tusks R/L	1½ / 1½
	5½/5½	Mammary gland	120
Lactating		Ovaries R/L	20/15g
Anoeterus	✓	Uterus +	575g
Pregnant		Uterus -	n.a.
Foetus: sex		Conceptus	
length		Placenta	
weight		Foetus	
umbilicus			
Sperm smear		Testes R/L	
		Seminal vesicles	
Collected:	✓	Bulbo-urethral gl.	
Mammary gland		Carcase, total	
Ovaries R/L	✓/✓	Viscera, total	
Uterus	✓	Total weight	
Vagina		Live weight	
Embryo		NOTES:	
Thyroid			
Adrenal R/L	✓/✓		
Pituitary			
Testis/ epididymis			
Lens	✓		
Lower jaw			
Stomach contents	✓		

previously used to track clinical trials and was reengineered to track librarian-mediated literature searches.

With this methodology in hand, the African studies curator contacted one of the HSCL librarians who had worked on the Librarian-Mediated Literature Searches project, serving as the liaison librarian for veterinary medicine. The two formed a team to plan the elephant database project using REDCap to contain the transcribed data handwritten on the thousands of data sheets. The team determined that it would require a cadre of student employees to be trained to transcribe these difficult-to-read records for input into the REDCap system.

Proposal Summary

The Parker Elephant Data Sheets ($5,000 cash request; $5,247 cost share contribution)

The project team will (1) provide convenient open access to a unique, historic, and scientifically significant dataset; and (2) demonstrate and prepare the Libraries for future projects that preserve and curate data collections for open access. Data from a recently digitized collection of field data sheets collected in the 1960s will be transcribed into machine-readable formats (spreadsheet, comma-delimited file, etc.) to facilitate easy online discoverability, examination, and analysis by students, researchers and practitioners, for example in conservation, biology, zoos, and veterinary medicine. The team will employ the free, browser-based REDCap (Research Electronic Data Capture) application to facilitate the data entry of these manuscript records and to control quality. The use of REDCap for this project builds on a previous SOP awarded to the HSCL team, *Analyzing Librarian-Mediated Literature Searches in the Health Sciences*. These data sheets are part of the Ian Parker Collection of East African Wildlife Conservation. The Elephant Data Sheets (3,175) are unique in several ways: the large number of individuals is unlikely to be reproduced; the sampling represents natural (albeit environmentally stressed) family groups rather than trophies or weak individuals; and until now the records have been unavailable to the public. The data sheet images were digitized with funds from the Center for African Studies' Title VI National Resource Center grant. Project team includes the African Studies curator (PI) and HSCL liaison librarian (Co-PI) (one year: 2013 to 2014).[29]

Epilogue

The proposal was fully funded. The project team created appropriate database fields and then tested their training process on some of the Libraries' employees. After fine-tuning their training methods, the African studies curator was able to recruit seven qualified students for the project. Ultimately all of the data sheets were digitized.[30] All of the data about each elephant was entered into the customized REDCap database, making them available to researchers for the first time.[31]

The completion of the project demonstrated the Libraries' commitment to making such rare and important donated collections available for public use, rather than leaving them as unprocessed backlogs for long stretches of time—which is often the case with donated materials. The Ian Parker Elephant Data Collection was combined with other related contributed collections to form

FIGURE 2.13
Photograph of Bob Campbell with orphaned gorillas Coco and Pucker and Dian Fossey's dog Cindy, Rwanda, Central Africa

Photo by Bob Campbell, https://ufdc.ufl.edu/ AA00055915/00001/1x a cluster of research materials on African wildlife conservation. The public exposure of the contents of this collection inspired other donors to contribute their collections to the Libraries, including Alistair Graham's survey data and maps documenting African crocodile populations. Another important gift, the photographic slides and diaries produced by the *National Geographic* photographer Bob Campbell, who documented Dian Fossey's gorilla research work in Mount Karisoke, Rwanda, was donated by Campbell's wife.

Some of these images were included in an issue of *National Geographic* magazine published in 2017, and also in a three-part National Geographic documentary film series in honor of the fiftieth anniversary of Dian Fossey's work, *Dian Fossey: Secrets in the Mist*. National Geographic Kids books editors are working on a biography of Fossey to be part of a set of books written for eight- to twelve-year-olds, completing a three-part series titled *The Trimates* that would include Jane Goodall and Birute Galdikas.

PLANNING

George A. Smathers Libraries / Strategic Opportunities Program

Prologue

The Baldwin Library of Historical Children's Literature contains more than 130,000 books and serials published in Great Britain and the United States from the mid-seventeenth century to the present. Its holdings of more than 800 early American imprints is the second-largest such collection in the United States.[32] In 2012, the new Baldwin Library curator arrived at UF with a couple of years of archival experience in children's literature at Wayne State University, although her focus then had been liaison to social sciences disciplines. It was her priority to get to know colleagues at UF who were interested in using the Baldwin Library collection in their own research and to promote the collection for use by students. Along with the digital scholarship librarian, the two asked the question: How do we increase collaboration to combine forces with the English Department and acquire expert advice to make collection-related planning decisions? During a meeting with two faculty members from that department, an idea emerged to create an advisory board composed of both UF and non-UF participants. While reviewing the idea, the curator discovered that a growing research trend to assist in collection development decision-making is to convene content experts to serve on advisory boards. This allows curators and librarians to seek collection development advice on a regular basis. Some of the duo's questions that could benefit from external guidance included: What books or types of books should be the priorities for future purchases related to meeting instructional needs? What grant opportunities should be investigated and pursued? The dean of the Libraries, however, advised against creating a formal advisory board because this might encourage the perception that library decisions would be made by an external group rather than by library staff. With advice from the grants manager, the duo proceeded to develop a grant proposal to fund planning activities related to the Baldwin Library to determine the feasibility of creating an Advisory Council.

Proposal Summary

Forging a Collaborative Structure for Sustaining Scholarly Access to the Baldwin Library of Historical Children's Literature ($4,983 cash request; $5,502 cost share contribution)

This project seeks to leverage relationships in the Department of English (partner), other humanities departments, and with nationally recognized scholars in (1) establishing a scholars council with local and national participation, and the Libraries' endorsement; (2) increasing multidisciplinary research by local, national, and international scholars and graduate students; (3) preparing for submission to external federal and private funding agencies, including planning for a collaborative digital collection of Early American and British Juvenile Literature and Religious Tracts; (4) creating protocols and testing a distributed digitization process based on the successful dLOC model; (5) assisting and informing the curator of the Baldwin Library of scholarly trends in children's literature and related fields for program development, digitization priorities, and other related activities; and (6) formalizing guidelines for paid and volunteer positions that provide support to enhance scholarly access. Project team includes the curator of the Baldwin Library of Historical Children's Literature (PI), with the digital scholarship librarian, education librarian, science and agriculture librarian, and metadata librarian (one year: 2013 to 2014).[33]

Epilogue

The proposal was fully awarded. The team convened to develop a detailed agenda, determine meeting dates, and draw up a list of participants to invite. Most of the awarded funds were budgeted for travel and honoraria to defray the costs for visiting experts. Participants included representatives from the University of North Carolina–Charlotte, University of Southern Mississippi, University of South Carolina, University of North Texas, and the College of Brockport–SUNY. The planning meeting was completed in 2014 and set forth the initial members of an Advisory Council, with a two-year option to renew and then rotate off. Subsequent meetings were convened with funding from the collection's endowment interest. The council, for instance, provided expertise on the refinement of a National Endowment for the Humanities grant proposal, and some members agreed to contribute

FIGURE 2.14
Online student exhibit created for the undergraduate course "Cradle and Grave: Childhood and Death in the Baldwin Archives."

Exhibit creators: Kalene Jones, Josie Urbina, Daniel Bryant, https://cradleandgrave.omeka.net/exhibits/show/grieving -and-child-s-literatur/animals-and-death

to metadata development services for this proposed digitization project, should it be awarded. Advisory Council members continue to offer guidance and ideas for opening the Baldwin Library to new partnerships, and new users for creative research purposes.

In another instance, Advisory Council members generated the idea for creating a new course for UF undergraduates to perform research using the Baldwin Library's content. After meeting with one of UF's English professors who serves on the Advisory Council, the curator and the professor began exploring the possibility of proposing a new course in the English Department. The English professor was working with an intern to integrate a special collection into the course. They learned that UF courses focused on children's literature were only available for graduate students, and so they set out to create a proposal to fund the planning and design of curriculum for a children's literature course for undergraduate students to be taught by a graduate student working in children's literature. It turned out that there is a history of graduate students in the English Department creating and teaching general education courses designed for undergraduate students. A subsequent Strategic Opportunities grant proposal, *Expanding Undergraduate Research in the Baldwin: Academic and Library Faculty Collaboration in Course Development,* was awarded, and the new course, "Cradle and Grave: Childhood and Death in the Baldwin Archives," was developed collaboratively and successfully taught by a doctoral student from the English Department to twenty-five under-graduate students.[34]

OUTREACH/COLLECTION DEVELOPMENT

George A. Smathers Libraries / Strategic Opportunities Program

Prologue

This unusual partnership project began at a performance of *Composing a Heart*, an original performance piece for clarinet, piano, spoken word, and multi-media created by the grants manager and composer/pianist Craig Ames in 1996. In 2012, the grants manager (a classically trained clarinetist) arranged to perform the piece without piano at the Civic Media Center in downtown Gainesville, in partnership with the curator of the UF Price Library of Judaica. Their goal was to increase awareness of the Price Library's holdings and programs, especially because of the curator's new arrival from Cambridge, England. The performance was preceded by the curator's talk about the Price Library. During the performance, the new curator observed how the audience was moved after hearing the immigrant stories of the grants manager's Jewish parents' emigration to the United States from Poland and Argentina. A few months later, the curator was contacted by an audience member who described its emotional impact on her. The performance sparked a recollection of family items that she wanted to donate to the Price Library.

Thinking along these lines, the grants manager and the curator wondered whether using *Composing a Heart* as a model for another live dramatic performance, depicting the personal stories of immigrant journeys held in the Price Library, could spark other audience-member contributions of primary materials to the library's collection. Through her connections in UF School of Music, the grants manager was referred to the School of Theatre and the director of the Center for the Arts and Public Policy, who was intrigued about the opportunity and spent time looking through selected diaries in the Price Library's collection for appropriate material on which to base a new play. Although the director had produced many original works, he was unaware of the variety of primary materials held in the collection. After discovering this treasure trove of first-person historical accounts, he agreed to produce a new theater work with student actors based on a few personal diaries. Lastly, the team invited the assistant director of the Center for the Humanities and the Public Sphere to join the project as the qualitative evaluator, and she accepted. Her background in theater and cultural sociology sparked her interest in participating.

Project Summary

A Performing Arts Approach to Collection Development ($3,769 cash request; $1,137 cost share contribution)

The project team will facilitate an innovative, collaborative research project to develop and test the efficacy of an alternative form of collection development using the performing arts, in partnership with the Center for the Arts and Public Policy (CAPP) and the Center for the Humanities and the Public Sphere (CHPS). The project will generate three performances linked to and based on materials in the Isser and Rae Price Library of Judaica. The performances will be held at three separate venues (UF McGuire Pavilion studio, UF Digital Worlds Institute, and the Jewish Community Alliance theater, Jacksonville). The project will test the hypothesis that transformative performances linked to objects in a collection will create a durable, emotional connection to the objects and through them to the collection. It will attempt to prove that a marketed performing arts program created by leveraging existing material and personnel expertise and aimed at targeted audiences creates outreach efficiency. Project team includes the curator of the Price Library (PI) with grants manager, director of communications, plus the theater director and the associate director of the CHPS (one year: 2012 to 2013).[35]

Epilogue

The project was fully funded. In addition to two performances of *Composing a Heart*, two immigrant stories from the Price Library's collection were selected by the theater director and curator for creating a new theater production:

Composing A Heart and other immigrant stories
...collecting and studying the fragments of a life

Rebecca Jefferson, curator, Price Library of Judaica
Bess de Farber, clarinetist and storyteller
Craig Ames, composer and pianist

October 6, 2013 3:00 p.m.

Jewish Community Alliance Theater
8505 San Jose Blvd.
Jacksonville, Florida

FIGURE 2.15
Postcard promoting a performance featuring archival materials from the Isser and Rae Price Library of Judaica
Design by Barbara Hood, https://ufdc.ufl.edu/IR00011033/00001

those of Leah Stupniker, a fourteen-year-old girl whose family sailed from Palestine to Ellis Island and who died of tuberculosis just days before reaching the United States;[36] and Emanuel Merdinger, a professor of chemistry at UF, who survived Nazi persecution in Romania by making beer for German troops.[37] The stories were combined to produce one theatrical piece.

The production, *A Handful of Leaves,* premiered at the UF Digital Worlds Institute in 2013. Follow-up interviews with audience members and student actors noted the many positive and personal benefits the performances produced. Beyond exposing the Price Library to over 300 new potential supporters, this collaborative artistic project resulted in donations to the University of Florida and presentations at the Qualitative Report Conference, the Imagining America Conference, and the Arts in Society International Conference in Budapest. The theater director subsequently produced another premiere, *Gator Tales,* a theatrical presentation based on first-person stories held in the Samuel Proctor Oral History Program collections at UF.[38] These stories recount the experiences of UF minority alumni during the Civil Rights movement of the 1960s—presenting hidden accounts and voices of dramatic events that occurred in Gainesville, Florida. The world premiere of *Gator Tales* was presented at the 2015 Fringe Festival in Edinburgh, Scotland.

Elements of the *Performing Arts Approach to Collection Development* project were subsequently included in an NEH Challenge Grant application, titled *Repositioning Florida's Judaica Library: Increasing Access to Humanities Resources from Florida, Latin America, and the Caribbean Communities* (see chapter 5). The team modified the *Composing a Heart* performance content to include various immigrant stories from the Price Library collection narrated by the collection's curator, along with photographs and maps depicting each immigrant's story. The resulting production of *Composing a Heart and Other Jewish Immigrant Stories* continues to provide a means for exposing and promoting the Price Library's holdings to potential donor audiences and motivating new contributions to the Library.

DIGITAL HUMANITIES

George A. Smathers Libraries / Strategic Opportunities Program

Prologue

In 2011, the Romance languages librarian, whose second language is French, became interested in exploring the possibilities of an upcoming commemoration of the 450th anniversary of the French presence in Florida through a proposed partnership with the French consul general's office in Miami under the auspices of the France Florida Foundation for the Arts and the VIVA Florida campaign, which promotes Florida's history and culture. The librarian attended meetings with these players, who were organizing commemorative events that had inspired his participation. He was aware of a set of rare engravings created by Theodor de Bry from original sketches by Jacques Le Moyne de Morgues, who was the official artist sent to visually chronicle France's effort to colonize Florida. In the 1560s this expedition, led by Jean Ribault, sailed from France to colonize Florida at a site near present-day Jacksonville. The librarian's idea was to animate the engraved prints digitally as a way of telling the story of Florida's first colonists through a short documentary film.

Although his idea had merit, the Romance languages librarian lacked a plan to create the film. He had spoken to a colleague, the literary collections archivist, who is fluent in French and was interested in supporting the project. Through this contact, the grants manager encouraged the librarian to contact the director of the UF Digital Worlds Institute, with whom she had worked on a Libraries partnership proposal to create a digital game to teach students about plagiarism. (See chapter 5.) The director accepted the invitation and provided an estimated budget to produce the animated documentary film. Other suggested resources included contacting the librarians specializing in the disciplines of psychology and history because of their notable skills in graphic design and script-writing. Both joined the team.

The last piece of the puzzle was to secure a narrator for the film. After discussions with others working in Special Collections, it was decided that a longtime Florida historian and UF emeritus professor would be the best candidate because of his outstanding speaking voice and his expertise in Florida's colonial history. He agreed to join the team, if funding could be secured.

Before submitting the proposal, the Romance languages librarian secured commitments from the UF France-Florida Research Institute to contribute $2,000 (to cover additional costs beyond those estimated by the Digital Worlds Institute related to narration, and project team travel to research relevant historical materials held at other Florida archives). One final decision needed to be made. The Romance languages librarian could not assume the leadership role for the project due to other grant project commitments he was leading at the time. Fortunately, the history librarian agreed to lead the project activities and manage the budget if the project was awarded.

Proposal Summary

French in Florida Online Video ($5,000 cash request; $6,955 cost share contribution, plus $2,000 donor contribution)

The goal of this project is to create an online video that celebrates the 450th anniversary of the French landing in Florida. The French were the first Europeans to colonize Florida. The proposed video will include the 1591 engravings by Theodor de Bry made from the forty-two original 1564 drawings sketched by Jacques Le Moyne, the first visual artist to visit the New World.

FIGURE 2.16
Home page for information about *The French in Florida* documentary film project
https://guides.uflib.ufl.edu/frenchinflorida

The illustrations will be animated, and UF Emeritus Professor Michael Gannon will narrate the tale of the brief stay of the French in Florida. An online LibGuide to support the video will be created. Objectives of the project include (1) introducing the Florida community to the little-known history of the French in Florida, the UF Digital Collections' online primary documents, and other resources relating to the history of Florida—the video will be available on the Libraries website and YouTube, and it will provide teachers/librarians with an instructional tool—and (2) the video will be a contribution to the statewide celebration of the 450th anniversary of the French in Florida. The Smathers Libraries has the opportunity to participate in a cooperative endeavor with other state institutions: the French consulate in Miami, UF France-Florida Research Institute, Florida Department of State, Viva Florida 500 project, Museum of Florida History, and various state parks. Project team includes the history librarian (PI), Romance languages librarian (Co-PI), with manuscript archivist, and psychology, sociology, and criminology librarian (one year: 2012 to 2013).[39]

Epilogue

The project was fully awarded. The team set out to complete the documentary. An agreement drafted for the Digital Worlds Institute (DWI) outlined the specific work its staff would perform and the payment schedule. The DWI director, a noted musical composer of major commissions, agreed to compose a score for the film to be performed by students in the UF School of Music.

The team secured the rights to use the de Bry engravings from the owner of them, and received permission to digitize the collection. The history librarian wrote the script based on her research of primary documents containing accounts of the French colonists' relations with the native Timucuan tribal members. She reviewed the engravings for sequencing the story, researched the time period, and accessed the French in Florida story through primary articles and history books. The manuscript archivist searched for and identified relevant archival material that focused on the French arrival, their meeting with the Florida natives, and interesting parts related to the battle with the Spanish at Fort Caroline and the Spaniards' ultimate slaughter of the French at Matanzas (both near what is now St. Augustine), which ensured the Spanish domination of Florida for the next two centuries.

DWI recorded all of the narrators, who included a male voice with a French accent. In the middle of the project one of the digital artists left for another job, leaving the animation of one of the soldier's arms to appear a little unnatural. There was a dispute over the French arrival year: whether it was 1562 or 1564. The French consul general from Miami attended the film's premiere, insisting that the year should be 1564, and an edit was made to satisfy the French consul. A large reception at the Tallahassee Museum of Florida History, sponsored by the museum, hosted the short *French in Florida* animated documentary, with live music performed by a string quartet made up of UF students. DWI sponsored the reception at the University of Florida to screen the film for a campus audience. The team developed a website to share information about the French in Florida historical information and planned celebrations, a LibGuide to provide links to the project's bibliography, and a link to view the documentary film, among other resources.[40]

OUTREACH

George A. Smathers Libraries / Strategic Opportunities Program

Prologue

Upon arriving at the UF Education Library, the new chair asked each staff employee for any ideas they had for making the library better. In particular, he was interested in ways of reaching deeper into the College of Education (COE) faculty and students to generate more library involvement and excitement. A few of the Education Library's staff—two librarians and two paraprofessionals—had been in the process of developing an idea proposed by a COE undergrad in a competitive essay for a library scholarship coordinated by the Libraries' Human Resources Department. To increase students' knowledge of the Libraries' many services, available equipment, and other valuable resources, the essay suggested creating a student ambassador program whereby students would receive training to represent the Libraries' resources to their peers. The team convened members of COE student associations for conversations to determine how they would envision such a program. Their major recommendation was that those chosen to participate as ambassadors should receive a $500 stipend. This would contribute to incentivizing recruitment and requiring participant accountability.

The team, led by the new chair, determined that securing Strategic Opportunities Program (SOP) funding would be the best option for covering the costs related to initiating a small pilot student ambassador program at the Education Library. One of the questions on the SOP application requires applicants to identify whether or not the project idea has been executed elsewhere, as a means of determining the degree of innovativeness of the idea. After a literature review, which searched for student ambassadors and student liaisons, the team discovered a few examples that could serve as possible models. At the University of Connecticut, student ambassadors had been hired by Elsevier to promote the use of academic databases, and the publisher provided them with training, marketing materials, and stipends. At Eastern Washington University, an undergrad had served as the official liaison for the library administrators and the student body. At Missouri University, student volunteer ambassadors had been recruited, through an online application, to serve for five to ten hours per month. Each of these examples suggested the various roles played by the ambassadors and liaison, and this ultimately led to the Education Library's team establishing a hybrid ambassador/liaison role—an innovation resulting from the team's investigation.

The team agreed that student "ambassador-liaisons" could be effective at communicating with their peers about the Education Library's services that they felt were most important and were enthusiastic about sharing. Beyond serving as conduits of information, the team wanted to give the student ambassadors they recruited the added opportunity to include this type of meaningful service work in their resumes. During their proposal planning, the team determined that students applying to become ambassadors would be required to submit letters of recommendation from faculty members, and if selected, would receive $500 stipends for their service.

Project Summary

Education Library Student Ambassador Program ($3,370 cash request; $2,482 cost share contribution)

The Education Library staff are developing a program to train College of Education (COE) students to act as ambassadors-liaisons between the various student organizations and the Education Library. After a short training period, they will lead/participate in outreach at student events in classes, at library-sponsored events, and through outreach campaigns. The ambassadors

Graduate student in School Psychology

Being a frequent library user who would often refer her classmates to library resources, Kimberly saw this as an opportunity to learn and share more

FIGURE 2.17
Slide from presentation: "Reaching Students: Developing a Library Ambassador Program," 2013 Annual Conference of the Florida Library Association, Orlando, Florida, May 2, 2013

Source: https://ufdc.ufl.edu/IR00011033/00001, Slide by Tiffany Baglier and April Hines

will suggest material purchases, present with librarians at campus events, and evaluate new programs for the library. Each ambassador (five total, both graduate and undergraduate) will serve for one year (non-recurring) and will be awarded a $500 stipend, at program conclusion, for their service. Students will have to apply and interview for the positions. Project team includes the Education Library chair (PI), daytime circulation supervisor (Co-PI), with two education librarians, and the spring 2012 student essay winner (one year: 2012 to 2013).[41]

Epilogue

The proposal was fully awarded. The team created an online application form with guidelines for eligibility. The preferred qualifications included public speaking experience and participation in student organizations. The team searched for self-starters who would require less oversight. Nine applicants were interviewed. The five selected ambassadors represented a wide variety of COE academic disciplines, including those studying educational technology, psychology, and bilingual education. Although the team succeeded in recruiting self-starters, several of these were already heavily involved in other activities that competed with their Library ambassadorships. Regardless, assignment logs, regular student-led meetings, and outreach activities to the COE student body all contributed to instilling accountability and increasing the Library's dissemination of student resources information. Each ambassador planned their own contributions to make meaningful connections between the campus Libraries' resources and COE students.

In retrospect, the team noticed indicators that participating students did gain a deeper knowledge of the Libraries' services in general and became more aware of themselves as information users. The ambassador program led to ideas about improvements that could be made in the Education Library (e.g., a furniture rearrangement to make more study space available).

During the grant period, the Education Library experienced several personnel changes, and the program could not be sustained beyond its end date. But the project's methodologies and results live on in a chapter coauthored by three team members, "Getting on the Inside: Developing a Discipline-Based

Student Ambassador Program" (pp. 147–64), in the book *Students Lead the Library: The Importance of Student Contributions to the Academic Library* (2017). A conference presentation, "Reaching Students: Developing a Library Ambassador Program," was shared at the 2013 Annual Conference of the Florida Library Association.[42]

RESEARCH

American Library Association / Carroll Preston Baber Research Grant

Prologue

For a couple years prior to 2010, the chair of the Cataloging and Metadata Department had observed changes in the Libraries' workplace environment while serving on several employment search committees. She learned that an MLS or other equivalent degree was not necessarily a required qualification, and that advanced degrees in a related field were becoming more accepted. She noticed that hiring non-MLS-degreed library faculty was increasing, although those hired still comprised a relatively low percentage of the overall UF librarian population. At UF, librarians are considered non-teaching tenure-track faculty, with ranks identified as assistant, associate, and university librarian. Once hired, no distinctions are made regarding non-MLS faculty members who hold positions that were advertised as requiring an MLS or a related advanced degree. The Libraries' personnel fully embraced these new hires regardless of their particular advanced degree.

A pervasive notion in the Libraries is that new hire searches for very specialized positions result in higher failure rates due to the difficulties of finding an MLS-degreed professional who also possess the other requisite knowledge in a discipline (e.g., Jewish Studies), a technical area (e.g., digital services), or an administrative function (e.g., grants management). The belief is that it would be easier to learn those aspects of librarianship that are typically included in an MLS degree through on-the-job experience, rather than having to learn a new field of expertise as described in the previous examples.

However, during interactions with non-MLS librarians, the department chair of Cataloging and Metadata considered that a more in-depth orientation to the field of librarianship, beyond the typical library orientation provided to all new employees, would accelerate the assimilation of new non-MLS employees into the Libraries. Because of the evolving demands placed on her own department, which at the time included supervising a cadre of librarians and paraprofessionals, the department chair was motivated to investigate national trends in hiring non-MLS employees, and to discover the unidentified and unaddressed needs of onboarding non-MLS librarians. For example, hiring an MLS graduate who is well-versed in programming can lead to quicker new staff onboarding for filling an open metadata position. But requiring the MLS degree can also produce a failed search, leaving an open position vacant for an extended period of time. Thus, the option for encouraging non-MLS applicants appeared to be the best course of action. This hypothesis is what the department chair planned to investigate through her proposed research project.

With mentorship from the grants manager, the two developed the narrative for the research project idea and timeline, and created the budget. The project needed human resource and research expertise to assist with survey design and statistical analysis. The Libraries' assistant dean of administrative services and faculty affairs had worked successfully with the department chair on various committees and Cataloging Department business, and possessed the skills and knowledge that the project required. He served as a sounding board who actively supported the project, and he agreed to provide consultation throughout the research project if the project were to be awarded.

Project Summary

Shifting Patterns: Examining the Impact of Hiring Non-MLS Librarians ($3,000 cash request; $3,080 cost share contribution)

This project plans to develop an understanding of the dynamics involved in hiring practices and to identify essential elements for initiating non-MLS degreed librarians into the librarian profession. The data gathered will be used to create a framework for a model orientation program that libraries can adapt to their local environment. Ensuring that non-MLS degreed librarians have a meaningful introduction to the theoretical and practical foundations of the field will greatly enhance their ability to collaborate and contribute to the library enterprise. Project team includes the chair of cataloging and metadata (PI), with support from the assistant dean of administrative services and faculty affairs (one year: 2010 to 2011).[43]

Epilogue

The project received full funding. In summer 2010 a former Libraries staff member of the Acquisitions Department, who was then a graduate student in the School of Library and Information Science at the University of South Florida, was hired to work with the department chair on executing the project. This partnership was destined to work well because the two had previously collaborated on library tasks and committees, and the graduate student was highly motivated and intellectually engaged in the project because of his commitment to the field. He gathered contact information for survey distribution and examined library job ads.

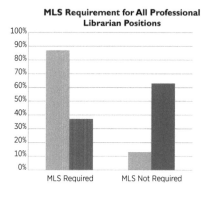
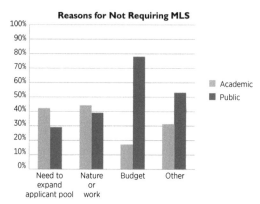

FIGURE 2.18
Slides from presentation: "Hiring Non-MLS Librarians, Trends and Training Implications,"
sponsored by the LLAMA Human Resources Section, ALA 2011 Annual Conference
Source: Slides by Betsy Simpson, https://ufdc.ufl.edu/IR00000459/00001/24j, 21, 24

The team collected 1,370 survey responses contributed by academic
library directors and human resource officers, and public library directors. The
findings were presented during a two-hour presentation, "Hiring Non-MLS
Librarians: Trends and Training Implications," sponsored by the Library Leadership & Management Association's Human Resources Section at the ALA's
2011 Annual Conference. The presentation included individual reflections
on the topic from an academic library human resources director, a non-MLS-
degreed librarian, and a public library director.[44] A journal article, "Hiring
Non-MLS Librarians: Trends and Training Implications," published in *Library
Leadership & Management* 28, no. 1 (2013), outlines the research findings and
data gathered.[45]

The challenges experienced by the department chair during the project
grant period were less about the research itself than about balancing the
workload, compounded by other professional and personal obligations. The
plan for the final phase of the project was to develop a framework for an orientation program that was geared toward serving non-MLS librarians and which
would be customizable at the local level. This phase was postponed due to
many other pressing matters—staff shortages and reductions, a department
move to a new floor, and other department and library work priorities. Then a
family health emergency led to the department chair's early retirement, with
the prospect that in some small measure, the output from the research project
had nevertheless contributed to a national dialogue on the topic.

CHAPTER 2 TAKEAWAYS

- *A very small grant funded project can produce unexpectedly broad impacts locally, nationally, and internationally.* Many of the projects described in this chapter's stories illustrate this point. For instance, the project to expand an oral history project capturing the stories about the country's first public bilingual educational program inspired one of the project team members to author and seek publishing (in Great Britain) for a book exposing this hidden history the first time. It happens that many bilingual educators around the world are aware of the Coral Way Elementary School "experiment" in the early 1960s, but not its history. Likewise, transcribing and digitizing the datasheets of the Parker Elephant Collection at UF prompted the donation of a National Geographic photographer's collection chronicling Dian Fossey's work mountain gorillas. And *A Performing Arts Approach* inspired one of the project team members to write and produce a play, *Gator Tales*, using a collection of UF's oral histories that eventually was performed in Edinburgh, Scotland.
- *One awarded application by a particular sponsor's program can easily inspire a subsequent proposal to the same program because a successful model is available and how-to expertise is accessible.* The Libraries were fortunate to receive two awards from the Carnegie-Whitney Program sponsored by ALA to create online bibliographies of historical children's books (*Women Authored Science Books for Children 1790–1890*), and out-of-sight books and resources about the popular topic of makerspaces (*Building Makers*).
- *Planning grant projects are often overlooked as viable first steps to create subsequent grant awarded projects.* Many benefits were derived by the project team who sought funding to create a scholars council to offer advice on future planning strategies for promoting and developing the Baldwin Library of Historical Children's Books. The same is true when considering the subsequent implementation grant (*Decolonizing Digital Childhoods*) awarded to the University of Cambridge partnership as a result of completing a successful planning grant project (*Digital Collections in Children's Literature*) with U.S. partners. In a rare twist of fate, the project team who applied for an IMLS planning grant (see the grant *Researching Students' Information Choices* in chapter 5) for researching student choices of various Google results was invited to submit an implementation grant proposal instead because its planning grant application was sufficiently developed to offer a plan for executing the entire project.

- *New grantseeking ideas can be generated through a variety of means:*
  - Attending an intensive workshop with participants from around the country can inspire a method and impetus for reconceiving the same workshop at a local level (*Digital Collaborations on Black History in Florida*).
  - Performing a function within an organization that requires repetitive content (tours for new employees), as presented in the *Advancing Accessibility* project, can inspire the staff member with this responsibility to search the internet for alternatives (3D academic library tours).
  - A request for collection information (Which books include maps of Cuba?) from the dean or director of a library can pose an insurmountable dilemma for a project team when the answer is buried in hundreds of books lacking sufficient metadata. Searching for other academic library personnel who have had the same dilemma can reveal an awarded grant application (NEH) that can be a model for a much smaller grant project (*Buried Treasure*).
  - Newly acquired historical collections of primary materials that are unusually challenging to access (audiotape recordings, stereographs, or elephant data sheets) can puzzle library staff who seek to make this valuable information accessible. The answers to the puzzles can emerge as applicants brainstorm solutions that can be achieved at reasonable costs through grantseeking (*Panama Canal Museum Collection*, *The Legacy of Stetson Kennedy*, and *The Parker Elephant Data Sheets*).

NOTES

1. University of Florida, Center for the Humanities and the Public Sphere, https://humanities.ufl.edu.
2. Megan Daly, Vasudha Narayanan, and Jonathan Edelmann, "Library Enhancement Grant for Hindu Studies," George A. Smathers Libraries, University of Florida Digital Collections, https://ufdc.ufl.edu/IR00011009/00001.
3. Ali Altaf Mian and Megan Daly, "Collection Enhancement in Islamic Studies," George A. Smathers Libraries, University of Florida Digital Collections, https://ufdc.ufl.edu/IR00011030/00001.

4. Suzan Alteri, Laurie Taylor, and Bess de Farber, "Digital Collections in Children's Literature: Distance Reading, Scholarship, Community," George A. Smathers Libraries, University of Florida Digital Collections, http://ufdc.ufl.edu/IR00010702/00001.

5. Digi ChildLit, "Digital Children's Literature" (playlist), YouTube, www.youtube.com/channel/UCiSw8eS04ifmtw1nOxEcXmQ.

6. AFRO Publishing Without Walls, https://pww.afro.illinois.edu/AFRO_PWW-incubation.html.

7. Florida African American Heritage Preservation Network, http://faahpn.com.

8. Stephanie Birch, Bess de Farber, Laurie Taylor, et al., "Digital Publishing on Black Life and History Collaborative Meeting," George A. Smathers Libraries, University of Florida Digital Collections, https://ufdc.ufl.edu/IR00010684/00001.

9. Stephanie Birch, "Digital Collaborations on Black History in Florida" (program), George A. Smathers Libraries, University of Florida Digital Collections, https://ufdc.ufl.edu/IR00010952/00001.

10. Brittany Kester, Maria Coady, Bess de Farber, et al., "The Coral Way Bilingual Experiment Digital Collection (1961 to 1968)," George A. Smathers Libraries, University of Florida Digital Collections, https://ufdc.ufl.edu/IR00010685/00001.

11. Maria Coady, Bess de Farber, Brittany Kester, et al., "Revealing a Hidden History: The Coral Way Elementary School Bilingual Experiment (1962–1968)," George A. Smathers Libraries, University of Florida Digital Collections, https://ufdc.ufl.edu/IR00010782/00001.

12. Maria R. Coady, *The Coral Way Bilingual Program* (Bristol, UK: Multilingual Matters, 2019).

13. Brittany Kester, Margarita Vargas Betancourt, and Pia Molina, "Pioneering Bilingualism," George A. Smathers Libraries, 2019, http://exhibits.uflib.ufl.edu/coralway.

14. Sara Russell Gonzalez and Bess de Farber, "Building Makers: An Annotated Bibliography of Maker Resources for Libraries, Schools, and Museums," George A. Smathers Libraries, University of Florida Digital Collections, https://ufdc.ufl.edu/IR00010963/00001.

15. Sara Russell Gonzalez, "Makerspace Bibliography," https://makerbooks.domains.uflib.ufl.edu/.

16. Vassar College, "Vassar College 360 Tour," https://360tour.vassar.edu.

17. Danielle Sessions, Bess de Farber, Lisa Campbell, et al., "Advancing Accessibility: Smathers Libraries 360-Degree Virtual Tours," George A. Smathers Libraries, University of Florida Digital Collections, https://ufdc.ufl.edu/IR00010481/00001.

18. George A. Smathers Libraries, https://cms.uflib.ufl.edu/.

19. Hannah Norton, Mary Edwards, Ariel Pomputius, et al., "Creative Campaigns to Promote HIV/AIDS Awareness among UF Students," George A. Smathers Libraries, University of Florida Digital Collections, https://ufdc.ufl.edu/IR00009328/00001.

20. Lisa Klug, Ariel Pomputius, Kelena Kippel, et al., "Graphic Novel / Zine Contest – Creative Campaigns to Promote HIV/AIDS Awareness among UF Students," George A. Smathers Libraries, University of Florida Digital Collections, http://ufdc.ufl.edu/IR00010220/00001.
21. Digital Library of the Caribbean, "Celebrating Cuba!" www.dloc.com/cuba.
22. Carol McAuliffe, Paul Losch, Margarita Vargas-Betancourt, et al., "Buried Treasure: Hidden Collections of Cuba Maps," George A. Smathers Libraries, University of Florida Digital Collections, https://ufdc.ufl.edu/IR00009327/00001.
23. National Endowment for the Humanities, "Funded Project Query Form," https://securegrants.neh.gov/PublicQuery/main.aspx?f=1&gn=PW-50904-11.
24. Suzan Alteri, Alan Rauch, and Bess de Farber, "Women Authored Science Books for Children 1790–1890: An Annotated Bibliography," George A. Smathers Libraries, University of Florida Digital Collections, https://ufdc.ufl.edu/AA00027007/00001.
25. George A. Smathers Libraries, "Guiding Science," cms.uflib.ufl.edu/guidingscience/bibliography.
26. James Cusick, "The Legacy of Stetson Kennedy: A Digital Archive for Social Justice," George A. Smathers Libraries, University of Florida Digital Collections, https://ufdc.ufl.edu/AA00027401/00001.
27. Jessica Belcoure and Rebecca Fitzsimmons, "Panama Canal Museum Collection: Digitization Metadata Capture, Outreach and Educational Tool Creation for a Set of Panama and Canal-Focused Stereographs," George A. Smathers Libraries, University of Florida Digital Collections, https://ufdc.ufl.edu/IR00003179/00001.
28. George A. Smathers Libraries, University of Florida Digital Collections, "Panama Canal Stereographs," https://ufdc.ufl.edu/ps.
29. Dan Reboussin and Hannah Norton, "The Parker Elephant Data Sheets," George A. Smathers Libraries, University of Florida Digital Collections, https://ufdc.ufl.edu/IR00003175/00001.
30. Ian S. C. Parker, "Ian Parker Collection of East African Wildlife Conservation: Elephant Data Sheets," George A. Smathers Libraries, University of Florida Digital Collections, https://ufdc.ufl.edu/AA00013409/00007.
31. Dan Reboussin and Hannah Norton, "The Ian Parker East African Elephant Data Sheets: A Handbook for the Transcribed Biological Data Set," George A. Smathers Libraries, University of Florida Digital Collections, https://ufdc.ufl.edu/IR00004209.
32. George A. Smathers Libraries, "Baldwin Library of Historical Children's Literature," https://cms.uflib.ufl.edu/baldwin/Index.
33. Suzan Alteri, Val Minson, Bess de Farber, et al., "Forging a Collaborative Structure for Sustaining Scholarly Access to the Baldwin Library of Historical Children's Literature," George A. Smathers Libraries, University of Florida Digital Collections, https://ufdc.ufl.edu/IR00003577/00001.

34. Suzan Alteri and Terry Harpold, "Expanding Undergraduate Research in the Baldwin: Academic and Library Faculty Collaboration in Course Development," George A. Smathers Libraries, University of Florida Digital Collections, https://ufdc.ufl.edu/AA00032965/00001.

35. Rebecca Jefferson and Bess de Farber, "A Performing Arts Approach to Collection Development," George A. Smathers Libraries, University of Florida Digital Collections, https://ufdc.ufl.edu/AA00013460/00001.

36. Leah Sputniker and (trans.) Rebecca Jefferson, *A Handful of Leaves*, George A. Smathers Libraries, University of Florida Digital Collections, https://ufdcimages.uflib.ufl.edu/IR/00/00/07/18/00001/A.Handful.of.Leaves.pdf.

37. George A. Smathers Libraries, "A Guide to the Emanuel Merdinger Papers," April 2016, http://www.library.ufl.edu/spec/manuscript/guides/merdinger.htm.

38. Brittany Valencic, "Gator Tales Examines Past Struggles of UF Students," *Gainesville Sun* (Gainesville, FL), February 12, 2015, https://www.gainesville.com/article/LK/20150212/Entertainment/604152277/GS.

39. Shelley Arlen, Matthew Loving, Bess de Farber, et al., "French in Florida Online Video," George A. Smathers Libraries, University of Florida Digital Collections, https://ufdc.ufl.edu/IR00001114/00001.

40. Cindy Craig, "The French in Florida 1562–1566," George A. Smathers Libraries, University of Florida, https://guides.uflib.ufl.edu/frenchinflorida.

41. Ben Walker, April Hines, Tiffany Baglier, et al., "Education Library Student Ambassador Program," George A. Smathers Libraries, University of Florida Digital Collections, https://ufdc.ufl.edu/IR00001115/00001.

42. Tiffany Baglier, April Hines, Marilyn Ochoa, et al., "Reaching Students: Developing a Library Ambassador Program," presentation at the Florida Library Association 2013 Annual Conference, Orlando, FL, May 2, 2013, https://prezi.com/flxhxrpslp6h/reaching-students-developing-a-library-student-ambassador-program/.

43. Betsy Simpson, Brian W. Keith, and Bess de Farber, "Shifting Patterns: Examining the Impact of Hiring Non-MLS Librarians," George A. Smathers Libraries, University of Florida Digital Collections, https://ufdc.ufl.edu/UF00095937/00001.

44. Betsy Simpson, Robin Wood, and Laura Blessing, "Hiring Non-MLS Librarians: Trends and Training Implications," presentation at the American Library Association 2011 Annual Conference, New Orleans, LA, June 23–28, 2011, George A. Smathers Libraries, University of Florida Digital Collections, http://ufdc.ufl.edu/IR00000459.

45. Betsy Simpson. "Hiring Non-MLS Librarians: Trends and Training Implications," *Library Leadership & Management* 28, no. 1 (2013), https://journals.tdl.org/llm/index.php/llm/article/viewFile/7019/6260.

3
Grant Partnership Proposals from $5,001 to $25,000

This chapter features fifteen stories about funded grant projects with budgets ranging from $5,431 to $23,980 awarded to the George A. Smathers Libraries and its partners from 2011 through 2020. The types of projects described in this chapter include technology, research, course development, public programming, preservation, digitization, research and development, digital humanities collaboration, professional development training, and outreach. The stories are organized in reverse chronological order, from those most recently submitted to those submitted earlier.

Included in this chapter are awarded proposals funded by the following sponsors and respective programs:

- Association of Research Libraries
- Center for Research Libraries / Latin American Materials Project
- Center for Research Libraries / Latin Americanist Research Resources Project
- Center for Research Libraries / Project Ceres
- Northeast Florida Library Information Network / Innovation Project

- Procter & Gamble / U.S. Higher Education Grant Program
- University of Florida, Academic Technology / Technology Fee
- University of Florida, Center for the Humanities and the Public Sphere / Library Enhancement Program in the Humanities
- University of Florida, Creative Campus Committee / Catalyst Fund
- University of Florida, George A. Smathers Libraries / Emerging Technologies

TECHNOLOGY

University of Florida / Technology Fee

Prologue

Since arriving at the Humanities and Social Sciences Library, the librarian for classics, philosophy, and religion had heard of the importance of pursuing Technology Fee grant funding. She was particularly inspired by her supervisor, who had been awarded a Technology Fee grant for a project to purchase and loan out GoPro cameras and other electronic tools to assist UF students and faculty with their field research needs. A brainstorming meeting was announced by the grants manager for those Libraries' personnel who were interested in generating new proposal ideas for Technology Fee funds. Because the librarian didn't have any ideas about what she might suggest during the brainstorming, the day prior to the meeting she searched for the top ten rated technologies used by university students.

One search result that appeared repeatedly was "smart pens." This sparked memories of all the times the classics librarian could have used a smart pen during her graduate and doctoral courses at UF as a student in the Classics Department. She recalled discarding all of her many handwritten notebooks because of the amount of labor she believed it would require to transcribe them for electronic preservation. The smart pen idea also aligned with her work as a co-convener for the Digital Humanities Working Group. One of her responsibilities was to experiment with new technology, specifically technology that creates efficiencies in the time-intensive discipline of the digital humanities.

Prior to the brainstorming meeting, the librarian gained a better understanding of the potential benefits yielded by offering students the ability to check out these pens. The next day during the brainstorming, she shared her idea to acquire smart pens for circulation on campus and was surprised by two other librarians who requested to join her project team to pursue Technology Fee funding (one from the Health Science Center Library and another from the Architecture and Fine Arts Library).

While exploring the opportunity to apply for these funds, the classics librarian learned that the campus Disability Resource Center (DRC) had purchased four smart pens to loan to students who required assistance with note-taking during their classes. She initiated conversations with staff members at the DRC who told her that they had applied for Technology Fee grant funds for purchasing smart pens in the past but had been declined. The DRC staff felt there was sufficient need on campus among those students they served by the DRC and others to justify a request to purchase 300 smart pens for circulation, ensuring that priority would be given to students with disabilities, and with an extended checkout period for those students. The DRC staff provided statistics related to the circulation of the four pens, the number of students who needed note-taking assistance in classrooms, and the total number of DRC students served annually. This provided evidence of need.

Beyond serving students with disabilities, the librarian sought to discover all of the various barriers that smart pens could overcome: capturing drawings during art class or architecture classes, avoiding having to type in Greek (which is incredibly difficult), notating hieroglyphics in an Egyptian history course, and recording chemistry formulas . . . there was no end to how many limitations could be overcome through the use of smart pens. As she planned the development of the proposed concept paper (the first-round preliminary submission) with her team members' input, the librarian eventually attracted partners from four of UF's libraries, in addition to the DRC, who expressed a desire to offer the lending of smart pens to their student and faculty patrons. After submitting the concept paper, the team received an invitation to submit a full proposal.

Proposal Summary

Facilitating Learning through Smart Pens ($71,940 cash request)

In partnership with the Disability Resource Center (DRC), the project team seeks to purchase 300 Livescribe pens, protective cases, paper, and ink to enhance note-taking capabilities for students, faculty, and staff. The proposers seek to offer Livescribe pens to aid in writing and preserving lecture and reading notes in classrooms, at home, and on the go. Students will be able to check these out from the circulation desks at Library West, the Marston Science Library, the Architecture and Fine Arts Library, the Education Library, and the Health Science Center Library. DRC students have been using Livescribe pens for assistance with note-taking for approximately two years. These pens can record audio and written notes to digital form and thus help students create more accurate and organized notes, potentially leading to better comprehension, retention of information, and higher performance in classes. Project team includes the classics librarian (PI), with director of DRC, assistant director of DRC, associate chair of the Humanities and Social Sciences Library, chemistry librarian, chair of the Architecture and Fine Arts Library, and bioinformatics librarian (one year: 2019 to 2020).[1]

Epilogue

After the full proposal was reviewed, the program director managing Technology Fee grants convened with the classics librarian and the grants manager to recommend that the team revise the proposal to focus on circulating fifty smart pens, rather than 300, and restricting the use of pens to DRC students. The review committee, which mostly consisted of students serving in student government, was only willing to support a reduced award amount of $11,990. Through e-mail communication, the librarian confirmed her team's support for accepting the reduced award with the accompanying restrictions limiting lending to DRC students, with distribution only occurring in the Humanities and Social Sciences Library. This alternative plan reduced much of the stress the librarian was feeling in anticipation of managing, maintaining, and circulating 300 smart pens. It also provided a manageable research study opportunity to monitor a smaller project for measuring impacts on student borrowers. The revised project thus has the potential to inform future Technology Fee grant projects.

RESEARCH

Northeast Florida Library Information Network / Innovation Project

Prologue

For many years, a team of librarians in the Marston Science Library dreamed of creating a sustainable 3D printing program, in which discarded printing projects and left-over filament could be recycled on-site. This program would include not just the recycling of waste generated by Science Library users, but also that of anyone on campus or in the community who wanted their own 3D printing waste to be recycled. In fall 2018, the makerspace supervising librarian and the engineering librarian who actively manages the 3D printing program attended a 3D-themed conference in Atlanta and participated in a presentation on how to create a sustainable 3D service. Rather than sharing solutions to the 3D waste recycling challenge, the presenter focused on how to calculate the costs associated with 3D production labs and ways to sustain these labs financially. Other participants, including professionals from museums, academic institutions such as Georgia Tech, makerspace staff, and material science researchers, asked questions about 3D waste recycling. But no one had any answers. This marked the moment that pointed the team in the direction of trying to solve the problem themselves. They only lacked time and money.

In January 2019, a call for proposals advertised by the Northeast Florida Library Information Network (NEFLIN) for innovation project applications

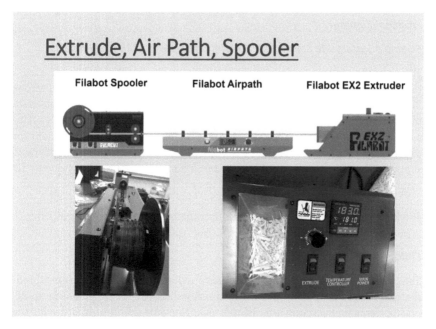

FIGURE 3.1
Slide showing the 3D printing filament recycling process, from a presentation at the 2019 Annual Meeting of the Northeast Florida Library Information Network
Image by Jean Bossart, https://ufdc.ufl.edu/IR00011033/00001

was distributed to Libraries staff. With some advice from the grants manager, the Marston Science Library team decided to submit a proposal to fund the creation of 3D recycling methods, and include NEFLIN as a potential partner (to receive any of the recycled filament resulting from the project for redistribution to smaller libraries that needed it). Because this team had been ahead of the curve, nationally—in terms of 3D printing adoption and being the first to loan out portable 3D printers to faculty and students—it wanted to continue its innovative trajectory with the creation of a recycling solution. The engineering librarian searched for web content shared on web forums or posted by hobbyists about ways to grind plastic. The 3D emerging technologies services manager found a series of YouTube videos called *Will It Blend?* that is followed by those interested in watching food processors in the act of blending unusual objects like electronics. The team hypothesized that by using a paper shredder that also shredded credit cards, or by using a blender to grind larger plastic into small pellets, the plastic pellets could be fed into an extruder for re-creating filament for spooling onto empty filament spools.

Proposal Summary

Finding a Sustainable Solution for 3D Printing Waste ($6,728 cash request)

The project proposes to develop a 3D plastic waste-recycling program using a Filabot EX2 extruder system. Many college and public libraries offer their patrons 3D printing services, but failed prints generate substantial amounts of waste plastic that is simply discarded. Through this grant project, the team will explore a more sustainable alternative that recycles the waste PLA into 3D filament for use in new 3D prints. Exploring the feasibility of recycling 3D filament waste supports the team's goal to provide outreach and materials to libraries with 3D printing capabilities that wish to make their 3D printing service more sustainable. Project team includes the engineering librarian (PI), with physics librarian, and 3D and emerging technologies services manager (seven months: 2019).[2]

Epilogue

The proposal was fully awarded. The team purchased the proposed paper shredder and other related supplies. They quickly discovered that grinding up 3D plastic items for recycling is a difficult task. Not only that, but in order for the extruder to perform correctly the plastic must be dry, clean, and approximately pebble-sized. The team created some recycled white filament, but it was not of the quality appropriate for use in a 3D printer. It contained too much moisture, so they removed the moisture using a dehydrator. The team was able to fuse together short sections of filament at the end of rolls to create reusable filament wrapped on spools by employing a winder purchased with project funds.

Recycling the bulky rejected 3D-printed plastic pieces became the final focus. Grinding them in a blender, purchased with project funds, while adding pressure from a plunger to allow a lightweight object to encounter the blades, only produced plastic dust, not pellets. Next the team experimented with a toaster oven, donated by a Libraries staff member, to melt the printed objects so that they could be flattened and fed through the paper shredder. In the end, the team was able to produce recycled filament suitable for 3D printing to ship to NEFLIN. In November 2019, the team presented its resulting methodologies to participants at the NEFLIN annual meeting.

OUTREACH

Creative Campus Committee / Catalyst Fund

Prologue

The idea for this project emerged during a medical humanities conference presentation attended by the director of medical humanities, who works in

UF's Health Science Center Library (HSCL). The presenter was an undergraduate student who had taught a course about "monsters" using narratives from health-related topics. The director had some questions following the presentation: Could undergraduate students develop their own courses within the UF Honors Program that would create a model for an undergraduate course that would be proposed, designed, taught, and graded by undergrads? Could the content of the new course be focused on medical humanities related to monsters? What kinds of images are identified as being monstrous? Do these ideas change over time? How does one define a human monster? Could the novel *Frankenstein* by Mary Shelley serve as literature for the new course? Would it be possible to coordinate an exhibit at UF's Harn Museum of Art, where the students in the course could curate the exhibit based on *Frankenstein*?

First, the director put out a call for undergraduate students who wanted to design the course. Four students were secured. As a means for planning two grant applications—one to the Creative Campus Committee's Catalyst Fund and the other to the Center for the Humanities and the Public Sphere's one-time series or event sponsorship—the director and her student partners began conversations with resource owners on and off campus about the various possibilities outlined in her questions. She envisioned a campus-wide program built around the timing and activities of the course. It happened that 2018 marked the 200th anniversary of the publication of *Frankenstein*. This coincidence served as the glue to hold together all of the components that the director envisioned, such as recruiting students to take the course, and attracting others interested in the topic on campus.

Plans started falling into place far in advance of the deadlines for submitting funding proposals due in early 2019. The director of the Honors Program agreed to the new course proposal serving honors students. The director of education programs and academic programs at the Harn Museum agreed to the timing of the exhibit (these are planned two years in advance) and the contributions of honors students as curators of the exhibit. Working with the four student volunteers, the team created a syllabus, selected material for assignments, designed lectures and discussions, planned to set up the Canvas online site for student engagement, and planned to be prepared to grade the students in the course.

Proposal Summary

From Godzilla to Someone with a Stigmatized Illness to a Serial Killer (a.k.a. What Makes a Monster?) ($18,212 cash request)

This project will explore our relationship to monsters, and the idea of monsters—whether they are the fantastic and threatening creatures of legend and imagination, biologically different or disabled people, or humans whose behavior goes beyond the bounds of the acceptable. Our monsters can change

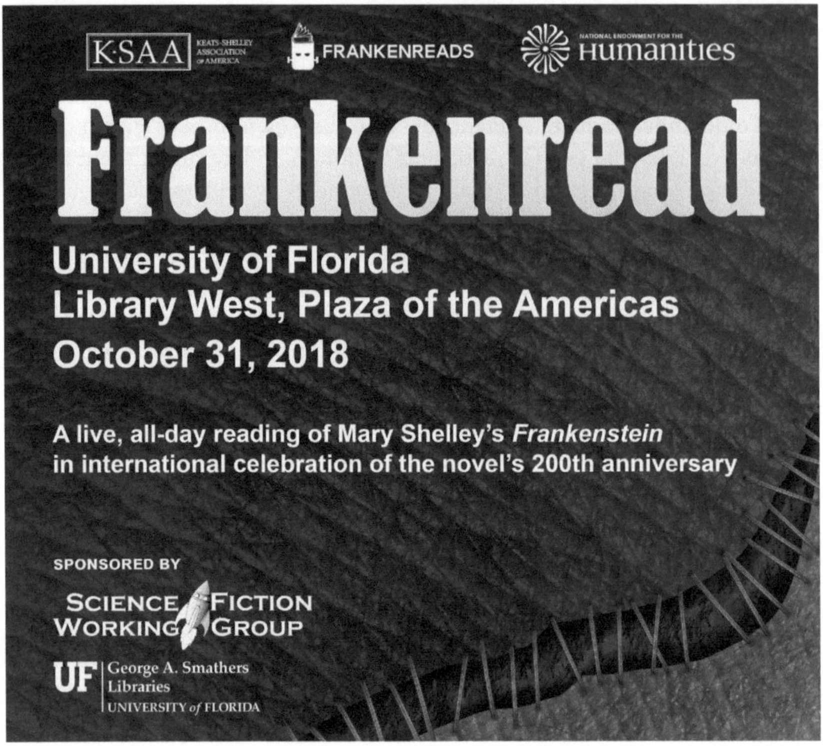

FIGURE 3.2
Poster promoting the Frankenread event. Image by Stephanie Birch.
Source: https://ufdc.ufl.edu/IR00011033/00001

over time as society changes its definitions, becomes familiar with the threatening unknown, or redefines and highlights monstrous behavior. The process of identifying monsters also occurs in response to societal stress and can serve to stigmatize individuals or reinforce behavioral norms. Funding will cover elements of a larger program, including a speaker series, film showing, and a graphic narrative contest supporting this discussion of how and why society identifies monsters—and what it means to be considered monstrous. Project team includes the director of medical humanities (PI), with the community engagement and health literacy liaison librarian, reference and liaison librarian, health sciences liaison librarian, and associate director of HSCL (one year: 2018 to 2019).[3]

Epilogue

The project was partially awarded, receiving $11,897. The director of medical humanities prepared a revised budget, with assistance from the grants manager and accountant, to accommodate the reduced award, focusing on the essential expenses required to complete the project while eliminating expenses that the reviewers wanted removed. To enhance the Honors course offerings and promote the project more broadly to other campus audiences, grant funds supported the speaker series, including the author of *Monstrous Progeny*; the author of a work in progress based on "What Do We Do with the Art of Monstrous Men?" (a 2017 essay for the *Paris Review*); and a film screening of the *Bride of Frankenstein* at the Harn Museum of Art which coincided with the 200th anniversary of Mary Shelley's *Frankenstein*. Another campus activity, "Frankenread," presented in partnership with the campus Science Fiction Working Group, was the live reading of the entire *Frankenstein* novel in one day by the English literature librarian, two English professors, and the mayor of Gainesville, among many others, in the outdoor plaza in front of the Humanities and Social Sciences Library.

Twelve students completed the Honors course taught by the four undergraduate students in August 2018, and three participated in a poster session at Stanford University for the Health Humanities Conference which featured a Frankenstein theme to commemorate Shelley's *Frankenstein* anniversary. The project team organized a Monsters Graphic Novel Contest that closed at the end of September 2019, to celebrate Shelley's *Frankenstein* anniversary.[4] The winners received $75 or $50, and their entries were displayed in the Health Science Center Library's new art display grids.

The Harn Museum exhibit, "Monsters and the Monstrous," opened in early 2019. Students in the course did projects to promote the exhibit, wrote Twitter and Instagram posts, and created a binder describing the exhibit content. One student composed a musical piece for the final course project.

TECHNOLOGY

University of Florida / Technology Fee

Prologue

MADE@UF, located in the Marston Science Library, is a virtual reality (VR) development space that is available to all students at the University of Florida. Over the past few years, student interest in learning and working with VR has grown exponentially as the cost of the technology has plummeted. In an effort to support student development, the MADE@UF Library team, which provides VR technology access and training, initially applied for funding to purchase VR technology for students to create VR experiences. These funds were granted from the UF Technology Fee grants program, which uses student technology fee funds to enhance students' access to state-of-the-art technology on campus.

The two main partners for the MADE@UF program are the VR for the Social Good Initiative, which is directed by professors in journalism and computer science, and UF Housing, which offers a makerspace area in student housing (Infinity Hall) containing duplicates of equipment and supplies available at the Science Library. These partners looked to the science librarians to identify the necessary resources and provide several locations at which students could create VR projects. Science librarians have worked with UF Housing to develop MADE@UF resources in the dorms, where students can learn and create computer applications. VR for the Social Good Initiative, on the other hand, supports a student group, Gator VR, which meets weekly in MADE@UF at the Science Library to create a variety of apps.

Using a whiteboard to poll students' technology needs, the science librarians noticed that many students were requesting borrowing privileges for checking out VR equipment to use off-site. The librarians, inspired by these multiple requests, joined MADE@UF partners to submit a new proposal requesting funding to purchase VR equipment for circulation.

Project Summary

VR/AR Development for Student Learning at MADE@UF ($16,620 cash request)

This project seeks to purchase virtual reality (VR) and augmented reality (AR) supplies, including nine Leap Motion Universal VR Bundles with cases, four PlayStation 4 VRs with cases, two Emotiv EPOC+ 14 Channel Mobile EEGs, two HP Z VR Backpack G1 Workstations, four Magic Leap Ones with cases, and six HTC Vive Wireless Adapters for MADE@UF. These items will increase access to new technology in MADE@UF at the Marston Science Library to enable development that incorporates gesture control, brain computer interface (BCI), and wireless VR by fall 2018; and expand student access to VR/AR technology beyond the Libraries by circulating VR backpacks, VR gaming systems, and AR headsets by fall 2018. Project team includes the engineering librarian (PI) with the librarian who supervises the makerspace, senior director of student retention and success initiatives in the UF Division of Student Affairs, and the co-directors of the VR for Social Good (one year: 2018 to 2019).[5]

Epilogue

The proposal was fully awarded. The team's first step was to reevaluate the technology budget items on the original application to make sure the list of items to be purchased were still relevant. Seven months after submitting the proposal, team members checked with appropriate Information Technology

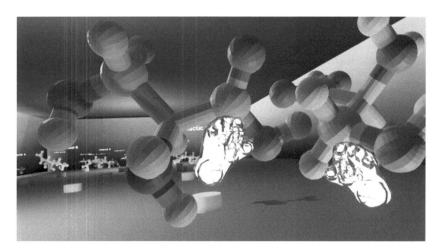

FIGURE 3.3
Image of the chirality of chemistry VR experience
Image by Sam Putnam, https://ufdc.ufl.edu/IR00011033/00001

and Access Services staff in the Libraries to ensure the proper distribution of equipment. Preparing technology to be distributed to partners and for circulation in general can be difficult because each piece of technology is unique and has its own idiosyncrasies.

A social media plan was implemented to promote the availability of this new technology. To jump-start the process, the engineering librarian took over management of the Science Library's Instagram account in an effort to build a UF community of VR and AR users. The Instagram account grew by 400 new followers with a total of over 1,100 followers who actively share within the community. Users are routinely informed through Instagram of the availability of VR equipment based on reservation system information. In just two months of promotion during the fall 2019 semester, the PlayStation headsets had been checked out 67 percent of the available time.

The program's broadening user base has attracted faculty and students in the Chemistry Department. They have begun to delve into creating immersive experiences in partnership with science librarians. For instance, some molecules are challenging to understand when viewing physical models or two-dimensional images of them. But in a VR environment, users are able to superimpose the molecules, which facilitates understanding of their chemical structures. This work led to a conference presentation by the chemistry professor for the American Chemical Society and an accompanying journal article submission. Another professor in German and Medieval Studies brought his entire class to the Science Library to learn to use the oculus headset for a virtual visit to Munich using Google Earth, and then students wrote about their

VR experience in the city. The increased interest in VR at the University of Florida has motivated the team to continue exploring ways to extend VR for teaching and learning.

DIGITIZATION/PRESERVATION

Center for Research Libraries / Project Ceres

Prologue

A retired folklorist and musician who performs Cajun music with the husband of an agriculture librarian writes a regular column featuring elder cattlemen, accompanied by his photographs (to capture these histories), for the *Florida Cattleman and Livestock Journal*. He intimated that the best source of information about these cattlemen lies in past issues of the magazine, and how great it would be if all the issues of the magazine dating back to the 1930s were made available (to him) online. The agriculture librarian, who oversees digital projects, consulted with the curator of UF's P.K. Yonge Library of Florida History, who had not seen the value in retaining the back issues of the magazine held in the collection, and had considered culling them. A former agricultural extension agent, the agriculture librarian was well-versed in the publication's content and extolled its virtues. As it turns out, the magazine contains articles about research results conducted by agricultural scholars at UF who knew the importance of sharing their findings about pasture management, breeds, pests, and other cattle-related topics with cattlemen throughout Florida. Scholars who authored articles for the magazine translated (or converted) their research findings for the benefit of the cattlemen who read the magazine. In effect, the magazine was used as an essential research dissemination tool. Beyond these benefits, the magazine chronicles the lives of cattlemen and cattlemen's families, forming a history of their lives in Florida. All told, its preservation and digitization would serve UF's Institute of Food and Agricultural Sciences faculty and students, and Florida historians, as well as the Florida cattlemen's constituents.

A meeting with the publication's board of directors created project buy-in. As the copyright owner, they granted approval to digitize the full run of the magazine, and confirmed that early issues of the magazine which were missing from UF's collection would be loaned for digitization purposes. With this in hand, the agriculture librarian created a proposal for submission to Project Ceres. In reviewing the sponsor's guidelines, the librarian noted that digitizing the magazine's issues from its inception (in 1934) until 1988 matched up with the funder's definition as "historic." The sponsor further stipulates that print versions must be preserved as well. It should be noted that Project Ceres funding is supported through a partnership with the U.S. Agricultural Information Network, the Agriculture Information Network Collaborative, and the Center for Research Libraries.

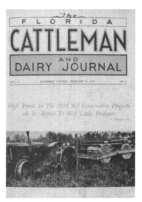  

FIGURE 3.4
Three covers of digitized magazines: *The Florida Cattleman,* 1936, 1937, and 1944

Source: https://guides.uflib.ufl.edu/floridacattleman

Proposal Summary

Preserving Florida's Agricultural History: Digitization of "The Florida Cattleman & Livestock Journal" ($9,258 cash request; $9,280 cost share contribution)

This project proposes to preserve and digitize *The Florida Cattleman & Livestock Journal*, from inception through 1988. The *Florida Cattleman* is a rare yet core Florida agricultural serial—digital versions do not exist. Full-text searchable issues with metadata revealing featured issue themes will be uploaded to the Florida historical agriculture and rural life collection hosted by the UF Digital Collections. Providing preservation and open access to this journal is of significant value to UF Institute of Food and Agricultural Sciences faculty and students, to Florida historians, and to the Florida Cattlemen's Foundation constituencies. Project team includes the agriculture sciences and digital initiatives librarian (PI), with the metadata and quality control coordinator, digital production manager, and cataloguing coordinator (one year: 2017 to 2018).[6]

Epilogue

The project was fully funded. The project was completed during the grant period to preserve and digitize 626 issues, for a total of 50,664 pages, of *The Florida Cattleman & Livestock Journal* from 1934 to 1988. Following the completion of the digitization and loading of files to the UF Digital Collections, the magazine's availability was promoted through an online website and social media posts, a published article, and a presentation at the U.S. Agricultural Information Network's Sixteenth Biennial Conference.[7] Along with the curator's agreement to preserve the original issues at the University of Florida, the magazine's publisher agreed to preserve the thirty-six issues held at the Florida Cattlemen's Foundation in Kissimmee, Florida, which had been loaned to the project team for digitization to complete the run. The plans to digitize the magazines literally saved the historic issues of the magazine. A vocational agriculture teacher at Yearling Middle School in Okeechobee, Florida, captured the essence of the project: "Now I can click a mouse and read a story about something that happened way back then, that we are reaping the benefits of today. So I think it's going to be a really neat deal that I think a lot of people will enjoy as much as myself."[8]

DIGITIZATION/PRESERVATION

Center for Research Libraries / Latin Americanist Research Resources Project

Prologue

This project's formation begins in 2004 when its primary collaborator, a researcher at the time and later UF's Caribbean Basin librarian, was attending a rare books conference where she first met her future project partner, a representative from the Centro de Documentación e Investigación Judío de México (CDIJUM, the Mexican Jewish Center for Documentation and Investigation). Although the librarian had grown up near Mexico City, she had not been aware of this organization, and now she filed it away mentally as a potential future partner.

In 2012, when the librarian learned of the Libraries' NEH Challenge Grant award, *Repositioning Florida's Judaica Library: Increasing Access to Humanities Resources from Florida, Latin America, and the Caribbean Communities* (see chapter 5), she shared information about this hidden resource with the Judaica Library curator, thinking that it would be good to explore a possible partnership with CDIJUM. The librarian, with funding from UF's Center for Latin American Studies – U.S. Department of Education Title VI award traveled to Mexico, visited CDIJUM, where she met with its representative, who now served as executive director. During the tour of this impressive archive, the librarian shared information about UF's successful distributed digitization collection, the Digital Library of the Caribbean (dLOC), and the potential for forming a partnership to digitize some of CDIJUM's primary materials for inclusion in that collection. If the Libraries could raise the necessary funding, she asked, would the executive director be interested in visiting UF to develop a possible partnership? A sports aficionado, the executive director was well aware of UF's Gator football team and was enthusiastic about accepting the invitation.

The trip was made possible with funds from the Libraries and the Center for Latin American Studies in January 2016. The executive director delivered a lecture on the history of Jewish immigrants in Mexico and the development of CDIJUM at the Judaica Library Suite at UF. His visit resulted in an international agreement between the CDIJUM and UF to begin digitizing the former's collections. During another trip to the United States to speak at the Society for American Archivists in Atlanta about CDIJUM's work on a new archive featuring legal topics, he was able to join the librarian and her family and attend an Atlanta Braves baseball game.

The first partnership idea was to digitize CDIJUM's holdings of 275 microfilm issues of *Kesher*, a Spanish-language Jewish Mexican newspaper with additions in Yiddish, Hebrew, and Ladino, published between 1987 and 2003.[9] A letter that the executive director secured to obtain permission from *Kesher*'s publisher to digitize these issues made this prototype project application to the Latin Americanist Research Resources Project (LARRP) possible.

Proposal Summary

A Prototype for the Digitization of Latin American Jewish Newspapers ($2,160 cash request; cost $1,353 cost share contribution)

In partnership with the Centro de Documentación e Investigación Judío de México (CDIJUM), the project team plans to digitize 275 issues of the Jewish Mexican newspaper *Kesher*. The Libraries hold 275 issues of *Kesher* on microfilm, published between June 1987 and December 2003. The digitized content will be made available in the freely accessible Digital Library of the Caribbean (dLOC) and featured in the newly developing Jewish Diaspora Collection. If awarded, this project will enable the Libraries to digitize the first such Jewish/ Latin American newspaper, thus providing easy access to an important publication that will contribute to the greater understanding and future scholarship of the Jewish communities in Latin America. Project team includes the director of digital project services (PI), with the Caribbean Basin librarian and the curator of the Price Library of Judaica (one year: 2016 to 2017).[10]

As the *Kesher* issues were being digitized, in January 2017, the two partners began discussing the submission of a second LARRP proposal to digitize all of CDIJUM's newspapers, which were only available in hard copy. The deadline was in April, allowing CDIJUM's staff ample time to prepare a spreadsheet of all its newspaper holdings with titles, issues, dates, and the status of complete published runs, and to obtain bids from digitization vendors in Mexico City (the collection was fragile and could not be transported to UF).

Proposal Summary

Digitization of a UNESCO World Memory Collection: Mexico's Jewish Heritage Newspapers ($14,630 cash request; $5,335 cost share contribution)

The Libraries, in partnership with the Centro de Documentación e Investigación Judío de México (CDIJUM), plan to complete vended digitization and in-house quality control related to digitizing 75,548 pages of CDIJUM's Jewish-Mexican newspapers *Di Tzait/Di Shtime, Der Weg, Prensa Israelita, Optimismo Juvenil, Tribuna Israelita, Fraiwelt,* and *Meksikaner Lebn.* The project also includes the completion of the digitization of *Kesher,* which LARRP funded in 2016. The digitized content will be made available in the freely accessible Digital Library of the Caribbean (dLOC) and featured in the newly developing Jewish Diaspora Collection (JDoC). If awarded, this project will enable the Libraries to digitize a UNESCO World Memory Collection: Mexico's Jewish Heritage Newspapers.[11] Project team includes the Caribbean Basin librarian (PI) and director of digital production services (Co-PI), with the director of CDIJUM, curator of the Price Library of Judaica, digital content management assistant, and digital production manager (one year: 2017 to 2018).[12]

Epilogue

The project was awarded full funding. An agreement was made with a vendor in Mexico City to execute the project, and 60 percent of the newspaper collection was delivered to begin the digitization process. The devastating 7.1 magnitude earthquake that hit Mexico City in September 2017, which killed over 300 people and damaged over 3,000 buildings, highlighted the vital need for such preservation projects. The CDIJUM archival facility suffered irreparable damage. The director risked physical harm entering the building with a few other workers to remove the remaining newspaper collection, along with all of the other threatened archives. Delays caused by the earthquake prompted the team to request an extension from the sponsor to complete the project.

A new challenge to overcome emerged from the quality of the vendor's work product. It happens that this particular vendor specialized in large contracts such as digitizing government documents. It had no previous experience performing boutique projects such as this one, in terms of metadata generation. This became an ongoing quality-control issue, with staff from CDIJUM enforcing the need for correct and complete metadata records. After several urgent calls from the vendor for payment of work performed, the partners agreed not to make payment until the job was performed to their satisfaction with the completed metadata. The unanticipated delays caused by the vendor prompted a second request to the sponsor for an additional extension.

FIGURE 3.5
Exterior and interior of the new facility for the archives of the Centro de Documentación e Investigación Judío in Mexico City
Photos by Bess de Farber, https://ufdc.ufl.edu/IR00011033/00001

In October 2018 the librarian, the grants manager, and the Judaica Library curator were in Mexico City to perform *Componiendo un Corazon y Otros Cuentos de Imigrantes Judias* (*Composing a Heart and Other Jewish Immigrant Stories* (see chapter 2) for CDIJUM's International Jewish Book Fair. After the performance, the chairman of CDIJUM's board of directors presented the team with the hard drives containing the completed project files. The hard drives were then delivered to the Libraries' Digital Support Services (DSS) staff and placed in the uploading queue, at which time staff determined the need for a password to open the encrypted files. Unfortunately, the password was lost, and duplicate hard drives had to be delivered to the team in Florida to complete the project. One final hurdle remained. As it turns out, the files were saved as PDFs and not as TIFF files. A third extension was requested by the project team and approved by the sponsor to convert all of the file formats and complete the loading of the digital collection. The newspaper titles that were digitized for the project include *El Tiempo, Hanoar Hazioni, Nuestra Vida, Vida Habanera, La Voz Israelita de Mexico, Der Weg – El Camino, Prensa Israelita, La Voz Sionista, Vida Judia en Mexico, Optimismo Juvenile, Tribuna Israelita,* and *Fraiwelt – Mundo Libre.*

RESEARCH

George A. Smathers Libraries / Emerging Technologies

Prologue

The chair of Special Collections and Area Studies at UF had an interest in adding experiential elements for patrons who visited the Albert H. Nahmad Panama Canal Gallery. Along with the UF map librarian, the two decided that adding sound to the visual experience would be a worthwhile endeavor, especially considering that many completed oral histories with former Zonians—American citizens who had lived in the Canal Zone—had yielded information on any number of topics. The map librarian had completed the Digital Humanities Bootcamp workshop (see chapter 3), during which she partnered with a faculty member from the UF Computer Information and Science and Engineering (CISE) Department who serves as the director of the SoundPad Lab. Together they brainstormed ideas about what was possible, given that the CISE faculty member was confident in her ability to work with her graduate students to develop and iteratively test the sound technology. A brainstorming workshop with interested Libraries staff provided the necessary feedback to inform the development of the project. A project team was created, including the Libraries' exhibit coordinator and exhibit assistant. They developed a synopsis of the project idea for vetting by the Grants Management Committee and the deans to verify its innovativeness, which was a key criterion of the Libraries' internal Emerging Technologies grants. With confirmation of the project's innovative components, the team proceeded to write and prepare the proposal in collaboration with the grants manager.

Proposal Summary

Sensing the Libraries: Sounds of the Panama Canal ($9,498 cash request; $2,092 cost share contribution)

This is a proof-of-concept project to assess the incorporation of 3D audio soundscapes into an exhibition visitor's experience. The project will use indoor location sensor technology to provide an immersive 3D audio experience for visitors to the Albert H. Nahmad Panama Canal Gallery. Initial feedback received during a demonstration of the technology during a temporary exhibit will be gathered during the Panama Canal Society Reunion. This will inform the Panama Canal Gallery's planning and presentation to visitors during demonstration times for groups and classes scheduled for visits. Pre- and post-evaluations will be gathered from each participant. Project results will be disseminated through a press release and conference presentations, and graduate students will be involved in presentation and publicity opportunities

96-A-2 (1084) A   Mrs. Richard M. Nixon meets pupils of Balboa High School, Canal Zone.   February 24, 1955.

FIGURE 3.6
Pat Nixon visits Balboa High School, February 24, 1955, a public school in the former Canal Zone. This is one of the photographs included in the Panama Canal Museum Collection at UF, featured in exhibits and online to acquire crowd sourced metadata.

Source: https://ufpcmcollection .files.wordpress.com/2015/07/ 2005-048-034-028.jpg and https://ufpcmcollection .wordpress.com/tag/balboa/

through the Libraries. Funds will be used for travel to the reunion, equipment, supplies, and for one OPS assistant. This project represents a collaboration between CISE and the Libraries and will provide a real-world setting for CISE faculty research. Ultimately, this project will bring innovative 3D audio technology to library visitors, expanding the boundaries of their interaction with historical materials and restoring dimensionality to the experiences of public history. Project team includes the map librarian, exhibits assistant, exhibits director, and assistant professor in CISE (one year: 2017 to 2018).[13]

Epilogue

The proposal was fully awarded. First, the team completed an initial test during a temporary exhibit at the Panama Canal Society's annual reunion in Orlando, Florida, where they received both critical and positive feedback. Weekly meetings created the necessary structure to convene the project team. After purchasing the supplies, the project relied heavily on progress made in developing the technology by the CISE faculty member and her students. The funding for student labor to assist with technology development in the

SoundPad Lab was completely spent. The CISE faculty member began funding the student workers through other sources, and of course there was significant turnover. A strategy by one of the students to develop the project's computer coding rather than purchasing proprietary software delayed the project considerably. Individual electronic elements worked well separately in the lab, but a lack of systems integration prohibited further testing in the exhibit area. One element tracks the patron's location in the exhibit while moving through the space using a wearable sensor powered by a Raspberry Pi; another dispenses the relevant audio to the patron during their exhibit experience; and the third is a graphical user interface (GUI) that allows the patron to connect with the other two elements.

Students working on the project successfully integrated the first two elements so that the 3D audio can be heard by the patron, and the sounds heard by the patron are dependent on where they are located in the space (while using a laptop). Next, they needed to make it functional by using a Raspberry Pi, which the patron can wear suspended around their neck, to replace the use of the laptop. The team wanted to experiment with wearable sensors as another option.

Not knowing when the technology would be ready to test in the exhibit space, the team developed scripts and gathered appropriate audio files from related oral histories and a mix of ambient sound customized to complement the exhibit materials. But the exhibits are only temporary, so to date, the process has been repeated three times, once for each new temporary exhibit. The unforeseen delays in technology development prompted the project team to request three no-cost extensions. The project is entering its third year, with a new completion date of June 2020. The team expects to request another extension due to UF's closure during the COVID-19 quarantine.

DIGITIZATION/PRESERVATION

Center for Research Libraries / Latin American Materials Project

Prologue

Upon first entering the Latin American and Caribbean Collection (LACC), which occupies an entire floor of the historic Smathers Library building, the preservation librarian was greeted by a distinctive and noticeable odor of vinegar. His background in preservation helped him to deduce that the odor was evidence of deteriorating acetate film, a phenomenon known as "vinegar syndrome." Once the deterioration of acetate film has begun, it cannot be reversed. To determine which films were actively deteriorating, the preservation librarian placed acid detector strips (Image Permanence Institute strips developed by the University of Rochester) of small paper that are coated with chemical agents. When in the presence of free acid molecules in the air, the strips will change color. The newspaper microfilm in the LACC was tested. A small number of reels tested positive for acetate deterioration, the largest and most damaged collection being one published in Spanish in the Dominican Republic. The next step was to answer the question: What should be done about it? Libraries personnel working in the mid-twentieth century had originally produced the microfilm—no other source existed. The reels that were damaged were those for patron use, not the originals stored in cold storage. As the preservation librarian perceived the situation, he had three options: (1) deaccession the user copies, (2) replace the user copies with new polyester microfilm reels at a cost of $50 per reel, or (3) digitize the master reels according to the National Digital Newspaper Program specifications published by the Library of Congress and upload them to the UF Digital Collections, while at the same time making a new copy of each reel on polyester film at a total cost of $200 to $250 per reel—this is the option he chose.

The Libraries' preservation mission is to make online access the most desirable option, whenever possible. In reviewing possible funding sources, the preservation librarian and the grants manager determined that the Center for Research Libraries through the Latin American Materials Project (LAMP) would be a feasible sponsor, especially because the deteriorating microfilm was of *Listín Diario,* historically the largest and most important newspaper published in the Dominican Republic's largest city, Santo Domingo.

The digitization of newspaper issues published before 1922 had already been completed. What remained were microfilm reels of issues published from 1923 to 1942. This period in the Dominican Republic's history was quite significant. It included coverage of the end of the U.S. military occupation, a major hurricane that hit the island in 1930, the political leadership transition to Trujillo, and the ultimate closing of *Listín Diario* in 1942. Global events included the Great Depression, the Spanish Civil War, Hitler's rise to power, and the early years of World War II.

Finally, the team created for this project reviewed other significant assets that would help demonstrate the feasibility of the digitization project. They chose to highlight ways in which the project could take advantage of the existing and often-used workflows developed to support the Libraries' many successful Florida and Puerto Rico Digital Newspaper Project. (See chapter 5.)

Proposal Summary

"Listín Diario": Preserving and Digitizing an At-Risk Dominican Republic Newspaper ($11,664 cash request; $9,184 cost share contribution)

The Libraries plan to complete reel preparation activities and vended digitization related to digitizing 70,800 pages of UF microfilm holdings of the Dominican Republic newspaper *Listín Diario* from 1923 to 1942. *Listín Diario* is a major daily paper published in Santo Domingo, DR. The master film for *Listín Diario* is held by UF, and the project will build upon earlier digitization efforts that captured the years 1909 to 1922. This project will complete the digitization of UF holdings of *Listín Diario* before the paper shut down under the Trujillo government in 1942. It should be noted that the existing access copies of the newspaper are on acetate film bases, which are rapidly deteriorating (vinegar syndrome). Digitization will ensure continuous access to the newspaper, while removing a preservation hazard from UF collection storage areas. The digitized content will be freely available to the public through the Digital Library of the Caribbean (dLOC) and the Caribbean Newspaper Digital Library (CNDL).[14] *Listín Diario* issues relating to the resettlement of Jewish refugees in Sousa, DR, published from 1938 to 1942 also will be added to the Jewish Diaspora Collection (JDoC). Project team includes the head of conservation and preservation (PI), digital support services director (co-PI), with digital content manager, digital workflow supervisor, digital production manager, and digital assets coordinator (one year: 2017 to 2018).[15]

FIGURE 3.7
Digitized newspaper cover of *Listín Diario*, December 23, 1909

Source: https://ufdc.ufl.edu/
AA00021654/00001

Epilogue

Phase I of the project (2017–2018) was fully funded. The team understood from this funding award that a subsequent proposal to digitize the Phase II portion of *Listín Diario*'s remaining microfilm could be anticipated to receive a second award if the Phase I project was successfully completed.[16] This supposition came to fruition in 2018, and both projects were successfully completed in 2019.

DIGITIZATION/PRESERVATION

Center for Research Libraries / Project Ceres

Prologue

In 1997, a science librarian and head of the Libraries' Preservation Department joined forces to create the "Bibliography of Florida Agriculture & Rural Life Literature" for the U.S. Agricultural Information Network and the national preservation program, Preserving the History of U.S. Agriculture and Rural Life, with funding and support from the NEH, the Food and Drug Administration, and the Institute of Food and Agricultural Sciences (Phase I).[17] These historical materials included topics related to agricultural economics (1820–1945), agricultural engineering (1910–1945), animal science (1820–1945), food and nutrition (1900–1945), forestry and natural resources (1820–1945), rural life (1820–1945), and soil, crops, and atmospheric science (1820–1945). The bibliography comprised more than 220 items. This project was not unique to the University of Florida—all of the land grant–designated universities were charged with prioritizing agricultural material intended for future digitization, as a means of preserving the country's agricultural records.

In 2015, two UF science librarians, one with a specialization in digital projects, were contacted by the librarian for the Division of Plant Industries (DPI, within the Florida Department of Agriculture and Consumer Services). The DPI librarian offered to provide the DPI's duplicates of issues of Florida agricultural journals identified in the Phase I project bibliography that were missing from UF's serials collections. During the first conversation, the DPI librarian requested that some of these rare documents be digitized, such as the minutes from the meeting that actually founded DPI. This request led the science-librarian team to consider whether or not Project Ceres funding (allocated by the Center for Research Libraries, with funding from the U.S. Agricultural Information Network and the Agricultural Network of Information Collaborative—a sponsor both librarians were aware of, for digitizing rare agricultural materials) would be a good match for such a project. Project Ceres funding is dedicated to preserving historical print materials through digitization for increased availability. This goal was the team's goal as well. They were excited about the prospect of exposing these rare agricultural serials to students, researchers, and those in the business of agriculture.

The partnership was expedited because the DPI librarian could easily see what serial issues listed in the "Bibliography" were missing from UF's collections (because the DPI collection holdings appear in the UF catalog). Commitment to the project partnership was established during a face-to-face meeting between the three librarians where the UF librarians learned more about DPI's collections to plan out which titles would be given to UF (duplicates at DPI) and which would be loaned to UF for such a project. They collectively decided to select historical agricultural serials based on their (1) limited availability, (2) high preservation need, and (3) publication date.

In making their selections, the team found two serial titles in the Jacksonville Public Library's Special Collections that matched the criteria. They had originally met up with the Special Collections librarian for the Jacksonville Public Library at a Northeast Florida Library Information Network Conference in Jacksonville. While in Jacksonville, she gave them an impromptu tour of the library's Special Collections. During the preparation of the Project Ceres proposal, the team reached out to the Jacksonville librarian to offer this digitization partnership opportunity. With her agreement, the team made arrangements to include (borrow) the *Florida Grove and Garden* and the early editions of the *Packing House News* for digitization. A revised workflow was developed for the Project Ceres proposal to include collections from the two external partners while ensuring long-term preservation of the print material, as required by the sponsor's guidelines.

Project Summary

Increasing Accessibility to Rare Florida Agricultural Publications – Phase II ($5,431 cash request; $8,538 cost share contribution)

This proposal will increase access to rare Florida agricultural publications by digitizing fifty-seven print serials (1,000+ items). Core historic serials were identified for digitization based on their limited availability and high preservation ranking. The team plans to provide greater detailed metadata for statewide extension serials previously identified as "miscellaneous publications," and enhance accessibility for researchers by converting the current bibliography into a dynamic and searchable format. Project team includes the agriculture science librarian (PI), agriculture sciences and digital initiatives librarian (Co-PI), with conservation associate, chair of the Marston Science Library, metadata and quality control coordinator, and digital production manager (one year: 2015 to 2016).[18]

Epilogue

The project was fully funded. Notably, it became the first Project Ceres award in its grantmaking history to feature external contributing organizations. Rather

FIGURE 3.8
Digitized covers of
The Bee-Keepers' Magazine,
May 1887, and *The Packing
House News*, January 1, 1924

Source: http://ufdc.ufl.edu/AA00052225/00005, http://ufdc.ufl.edu/AA00052231/00001

than digitizing fifty-seven print serials, only twenty-two titles were digitized. However, the actual number of items totaled 1,413, well above the proposed 1,000, comprising a total of 28,518 digitized pages. Agreements were signed by DPI and the Jacksonville Public Library, per the sponsor's requirements, with provisions to preserve the print serials in perpetuity, including the right of first refusal by UF to obtain the documents should physical weeding of any of the digitized items be undertaken by a partnering institution. Notes to this effect were added to each applicable item in the Jacksonville Public Library and DPI catalogs.

A one-year extension of the project was approved due to the unforeseen additional time needed to complete the metadata fields required by the sponsor, which were made more difficult because of inconsistencies and misprints in these old journals, not to mention the name changes in their titles and issues. The team had not anticipated the sponsor's requirements for detailed metadata, which was revealed in the metadata template delivered along with the award guidelines. Funding to create new metadata (by hiring a student to do this) was disallowed per Project Ceres guidelines, causing the team to request internal funds for student labor to complete the project. Training three students who each worked independently throughout the project also required additional effort by the team. Limited access to team members for answering subjective student questions about inconsistencies in the publications caused the students to make decisions in a vacuum, producing inconsistent metadata that had to be corrected.

The team soldiered on with student assistance until they completed all of the requirements for the list of twenty-two newly digitized titles, including the *Minutes of the State Plant Board of Florida, Annual Report, Florida Division of Fruit & Vegetable Inspection; Florida Department of Agriculture Bulletins* (monographic serial); *Bee-Keepers' Magazine, Beekeepers Item, Dixie Beekeeper, Florida Flower Grower, Florida Foliage Grower, Florida Market Bulletin, Florida Shipments of Seasonal Flowers, Florida Shipments of Seasonal Fruits and Vegetables, Florida Vegetables, The Harvester, List of Certified Nurseries and Stock Dealers, Packing House News, Plant Industry News, Plant Protection News, Publications of the Division of Plant Industry* from 1915 to 1972 (formerly the State Plant Board of Florida), the *Report of Green Fruit Inspection*, and the *Skinner Packing House News*. The team's presentation in 2017 at the Annual Meeting of the Agriculture Network Information Collaborative at the National Agricultural Library in Beltsville, Maryland, highlighted the project's workflows and the team's practices of working with external partnering organizations.

TECHNOLOGY

George A. Smathers Libraries / Emerging Technologies

Prologue

The Info Commons coordinator and the manager of the Humanities and Social Sciences Reference Collection regularly read online newsletters for reviews about materials and technology. They came across an article[19] about the ALA's "Cutting-Edge Technology in Library Services" award in 2014 to the One Button Studio (OBS), a user-friendly audio and video production studio installed at Penn State University.[20] This new technology in an academic library aroused their interest because they often search for ways to pursue technology projects, especially those that serve students with disabilities, that would enhance the offerings in the Humanities and Social Sciences Library (known as Library West). Penn State's OBS specifications and budget costs for the related equipment to replicate the project at UF were available through open-access documentation. Later, the dean of the Libraries visited an OBS in southern Florida, and as a result the librarians were encouraged to prepare and submit an Emerging Technologies (ET) grant application. This internal Libraries program supports innovative technology projects up to a maximum of $10,000.

At the start, the librarians enlisted the facilities manager to identify a prospective student study room that would make a good candidate for conversion into an OBS.

The selected student study room was the largest of its kind in Library West that met the specifications outlined by Penn State, with a location away from constant foot traffic. In fact, few students were aware of this particular study room. The total cost for technology appeared to be close to $10,000, although the repurposing of the room required additional funding which the deans agreed to cover if the ET grant proposal was successfully awarded by the Libraries' Grants Management Committee. Specifically, a wall had to be installed along with curtains to control lighting, a green screen was required, and soundproofing panels and retrofitted network drops would provide internet connectivity. Penn State's specifications called for Mac products, but UF is a Windows university, making the project unique among all of the existing OB Studios at the time.

Planning for the Windows-based project required expertise from the Libraries' Information Technology Department to assist in the development of a budget comparable to that of Penn State. Staff at the Penn State library manage a problem board on a discussion list where tech issues related to questions about how to install an OBS are handled. Through this discussion list, the librarians could see which other peer institutions had installed an OBS. This information was needed as a way to make comparisons with other similar projects to convey the innovativeness of the project in the grant application. Another aspect of the project that had to be researched was that UF's Health Science Center Library already had a green screen inside a study room that could be reserved. The team was charged with differentiating the existing study room's features from the proposed OBS room to compare the two and justify the innovative elements of the OBS proposal.

Proposal Summary

Library West One Button Studio ($10,000 cash request; $13,246 cost share contribution)

The project team plans to create a One Button Studio (http://onebutton.psu. edu/) in room 142, Library West. The One Button Studio (OBS) contains all of the benefits of a professional production studio, providing users with a green screen, lighting, and audio and cutting-edge camera equipment. This "all-in-one" setup can be used to produce high-quality video quickly and easily. The studio will use a free app in the Mac App Store paired with a list of off-the-shelf, third-party production equipment. Everything will be set up ahead of time (green screen, lighting, camera, audio, etc.). The amount of time spent operating the equipment is estimated to be less than twenty seconds— no recording experience is necessary. Students will be able to use the OBS

Basic instructions for beginners...

1 Login to the computer

2 Insert USB drive
(USB port located top of podium, near red button)

3 Push button to begin
(Lights will turn on. 15 second countdown before recording begins)

4 Begin filming

5 Push button to end
(must wait 2 minutes before removing USB drive or beginning another recording)

6 Want to record another?
Return to Step #3

7 Done? <u>Wait</u> 2 minutes.
Remove USB drive.
(shuts off system)

8 Logoff the computer

FIGURE 3.9
Infographic for how to use the One Button Studio
Graphics by Stacey Ewing, https://ufdc.ufl.edu/IR00011033/00001

to practice presentations for class, produce a green screen recording or video assignment, create e-portfolio introductions and content, deliver an introduction to an online course, present research papers, record a lecture, or create demonstration modules. The OBS will strongly support both student learning and professional development activities. After the One Button Studio project installation has been completed, all that a user will have to do will be to reserve the room for a two-hour slot using the Libraries' online D!BS reservation system, pick up the key at the circulation desk, enter the room, and plug in a USB drive (requires FAT format with a minimum one GB of space). Project team includes the associate chair of the Humanities and Social Sciences Library (PI), collection manager of the Humanities and Social Sciences Reference Collection, selector for Women's, Gender and LGBTQI+ Studies (Co-PI), with the facilities manager and chair of Humanities and Social Sciences Library, in partnership with UF Academic Technology (one year: 2015 to 2016).[21]

Epilogue

The project proposal was fully funded. In the middle of the project, management of the Humanities and Social Sciences Library's technology was migrated to the Academic Technologies (AT) unit on campus, which allowed AT staff to contribute some of that unit's own funds to the project. AT staff ultimately covered the costs of the green screen, a unique feature that is now available at no cost to students and faculty. The various construction activities to repurpose the study room required more time, and the team applied for and received a no-cost extension.

The "soft" launch of the new OBS occurred in summer 2016. This scheduling change allowed the team to monitor the OBS reservation system during the library's reduced summer hours. Many of the system's glitches were resolved during this time, when there were fewer patrons. The full OBS launch with ads, bookmarks, signage, and a news release took place in the fall of 2016. A LibGuide for using the OBS was created and promoted,[22] and news stories were circulated.[23]

Originally, the OBS was restricted to student use, but the policy has changed to include faculty users. A designated lab manager stationed at the library's front desk is assigned to periodically monitor the room, lower the camera if necessary, and provide other minimal assistance. Speakers were added after the launch because originally, the studio only recorded presentations, but not playback—students would have to view and listen to the presentation after leaving the studio, and return to make new recordings. UF's OBS has other versatile features; it offers the ability to view PowerPoint slides side-by-side with the presenter at the same time, or it can feature just PowerPoint slides with voice-over, or just the presenter without additional media. A user can deep-freeze their presentation so that they can access it during another visit, rather than losing the file after shutting down the system. The only requirement to use the OBS is having an encrypted flash drive for protection (a UF policy) with FAT32 formatting, or the flash drive can be formatted by the OBS equipment prior to recording.

PROFESSIONAL DEVELOPMENT

Creative Campus Committee / Catalyst Fund

Prologue

The UF Digital Humanities Working Group established in December 2011 is managed by the Center for the Humanities and the Public Sphere to support librarians, faculty, and graduate students who are engaged in learning this new methodology for humanities scholarship. The group meets monthly "to discuss current projects and topics at the intersection of digital technologies and core research needs and questions in the humanities disciplines."[24]

The group's members said that they wanted more time for training and practice using the tools and collaborative activities that could accelerate their individual and collective digital humanities (DH) initiatives. Because of the methodology's newness, scholars didn't know how to work in this genre or what was possible—and they didn't know what they didn't know. Moreover, many humanities scholars didn't even know that they were already "doing" DH work. To mitigate these barriers, the digital humanities librarian was asked to create an intensive workshop that would assist these scholars and their graduate students who were experimenting in DH. (Her goal expanded to include luring in those with little or no DH know-how as a means of broadening the impact of a proposed future workshop.)

Together with the grants manager, the digital humanities librarian assessed the possibility of submitting a preliminary proposal to meet the UF Catalyst Fund deadline. The Libraries previously had received Catalyst Fund awards for presenting two series of Collaborating with Strangers Workshops. These applications offered models for this new proposal. The DH workshop idea appeared to be a good match. The librarian prepared an agenda for a two-day intensive workshop to present experts who would share a few DH technologies, allowing scholars to plan and work in small groups to practice using the new technologies they would be introduced to. The proposed goal was to organize scholars and graduate students into groups that reflected various abilities and experience levels, so that group members could help each other complete the practice exercises. The librarian was familiar with other digital humanities experts who routinely presented at conferences or workshops such as this. She recruited a library partner, the chair of Special and Area Studies Collections, and submitted drafts of the proposal idea to key Libraries and humanities faculty to gain feedback, buy-in, and commitment to support pre- and post-DH workshop activities.

The grants manager/librarian team searched for a term that would represent the essence of the DH workshop and would communicate its innovative intensity over a short period of time. Rather than using the word "intensive" for the workshop, which was the other alternative, the term "bootcamp" conveyed more of the inherent nature of the workshop, and seemed more likely to attract participants. "Bootcamp" also offered a nontraditional image of the proposed workshop that might generate campus buzz, as well as appealing to the Catalyst Funds grant reviewers who would be more inclined to support a bootcamp than an intensive workshop.

The Catalyst Fund at UF is managed by the Creative Campus Committee and offers an annual preliminary application deadline, and a subsequent full proposal opportunity to address some of the committee's questions with additional information.

Digital Humanities Collaboration Bootcamp ($14,936 cash request)

Funds will support an intensive two-day Digital Humanities (DH) Bootcamp to grow a culture of radical collaboration across campus. The DH Bootcamp will serve sixty participants, with the majority being first-time DH practitioners, by providing multiple trainings for skill development, which will be used to create new instructional materials for infusing DH within courses. This initial start-up activity will train faculty and graduate students to enhance their teaching and research practices with new technologies and highly collaborative approaches. Small groups will be organized to reach a mix of disciplines and experience. Project team includes the digital humanities librarian (PI), with the chair of Special and Area Studies Collections, the Digital Humanities Working Group, Digital Humanities Library Group, and Research Computing (nine months: 2015 to 2016).[25]

Epilogue

The project was awarded $10,000, and a revised budget was submitted to match up with the awarded amount.[26] The bootcamp was successfully completed according to the planned timeline and intensive workshop agenda. Fifty-one faculty members and students participated in eight different teams, each with an assigned facilitator who was either a librarian or a high-performing computing staffer.

The librarian deliberately sought to recruit humanities faculty who had not participated in other DH activities. One major result of the bootcamp was a shift in consciousness among faculty and graduate students as to the meaning of DH. The original goal was achieved—to solicit participation from all over campus, beyond the humanities, as a way of introducing DH to other disciplines, which eventually would generate new multidisciplinary collaborations, something humanities faculty were eager to do. The bootcamp team sought to substantiate the cultural adoption of DH on campus. A longer-term result was expanded participation in DH on campus, and a sense of community around the field of DH scholarly activities, as a well-supported disciplinary methodology.

DIGITAL HUMANITIES

Association of Research Libraries

Prologue

The two initial leaders of this project, the Libraries' associate dean for administrative services and faculty affairs and the assistant program director for human resources, had been working on a new employee recruitment study to determine the most optimum places to advertise the Libraries' new open positions. Their goals were (1) to identify the best places to advertise library positions to generate pools of applicants, and (2) to have effective means for generating applications from underrepresented groups. During the study, they wondered whether a more useful solution would be to create a community of practitioners who work in libraries to recruit applicants for open job positions. The practitioners would collect data on their recruitment activities and track outcomes and share this with others involved in the same position recruitment activities.

With this community-based project in mind, the two leaders recognized a recurring need for libraries to share information on their positions—how academic library work was organized and defined. They asked themselves: How do we build an online repository where professionals who are all engaged in the same work administering libraries would be willing to contribute their library's recruitment documents (e.g., job descriptions)? The team's existing assets included access to an established network of human resource (HR) administrators that they had built over a few years and who were involved in the recruitment study.

At the same time, academic libraries were evolving and becoming more digitally focused, and professionals in the HR field began sharing each other's position descriptions (PDs). Given that the team was familiar with the nature of the ever-expanding UF Digital Collections, they arrived at the idea of creating a new digital collection where academic library community members could upload their libraries' position descriptions. This would provide an online collection—and an opportunity to curate, store, and manage a significant and diverse collection of PDs related to positions in academic libraries around the country. During conversations at conferences and meetings, the team learned that many academic libraries were struggling with maintaining data about new and changing positions over time. They believed that having a central national collection of PDs would help those working in the field to better understand it, and how the workplace in academic libraries was evolving. For example, users could determine how many Judaica librarian positions or library grants management positions existed in academic libraries, along with the various PDs for those positions; this could inform the development of other similar positions, or it might build a case for adding such new positions where there was a need. In the end, the team's goal was to create a collaborative community through voluntary participation that would share and learn from the information contained in a collection of PDs.

Although the Association of Research Libraries (ARL) does not solicit grant proposals for such collection-development activities, the team approached ARL administrators to determine their interest in supporting this endeavor. The team had developed relationships with ARL administrators through professional social networks. ARL, with its national presence, appeared to be a good potential sponsor/partner with which to create a mutual long-term sustainability plan in order to grow participation and contributions to the proposed collection. As a potential sponsor, ARL would likely encourage academic libraries to participate in building the collection.

Prior to submitting a sponsorship proposal, the team brainstormed a list of benefits that would be attractive to ARL's leadership. They set out to answer the question: What was in it for ARL? The team's list included (1) recognition for supporting the only digital collection of library position descriptions in

FIGURE 3.10
Home page of
the ARL Position
Description Bank

Source: https://arlpdbank.uflib
.ufl.edu/Search.aspx (requires
login to reach this page)

the country, (2) a reasonable and affordable cost to create the collection, (3) a centralized information database that would demonstrate ARL's support for meeting the needs of member academic libraries, and (4) the fact that the project leader's credibility offered ARL a trusted professional who had a good track record, had served in elected positions in the community of practice, was connected with HR professionals throughout the country, and had knowledge and access to personnel at UF who were successful creators of large and functional digital collections.

Project Summary

ARL: Position Description Bank, Phase I ($16,069 cash request; $27,223 cost share contribution)

The project team proposes to establish a centralized position description database for academic libraries that will improve the sharing of information between them. The project will create a browsable and searchable database that provides access to a national collection of position descriptions, and will include the long-term digital preservation of this archive. The proposed ARL PD Bank will be developed based on specifications determined by the ACRL's Personnel Administrators and Staff Development Officers Discussion Group through focus groups and other feedback channels. Project team includes the associate dean for administrative services and faculty affairs (PI), director of human resources (Co-PI), the digital scholarship librarian (Co-PI), and the UF Digital Collections programmer (one-year project: 2012 to 2013).[27]

Epilogue

The project was fully funded through a grant agreement. Most of the software design for the project had been completed when the programmer, who had created Sobek, the UF Digital Collections platform, left the Libraries to pursue commercial endeavors. The team approached administrators at UF Information Technology (UFIT) for a commitment to complete the project and sustain any future software development needs. Coincidentally, UFIT leaders had been searching for such collaborative projects at the time. Ultimately, the collection was created to be hosted by UF personnel within the Libraries' digital infrastructure, and ARL became the owner of the collection and system in terms of branding.

The digital scholarship librarian had extensive experience in growing the community of contributors to the Digital Library of the Caribbean (dLOC). As the third leader, she offered strategies that had been successful in developing an enthusiastic community of participating contributors to dLOC. To attract contributors to the PD Bank's collection, the team presented a series of webinars that were recorded and accompanied by tutorials—thus repeating the same content over and over again to new potential contributors. To promote the collection more broadly, team members presented the PD Bank through ARL webinars and ALA conferences. Approximately 120 institutions participated in sharing their position descriptions, and the PD Bank is now actively used in the academic library community.

OUTREACH/TRAINING

Florida Department of State, Division of Library and Information Services / Library Services and Technology Act

Prologue

In 2011, after completing two small, successful, internal SOP digitization and preservation projects to protect and expose hidden historical Jewish newspapers in the Price Library of Judaica collection, the curator determined the need to digitize microfilm reels of the *Jewish Floridian*. This newspaper documented the history of Florida Jewry from 1927 until the periodical was disbanded in 1990. Access to these microfilm reels required a visit either to the UF campus or to the Jewish Museum of Florida located in South Beach. Digitizing the microfilm reels would make the newspaper available online, and thus solve this problem. The project idea was a compelling one, especially for potential funding from the state library, given the large population of Jewish residents in Florida, and the fact that UF hosts the largest contingent of Jewish academic students in the country. Working with the grants manager, the curator developed a proposal to make this newspaper freely available to potential users, which included the 614,000 Jewish Florida residents at that time, making Florida the third most Jewish-populated state in the country.[28] However, several months later the project team learned of the proposal's declination.

Rather than surrendering to this defeat, the grants manager suggested broadening the appeal of the project and submitting a completely revised proposal.

The newly conceived proposal focused on providing how-to training for online users of the expansive Florida Digital Newspaper Library, especially for those living in the three most populous Florida counties, which coincidentally served the largest number of Jewish residents. In order to focus the training on a specific collection, the team sought funding to digitize the *Jewish Floridian* microfilm reels. These newly digitized newspapers were proposed to be the training's focused content. The partnership proposal again included the Jewish Museum of Florida, but this time added new partners—the library systems of Miami-Dade, Broward, and Palm Beach counties—to target the librarians working in that region.

Proposal Summary

The Florida Digital Newspaper Collection: Broadening Access and Users ($21,753 cash request; $12,721 cost share contribution)

In partnership with the Jewish Museum of Florida and three Florida county public library systems, the project team plans to provide technical assistance

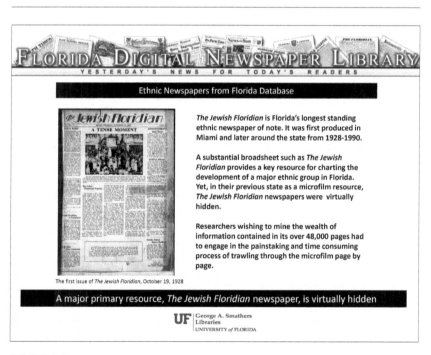

FIGURE 3.11
Home page for the Ethnic Newspapers from Florida Collection
Source: https://ufdc.ufl.edu/AA00016915/00001

and training to broaden access to the Florida Digital Newspaper Library (FDNL) and highlight "hidden" local and ethnic Florida newspapers. The project will (1) convert 127 reels of *The Jewish Floridian* from microfilm to digital format; (2) ingest digitized items in to the UF Digital Collections and create a distinct subcollection for Jewish and other ethnic newspapers within the FDNL; (3) provide training on how to access and use the FDNL, focusing on *The Jewish Floridian* as an example of a unique primary resource; (4) provide redundant storage for its preservation in perpetuity; (5) conduct post-project surveys; and 6) publicize and promote the digitized items to Florida citizens. Project team includes the curator of the Price Library of Judaica (PI), with history librarian, communications coordinator, digital media specialist, digital assets coordinator, and the chair of the Digital Library Center (one year: 2012 to 2013).[29]

Epilogue

The proposal was fully funded. The digitized version of over 100,000 pages of the *Jewish Floridian* was added to the Ethnic Newspapers from Florida subcollection.[30] The *Jewish Floridian* ultimately became the most popular newspaper in the Florida Digital Newspaper Library with over six million views, leading to the realization that Florida Jewish materials needed greater exposure. An electronic tutorial in 2013 was recorded and disseminated throughout South Florida by the Southeast Florida Library and Information Network for librarians who serve those looking to chronicle their family genealogical histories.[31] This generous coordination and promotion of the training, which took place at Florida Atlantic University's Library, added another partner to the project.

TRAINING

Procter & Gamble / U.S. Higher Education Grant Program

Prologue

In 2009, the Libraries' grants manager experimented with a facilitation process with faculty members of the UF College of the Arts known as the CoLAB Planning Series workshops, which was created for nonprofit organizations in South Florida, and later modified at the University of Arizona for students, faculty, and library employees. The experiment was successful in reducing the time it normally takes to initiate collaborations. The workshop attracted over 100 arts faculty members who generally work in their respective departments of music, theatre/dance, visual arts, and art history. One outcome was the creation of a transdisciplinary course, team-taught by faculty members in different disciplines who had not worked together previously. The dean said that more had been accomplished during the workshop to initiate collaborations than in the previous fifteen years.

With this success, the grants manager created a project team to further develop the methodology to serve UF's students, faculty, and administrators as a way of increasing cooperation, coordination, and collaboration on campus. The team, representing librarians from the Fine Arts, Social Sciences, and Science libraries, first applied for Catalyst Funding through UF's Creative Campus Committee, which was successful in securing funds for six Collaborating with Strangers Workshops, with funding for external evaluation services provided by a faculty member in the College of Education.

Proposal Summary

Collaborating with Strangers ($12,962 cash request)

The goal of this project is to promote, facilitate, and evaluate six "speed-meeting" sessions based on a facilitative process known as CoLAB Planning Series in partnership with arts, science, engineering, and various undergraduate programs. An average of thirty participants for each session will include faculty and graduate and undergraduate students; pre-registration is not required. External evaluation will determine effectiveness for future replication and expansion. The project goal is to use successful facilitation processes and online follow-up for eliminating barriers to networking and learning about extant campus resources. Project team includes the social sciences outreach

FIGURE 3.12
Students in the Public Relations Society of America participate in a Collaborating with Strangers Workshop at the University of Florida's College of Journalism and Communications
Photo by Barbara Hood, https://ufdc.ufl.edu/IR00011033/00001

librarian (PI) with the grants manager, communications director, science outreach librarian, and head of the Architecture and Fine Arts Library (one year: 2011 to 2012).[32]

Epilogue

The proposal was partially funded at $12,292. This initial project was successful: it attracted 149 enthusiastic participants from all over the campus (17 percent faculty, and 58 percent graduate students and 25 percent undergraduates, of which 42 percent were international students), and 91 percent of them responded positively about whether they would attend a similar workshop again. The project inspired subsequent submission and awards of these grant applications:[33]

- *Collaborating with Strangers Workshops* (2012)—$4,447 awarded by the Creative Campus Committee's Catalyst Fund for presenting and evaluating four workshops featuring different themes: grantseeking, sustainability, books and objects of study, and humanities.[34]
- *Collaborating with Strangers in and Outside Mass Communications* (2014)—$4,292 awarded by Procter & Gamble's U.S. Higher Education Grant Program for presenting and evaluating five workshops.[35]
- *Collaborating with Strangers in and Outside Mass Communications* (2015)—$4,342 awarded by the Smathers Libraries for presenting and evaluating five workshops.[36]

After completing these four grant projects with various project team members and facilitation provided by the grants manager, it appeared that the workshops had become routine. A team comprised of the director of communications, the journalism and mass communications librarian, and the grants manager decided to submit a proposal to ALA Editions to author a book to expand the use of these workshops to other libraries. The proposal was approved and a how-to training guide, *Collaborating with Strangers: Facilitating Workshops in Libraries, Classrooms, and Nonprofits*, was published in 2017.

With the book in hand, the grants manager decided to lead the development of a funding proposal to demonstrate the "CoLAB Planning Series – Collaborating with Strangers Workshop" methodology at other Florida academic libraries as a way to inspire others to facilitate similar workshops in their communities. Procter & Gamble's U.S. Higher Education Grant Program appeared to be the obvious choice for supporting such a project. This program's goal is to support programs that engage students as a means of improving their professional development skills for their future careers.

In reviewing a previously awarded P&G grant project, the grants manager identified the rationale for developing a new case for funding to expand

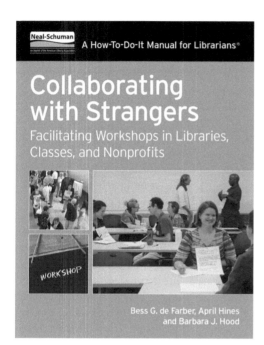

FIGURE 3.13
Book cover of *Collaborating with Strangers: Facilitating Workshops in Libraries, Classes, and Non-profits*

Cover image by ALA Editions

the workshops throughout Florida. The premise for P&G funding was that students increasingly lack the skills needed to converse with others they do not know. Studies have validated that born-digital students in academia prefer digital communication. In fact, the evaluation results of previously facilitated CoLAB Workshops indicated that most participants were uncomfortable talking to "strangers," and that the CoLAB Workshop experience improved their comfort levels.

Proposal Summary

Collaborating with Strangers Workshops: Broadening Impact through Florida Academic Libraries ($8,033 cash request)

This project seeks to train librarians (on five campuses in Florida) to facilitate Collaborating with Strangers (CoLAB) workshops, and to connect 150 students and librarians during CoLABs to demonstrate the process. CoLABs eliminate barriers to networking with strangers, while creating fertile ground for creative, entrepreneurial ideas that arise from focused conversations. Project team includes the grants manager (PI), journalism librarian (Co-PI), and the Libraries' communications director (Co-PI) (one year: 2017).[37]

Epilogue

The proposal was fully funded. First, the grants manager began re-contacting librarians at the five colleges and universities who had agreed to participate. Challenges began surfacing immediately. One librarian was in the process of looking for another job. Another was short-staffed and unable to commit to the project. As partners canceled for a variety of reasons, including lack of available time due to the impact and closures resulting from Hurricane Irma, the grants manager decided to submit two proposals for conference workshop sessions that could serve the same intent of the proposal: to train faculty members and librarians working in higher education to facilitate these workshops.

Both proposals were accepted, and CoLAB Workshops were held at the International Association of Facilitators' North American Conference in West Palm Beach and at the HASTAC (Humanities, Arts, Science, and Technologies Alliance and Collaboratory) Conference at the University of Central Florida, in Orlando. The participants in the CoLAB Workshops at both conferences included staff, faculty, students, and librarians from the University of Florida, University of Central Florida, University of Oregon, Florida State University, University of Minnesota, Indian River State College, North Carolina Central University (Durham), Arcadia University (Philadelphia), Oklahoma State University, City University of New York, and Middle Tennessee University. In addition to the two conferences, representatives from the Rollins College Endeavor Foundation Center for Faculty Development and librarians from the Florida State University Libraries coordinated two workshops at their campuses which included librarians, as well as students, faculty, and staff members from other campus departments who wanted to learn about and experience the CoLAB Workshops for themselves. Most participants found the process easy to replicate in their own environments. One Post-it note response to the question "What are your next steps?" shared: "Attempt this process in multiple groups and classrooms (tech writing). Could I offer this process for the next round of collab grantseekers?" Another participant shared, "Totally stealing this workshop for next THATCamp."

Since the completion of the project, the grants manager has worked with the assessment librarian to qualitatively code data produced by participants during CoLAB Workshops. The results have shown that these workshops can offer alternatives to traditional strategic planning activities, like collecting survey results or conducting focus groups, to generate data about specific audiences, including their interests and future aspirations. The patterns exposed by the analysis of this data can provide organizations that sponsor CoLAB Workshops with insights into the types of programs and supports that, if implemented, could benefit the workshop participants they serve. To date, over 3,500 students, faculty, administrators, librarians, and nonprofit personnel have participated in CoLAB Workshops.

CHAPTER 3 TAKEAWAYS

- *Find out which primary collection materials are threatened and then determine which sponsor might care about their digital preservation.* Several proposals described in this chapter were awarded grant funds to mitigate the loss of these precious resources. Projects funded through the Center for Research Libraries, whose funds for digitization and preservation largely come from organization membership dues, supported the digitization of agricultural materials (through its Project Ceres funding program), newspaper microfilm reels of a major Dominican Republic newspaper (through its LAMP funding program), and rare printed Jewish heritage newspaper pages held in a Mexican archive (through its LARRP funding program).

- *A clever title can capture the interest of grant reviewers.* In the year that the digital humanities (DH) "bootcamp" proposal was submitted, DH work on campuses was in its infancy—not many faculty members were actively embracing this new form of scholarship—it was a mystery. Using the term bootcamp aligned with reviewer's goal to fund innovative projects. How often have you heard the term used to describe an intensive workshop in an academic setting? Another grant project example of using a non-traditional yet attention-grabbing title, *Film on a Boat*, can be found in chapter 5.

- *If a project team fails to be successful with its first submission, it shouldn't resubmit the same proposal for a subsequent deadline without significantly addressing its weaknesses (obtained in reviewer comments or through commonsense).* In the case of the *Florida Digital Newspaper Collection* project, the project team failed to receive funding for its first proposal to digitize a beloved Florida newspaper, the *Jewish Floridian*. Determining that the project scope was too narrow, the team resubmitted the proposal the following year with three major metropolitan public library system partners to emphasize the need to train users of the entire newspaper collection, rather than just digitizing the one newspaper title for its own sake.

- *A successful project with an evidenced-based track record can offer a sponsor a fundable proposal idea to expand its reach to serve new audiences.* The *Collaborating with Strangers Workshops* project illustrates this example. After many different sponsors had supported CoLAB Workshops at UF—primarily funding CoLAB Workshop assessments performed by the UF College of Education faculty—the author and creator of these workshops determined that providing how-to CoLAB facilitation training to other academic libraries' staff and faculty members could offer a fundable project to the national sponsor, Procter & Gamble, for expanding CoLABs to other campuses.

NOTES

1. Megan Daly, Bess de Farber, Gerry Altamirano, et al., "Facilitating Learning through Smart Pens," George A. Smathers Libraries, University of Florida Digital Collections, https://ufdc.ufl.edu/IR00010795/00001.

2. Jean Bossart, Sara Russell Gonzalez, Bess de Farber, et al., "Finding a Sustainable Solution for 3D Printing Waste," George A. Smathers Libraries, University of Florida Digital Collections, https://ufdc.ufl.edu/IR00010703/00001.

3. Nina Stoyan-Rosenzweig, Jane Morgan-Daniel, Hannah Norton, et al., "From Godzilla to Someone with a Stigmatized Illness to a Serial Killer / What Makes a Monster? A Community-Wide Discussion," George A. Smathers Libraries, University of Florida Digital Collections, https://ufdc.ufl.edu/IR00010958/00001.

4. Health Science Center Libraries, University of Florida, "Guidelines for Monsters Graphic Novel Contest," https://guides.uflib.ufl.edu/graphic-novel-contest.

5. Samuel Putnam and Bess de Farber, "VR/AR Development for Student Learning at MADE@UF," George A. Smathers Libraries, University of Florida Digital Collections, https://ufdc.ufl.edu/IR00010432/00001.

6. Suzanne Stapleton, Bess de Farber, Laura Perry, et al., "Preserving Florida's Agricultural History Digitization of *The Florida Cattleman & Livestock Journal*," George A. Smathers Libraries, University of Florida Digital Collections, https://ufdc.ufl.edu/IR00009329/00001.

7. Suzanne Stapleton, "Preserving Florida's Agricultural History: Digitization of the *Florida Cattleman & Livestock Journal*," presentation at the 16th Biennial Conference of the U.S. Agricultural Information Network, Pullman, WA, May 13–16, 2018, George A. Smathers Libraries, University of Florida Digital Collections, http://ufdc.ufl.edu/IR00010422/00001.

8. Suzanne Stapleton, "Preserving Florida's Agricultural History at the University of Florida: *Florida Cattleman & Livestock Journal*," George A. Smathers Libraries, University of Florida, https://guides.uflib.ufl.edu/floridacattleman.

9. University of Florida Digital Collections, Jewish Diaspora Collection, *Kesher*, December 15, 2003, http://ufdc.ufl.edu/AA00065679/00001.

10. Margarita Vargas-Betancourt, Chelsea Dinsmore, Bess de Farber, et al., "A Prototype for the Digitization of Latin American Jewish Newspapers," George A. Smathers Libraries, University of Florida Digital Collections, https://ufdc.ufl.edu/AA00039438/00001.

11. UNESCO, "Collection of the Center of Documentation and Investigation of the Ashkenazi Community in Mexico (16th to 20th Century)," http://www.unesco.org/new/en/communication-and-information/memory-of-the-world/register/

full-list-of-registered-heritage/registered-heritage-page-2/collection-of-th e-center-of-documentation-and-investigation-of-the-ashkenazi-community-in -mexico-16th-to-20th-century.

12. Margarita Vargas-Betancourt, Enrique Chmelnik, and Chelsea Dinsmore, "Digitization of a UNESCO World Memory Collection: Mexico's Jewish Heritage Newspapers," George A. Smathers Libraries, University of Florida Digital Collections, https://ufdc.ufl.edu/IR00009776/00001.

13. Carol McAuliffe, Kyla McMullen, Elizabeth Bouton, et al., "Sensing the Libraries: Sounds of the Panama Canal (ET04)," George A. Smathers Libraries, University of Florida Digital Collections, https://ufdc.ufl.edu/IR00010054/00001.

14. Digital Library of the Caribbean, http://dloc.com.

15. Fletcher Durant, Chelsea Dinsmore, and Bess de Farber, "*Listín Diario*: Preserving and Digitizing an at-Risk Dominican Republic Newspaper," George A. Smathers Libraries, University of Florida Digital Collections, https://ufdc.ufl .edu/IR00009775/00001.

16. Fletcher Durant and Bess de Farber, "*Listín Diario*: Phase II: Preserving and Digitizing an at-Risk Dominican Republic Newspaper (1931–1942)," George A. Smathers Libraries, University of Florida Digital Collections, https://ufdc.ufl .edu/IR00010315/00001.

17. Vernon N. Kisling, Jr., "Florida Agriculture – Rural Life Bibliography," George A. Smathers Libraries, University of Florida Digital Collections, https://ufdc.ufl .edu/UF00076179/00002.

18. Melody Royster and Suzanne Stapleton, "Increasing Accessibility to Rare Florida Agricultural Publications—Phase II," George A. Smathers Libraries, University of Florida Digital Collections, https://ufdc.ufl.edu/AA00029271/00001.

19. Wendy Jo Girven, ed., "Special Academic Libraries and the Millennial Patron," *Journal of Library Administration* 56, no. 8 (2016), www.tandfonline.com/doi/ full/10.1080/01930826.2016.1231551.

20. Penn State University, "One Button Studio," https://onebutton.psu.edu.

21. Stacey Ewing and Colleen Seale, "Library West One Button Studio," George A. Smathers Libraries, University of Florida Digital Collections, https://ufdc.ufl .edu/AA00038093/00001.

22. George A. Smathers Libraries, "One Button Studio @UFLibrary West," http:// guides.uflib.ufl.edu/InfoCommons/onebutton.

23. UF Information Technology, "One Button Studio Opens in Library West," https://news.it.ufl.edu/education/one-button-studio-opens-in-library-west; J. W. Glass, "Library West Opens Video Filming Studio," Alligator, March 28, 2016, www.alligator.org/news/campus/library-west-opens-video-filming-studio/ article_b0fa05ce-f49a-11e5-afc5-f3cd8ad8f9ca.html.

24. University of Florida, "Digital Humanities Working Group," https://digital humanities.group.ufl.edu/dh-uf.

25. Laurie Taylor, Bess de Farber, Haven Hawley, et al., "Digital Humanities Collaboration Bootcamp," George A. Smathers Libraries, University of Florida Digital Collections, https://ufdc.ufl.edu/AA00028978/00001.

26. Laurie Taylor, Bess de Farber, Haven Hawley, et al., "Digital Humanities Collaboration Bootcamp, Team Meetings Notes, Oct. 19, 2015," George A. Smathers Libraries, University of Florida Digital Collections, http://ufdc.ufl.edu/AA00028978/00003.

27. Brian W. Keith, Bonnie Smith, and Laurie Taylor, "ARL: Position Description Bank, Phase I," George A. Smathers Libraries, University of Florida Digital Collections, https://ufdc.ufl.edu/IR00000787/00001.

28. Rebecca Jefferson, "The Florida Jewish Newspaper Project (LSTA Grant Proposal)," George A. Smathers Libraries, University of Florida Digital Collections, https://ufdc.ufl.edu/AA00000517/00001.

29. Rebecca Jefferson and Bess de Farber, "The Florida Digital Newspaper Collection: Broadening Access and Users," George A. Smathers Libraries, University of Florida Digital Collections, https://ufdc.ufl.edu/AA00010438/00001.

30. University of Florida Digital Collections, George A. Smathers Libraries, "The Florida Jewish Newspaper Project," https://ufdc.ufl.edu/jewishnewspapers.

31. Rebecca Jefferson and April Hines, "Ethnic Newspapers Database and the Florida Digital Newspaper Library," George A. Smathers Libraries, University of Florida Digital Collections, http://ufdc.ufl.edu/AA00016915/00001.

32. Missy Clapp, Bess de Farber, and Barbara Hood, "Collaborating with Strangers (CoLAB) Grant Proposal (2011)," George A. Smathers Libraries, University of Florida Digital Collections, http://ufdc.ufl.edu/AA00013651/00001.

33. M. David Miller, "CoLAB: Collaborating with Strangers Evaluation (Report)," George A. Smathers Libraries, University of Florida Digital Collections, https://ufdc.ufl.edu/AA00013651/00001.

34. Ann Lindell, Bess de Farber, Barbara Hood, et al., "Collaborating with Strangers (Catalyst Fund)," George A. Smathers Libraries, University of Florida Digital Collections, https://ufdc.ufl.edu/IR00000788/00001.

35. April Hines and Bess de Farber, "Collaborating with Strangers In and Outside Mass Communications," George A. Smathers Libraries, University of Florida Digital Collections, http://ufdc.ufl.edu/AA00019151/00001.

36. April Hines, "Mini Grant: Collaborating with Strangers In and Outside Mass Communications," George A. Smathers Libraries, University of Florida Digital Collections, http://ufdc.ufl.edu/IR00003574/00001.

37. Bess de Farber, April Hines, and Barbara Hood, "Collaborating with Strangers Workshops: Broadening Impact through Florida Academic Libraries," George A. Smathers Libraries, University of Florida Digital Collections, https://ufdc.ufl.edu/IR00008781/00001.

4

Grant Partnership Proposals from $25,001 to $100,000

This chapter contains nine stories about funded grant projects with budgets ranging from $30,000 to $86,431 awarded to the George A. Smathers Libraries and its partners from 2010 through 2021. It happens that this funding range features the least number of submitted proposals during the years covered by this publication.

The types of projects featured in this chapter include technology, collaborative research and teaching, digital publishing, digitization, preservation, and professional development. The stories are organized in reverse chronological order, from those most recently submitted to those submitted earlier.

Included in this chapter are awarded proposals funded by the following sponsors and respective programs:

- The Andrew W. Mellon Foundation / Higher Education and Scholarship in the Humanities
- Florida Division of Library and Information Services / Library Services and Technology Act
- National Endowment for the Humanities / Preservation and Access Education and Training

- National Endowment for the Humanities / The Andrew W. Mellon Foundation / Open Book Program
- National Historical Publications and Records Commission / Digitizing Historical Records
- National Library of Medicine / HIV/AIDS Community Information Outreach Project
- National Park Service / Saving America's Treasures
- University of Florida / Technology Fee

TECHNOLOGY

University of Florida / Technology Fee

Prologue

The project team had heard from student patrons in both the Architecture and Fine Arts Library and the Map and Imagery Library about the lack of access to a large-format scanner for scanning large pieces of artwork, historical and student-created architectural drawings, and large maps. The Libraries at the time offered 8.5" × 11" or 11" × 17" flatbed scanners, and up to 18" × 24" formats using the Kic Bookeye scanners. Librarians had observed the lengths to which students would go to scan large architectural drawings, artwork, and maps—taking multiple scans and then stitching them together using Photoshop, or paying for scanning services at a commercial printing company at about four dollars per scan.

The Technology Fee program reviewers mostly include members of student government who are elected to serve for one year. Student reviewers of these grant applications often have limited knowledge about the actual needs of the 50,000 students they serve. This is because of the nature of their positions and a lack of system-wide methods to access such information. Knowing this, the team comprised of the head of the Architecture and Fine Arts Library, the architecture librarian, and the head of the Map and Imagery Library were aware of past student reviewers' feedback that requested more evidence of need. To verify their project's need, the team solicited feedback via campus e-mail lists and whiteboards that asked students to share their needs for access to such a scanner. Nearly all the responses indicated that access would save students time and money. Photographs of the students' handwritten comments were included in the grant narrative to justify why on-campus access to large-format scanners was important to them. This made an impact on the reviewers. The comments shared included: "Yes, Yes, Yes, to *yes dear god!!* no more scanning my 36" × 24" drawings one piece at a time and then stitching them back together in Photoshop"; "Yes, I am always going to Target copy or spending hours trying to Photoshop my two scans together"; and "Will save time for everyone!"

The initial concept paper proposed the acquisition of two large-format scanners. After the first-round review, the team received an invitation to submit a full proposal. In between the concept paper and the full proposal submission, the team continued to ask students for input about what they needed in regard to the scanners. This new input, particularly from the architecture students, changed the full proposal application to include the purchase of one additional large-format scanner to be installed in the Humanities and Social Sciences Library, open twenty-four hours a day, seven days a week, to increase accessibility and serve the large population that frequents this popular library.

Proposal Summary

Large Format Scanning in the Libraries ($30,000 request)

This project team seeks to purchase three Image Access WideTEK 44 Scanners to be located at the Architecture and Fine Arts (AFA) Library, the Map and Imagery Library, and the Humanities and Social Sciences Library. This equipment features a drum/roll-fed color scanner that accommodates materials up to forty-four inches wide to improve access to digitization options for library collections and original works produced by students and faculty. Project team includes the head of the Map and Imagery Library (PI) and the head of the Architecture and Fine Arts Library (Co-PI) (one year: 2018 to 2019).[1]

FIGURE 4.1
A student uses the large-format printer in the Map and Imagery Library
Photo by Barbara Hood, https://ufdc.ufl.edu/IR00011033/00001

Epilogue

The project was fully funded. The three scanners were purchased and installed with a separate screen that allows patrons to edit the scan on the fly. The printers have experienced heavy use by UF-affiliated users. Architecture students in design courses use their scanner extensively to scan maps for the areas being investigated by the class, as well as for large-scale architectural drawings. Recently, unique maps and blueprints of a section of the Florida Barge Canal were scanned. The wide-format scanner was very useful to a Libraries-funded graduate student intern who was studying epigraphic squeezes—paper impressions taken of ancient Greek inscriptions. The scanner was able to handle these large pieces of paper without damaging them. Another project benefit was that when students were providing feedback on what they needed with regard to scanning equipment, some AFA Library users requested a large paper cutter. Using funds from another source, the AFA Library staff purchased a 50+ inch rotary trimmer and paper cutter that now serves many architecture and art students.

COLLABORATION DEVELOPMENT

The Andrew W. Mellon Foundation / Higher Education and Scholarship in the Humanities

Prologue

Applying for funding from private foundations often requires an invitation to apply. Typically, the invitation is delivered by a program officer (if the foundation supports that type of position), or by a board member if the invitation comes from a small or family foundation. This trend of "invitation-only applications" has grown over the years due to the many funding databases now available and the ubiquitous online presence of foundation guidelines, lists of past awardees, and contact information. The internet has essentially opened the floodgates to potentially thousands of applicants, easily overwhelming the capacity of small staffs or boards that are managing foundation review and award processes. Foundation boards are sensitive to the amount of funds expended on operational expenses, including staff, since this reduces the available grant funding.

In this case, the invitation arrived from the senior program officer for the Andrew W. Mellon Foundation's Higher Education and Scholarship in the Humanities Program, after learning about the dynamic work of the UF Center for the Humanities and the Public Sphere through the executive director of development of the UF Foundation. The Andrew W. Mellon Foundation's mission is to "strengthen, promote, and, where necessary, defend the contributions of the humanities and the arts to human flourishing and to the well-being of diverse and democratic societies."[2] To this end, the senior program officer was interested in receiving a proposal request to fund an implementation project that would (1) support the work of humanities faculty on campus in developing new curricula that would target undergraduate students, as a way of increasing the pipeline of students who chose to study humanities disciplines; and (2) increase the awareness of innovative programming supported by the Center for the Humanities and the Public Sphere.

The director and associate director of the Center, who were relatively new to requesting major private foundation funding, approached the Libraries grants manager for support in developing a fundable proposal. Although the grants manager is restricted to performing grantseeking activities that include Libraries personnel, this opportunity offered both parties a way to develop a strong proposal while including the grants manager's particular expertise as a certified professional facilitator and collaborative grants administrator in the proposal, thus creating a new partnership for the Libraries. In reviewing recent awards made by the Mellon Foundation, the project team learned of its interest in supporting cross-disciplinary faculty groups to perform research and offer curricula that would address contemporary public issues while employing the lens of the humanities.

The Center's director and associate director devised a plan to convene multidisciplinary humanities and non-humanities faculty members and doctoral students to form research groups that would (1) develop new syllabi for undergraduate courses around topics related to a grand challenge question, (2) identify other campus courses that would contribute to a designation of "Intersections Scholar" for undergraduates upon graduation, and (3) raise the visibility of the Center on campus and beyond through its sponsorship of public-facing programming that would present lectures, exhibits, published materials, videos, and other outlets for supporting the research of faculty group members as they contributed research to explore their grand challenge questions. Including the Libraries as a major partner provided access to several assets: multiple presentation venues of different types and sizes, an internal graphic design and printing department for publishing promotional materials, subject-specific librarians to support the work of the various faculty researchers, technological tools for supporting undergraduate students in new humanities courses, and knowledge about and access to primary materials related to the work of faculty groups to use in their research, programming, and courses. Beyond these assets, the grants manager offered facilitation expertise for the Intersections Groups to support successful completion of their projects, as well as grantsmanship assistance to create fundable proposals for future sponsors.

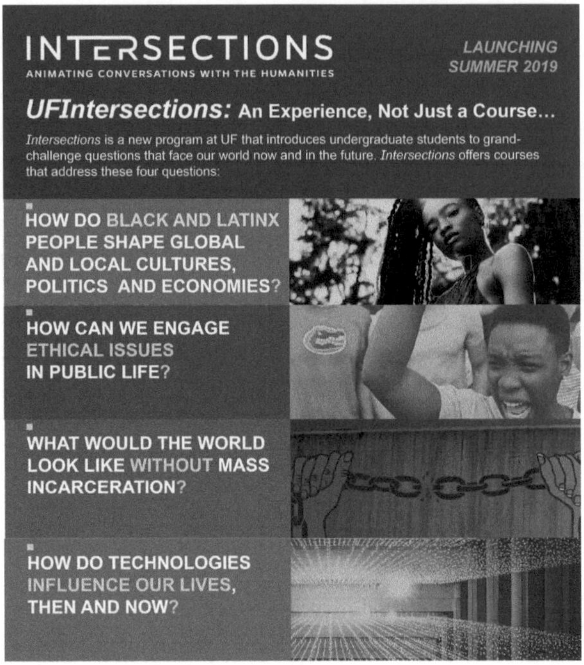

FIGURE 4.2
Poster promoting
Intersections
Scholars recruitment

Image by Barbara Hood,
https://ufdc.ufl.edu/
IR00011033/00001

Project Summary

Intersections: Animating Conversations with the Humanities ($400,000 total cash request; $59,686 cash request for Libraries subaward)

This proposal submitted by the Center for the Humanities and the Public Sphere (CHPS) requests three years of support to raise the visibility of CHPS by shaping undergraduate humanities general education and highlighting the contribution of humanities disciplines to solving local and global challenges. This proposed program is designed to harness the perspectives and methodologies of humanities disciplines to address grand challenge questions. The program will encourage faculty and doctoral students to work collaboratively, identify essential themes from a variety of disciplinary perspectives, and develop a research-based undergraduate curriculum that integrates scholarly approaches to these complex issues. Project team includes the CHPS personnel including director (PI), associate director (Co-PI), and incoming interim director of the CHPS (Co-PI), with grants manager (subaward PI), and consultation from director of the Honors Program, associate provost for undergraduate affairs, senior associate dean of scholarly resources and services, and associate dean for undergraduate affairs (three years: 2017 to 2020).[3]

Epilogue

The proposal was fully funded, and the Libraries grants manager joined the Intersections Leadership Team (which included the CHPS director and associate director) to oversee the facilitation and management of the program. Initially, the program required extensive communication to orient prospective participating faculty to this new opportunity for the funding of cross-disciplinary research and teaching groups. Two workshops called "Collaborating with Strangers on Intersections: Animating Conversations in the Humanities @ UF" brought over seventy faculty members, library faculty, and graduate students together to learn about the opportunity and each other's research interests. Two subsequent workshops called "CoLAB Idea Table Cafes Intersections: Animating Conversations in the Humanities @ UF" gave faculty and graduate students opportunities to develop ideas for research and teaching groups, and practice the development of grand challenge questions.

Eight groups eventually formed and submitted funding applications to CHPS to carry out new research, sponsor public events, develop new humanities courses, and practice collaboration activities. A peer review process selected four groups, each of which included a librarian, for Intersections Research-into-Teaching Grants totaling $120,000: (1) "Intersections on Ethics in the Public Sphere" (How can we think critically about the ethical dimensions of divisive public issues?); (2) "Intersections on Global Blackness and Latinx Identity" (How does blackness travel locally and across the globe?); (3) "Intersections on Mass Incarceration" (What would a future without mass incarceration look like and how do we get there?); and (4) "Intersections on Imagineering and the Technosphere" (How have technologies shaped our lives, and how can we draw on them to meet twenty-first-century challenges on a planetary scale?). A website featuring each of the groups was developed as a means of promoting Intersections and information about relevant courses to recruit undergraduate student enrollment.[4] At the time of this writing, over 140 undergraduates have enrolled, and forty have completed the course selection requirements for becoming Intersections Scholars.

COLLECTION DEVELOPMENT

National Endowment for the Humanities /
The Andrew W. Mellon Foundation / Open Book Program

Prologue

A new grant program was established by NEH in partnership with the Mellon Foundation in 2015. The goal of the program, which is called the Open Book Program, is to support the re-release of out-of-print books published in hard copy exclusively by university presses around the country. Much can be gained when a prospective applicant discovers a new grant program for which it is prepared to submit a fundable proposal. The number of competitive applications submitted to secure a grant award during the first round of a new funding opportunity is usually sparse. In this case, the Libraries' digital scholarship librarian was prepared to respond to the first call for proposals when the opportunity appeared on the NEH website. A relationship between the University Press of Florida (the Press) and the Libraries staff—the digital scholarship librarian in particular—had been cultivated over several years, largely through conversations related to determining the copyright clearance for previously out-of-print books published by the Press that were being considered for digitization and uploading by the UF Digital Collections.

The Press has a lean staff whose targeted responsibilities keep a complex publishing and marketing system running. To bring more visibility to the outstanding work of the Press staff, the digital scholarship librarian and the grants manager co-presented a CoLAB Workshop (see chapter 3), Collaborating with Strangers on Publishing, which introduced Press staff to librarians, faculty, and students as a means of building awareness on campus of the Press's mission and publishing programs. This effort to help the Press staff demonstrated that the Libraries' employees were genuinely interested in combining forces with the Press.

When the NEH/Mellon Foundation called for the first Open Book Program proposals, the Press and the Libraries staff members immediately met to determine the feasibility of working together to submit a fundable proposal. The Press staff voiced their collective aversion to managing both the grant preparation and the submission process, as well as the post-award management process if the application were awarded. The Press's small staff could not assume these responsibilities while simultaneously managing their workflows and workloads. After an initial meeting with Press administrators, and a call with the program director at NEH, the librarian and the grants manager were convinced that a collaborative and fundable project could be developed in time to make the deadline. It was determined that (1) the Libraries staff would prepare the application draft for review and input by the Press, (2) the applicant organization would be the Libraries in partnership with the Press, and (3) the awarded funds would be managed by the Libraries with a subaward to the Press, so that funds could be expended directly by the Press for vendor digitization expenses and compensation for a few staff members who worked on the project.

To extract a theme for the type of out-of-print books to be selected for digitization and open-access publishing, the digital scholarship librarian proposed topics that would most align with the Libraries' major objectives; namely, out-of-print books about Florida and Caribbean history. These foci would yield a plethora of potential out-of-print books previously published by the Press from the 1960s through the 1990s to be assessed for re-release. The grant application guidelines requested information about the titles and authors to be considered for digitization during the grant period, since the funder knew that some books would not be eligible for various reasons, the most significant being difficulty in obtaining copyright releases, not just from the author but also from photographer(s) who had contributed to the original books. A major strength that the Press staff brought to the proposal was their knowledge of the significance of each of the potentially viable out-of-print books. This narrative describing the selected books' significance, especially for supporting current and future humanities scholars as well as public school teachers who teach history throughout the state, was key to producing a fundable proposal.

Proposal Summary

Books about Florida and the Caribbean: From the University Press of Florida (UPF) to the World ($78,865 cash request; $69,843 cost share contribution)

In collaboration with the Press and a humanities advisory board, the project team will make thirty out-of-print books freely available online and in electronic formats. The project team plans to complete the following deliverables: (1) engage an expert Advisory Board to prioritize selections and plan for promotional and educational programmatic opportunities for university press and academic library collaborations; (2) secure rights and permissions for selected books about Florida and the Caribbean published by the Press from 1968 to 1992; (3) digitize and distribute with Creative Commons-licensing for books in the EPUB 3.0.1, PDF for print-on-demand, and Web PDF formats; (4) implement a marketing plan to broadly

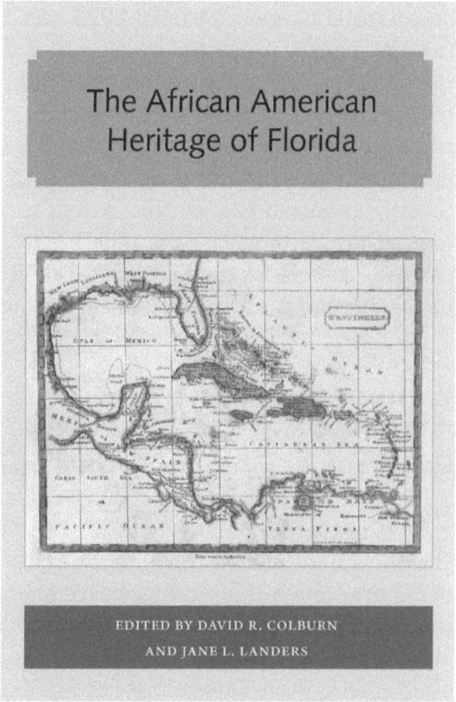

FIGURE 4.3
One of the digitized out-of-print books made available through the Open Books Program. *The African American Heritage of Florida*, published in Philadelphia, 1806
University Press of Florida, https://ufdc.ufl.edu/AA00061985/00001

promote the online availability of the books to scholars, educators, students, and the general public; and (5) produce a white paper that documents the project's processes, costs, and rights issues while serving as a guide for replicating its collaborative process for other university presses and academic libraries. Project team includes the digital scholarship librarian (PI), director of the Press (Co-PI), coordinator of digital production services (Co-PI), chair of Special Collections and Area Studies (Co-PI), and assistant dean of administrative services and faculty affairs (Co-PI) (two years: 2016 to 2018).[5]

Epilogue

The proposal was selected to be fully awarded by the Mellon Foundation. But to receive the award, the librarian and the grants manager were required to rewrite the entire NEH proposal to conform to the guidelines specified by the Mellon Foundation. The team found this both challenging and a learning experience that might come in handy for preparing future Mellon Foundation applications.

During the project, the Press experienced staff changes that required the team to request a no-cost extension to complete the project. Beyond completing the digitization and deposit of thirty-nine out-of-print books into the open-access UF Digital Collections, providing a print-on-demand option, and broadly promoting and distributing the free online availability of these books (total usage as of April 2020 was 159,653 views), the project yielded the opportunity to further develop staff relationships between the Press and the Libraries. The grant project activities themselves created the impetus for the Libraries and the Press team members to meet on a regular basis. As the staffs worked together to resolve workflows, rights, and budget issues, they developed a close working relationship. Upon completion of the project, both teams recognized the valuable assets each had brought to the project and wanted to continue working together in a similar fashion. To that end, the partners co-created the LibraryPress@UF to offer opportunities to combine forces through the formation of a new co-imprint.[6]

TECHNOLOGY

University of Florida / Technology Fee

Prologue

The 3D project team at the Marston Science Library was curious about a type of 3D printer which uses alternative filament—other than plastic—for environmental reasons, and about offering options for printing in different colors. They identified a company that uses paper fiber filament and felt they had a case for requesting Technology Fee funding to cover the purchase cost. One of the many benefits of using two types of materials for printing is the ability to print complicated models that require a lot of support material, which holds up complex geometries during the 3D printing process. The idea was to use a water dissolvable material for the support material.

Simultaneously, the team was considering ways that students and faculty could learn the 3D printing process directly and was considering requesting funds to purchase small 3D printers that students and faculty could check out and use outside of the Libraries. In 2016, the customary procedure was that 3D projects were dropped off at the Science Library, printed behind a glass printing lab, and fees were paid ($0.15/gram) by the patrons who used this printing service. No one outside of the lab was learning how to actually do 3D printing for their own projects. After extensive inquiries and searching, the team discovered that no other library at the time was loaning out 3D printers to patrons. Their rationale to justify the request and to validate the feasibility of this idea was that iPads were circulating at a higher cost per unit than a 3D printer that could be bought for under $300.

Proposal Summary

New Functionality for UF Libraries' 3D Printing Services ($86,431 cash request)

The team plans to expand the UF Libraries' 3D printing services to include multicolor printers, along with a fleet of small 3D printers that will circulate to students. The proposal requests the acquisition of four dual-extruder Fusion F306 printers that can 3D print models using two colors of plastic filament. Project team includes the engineering librarian (PI) and physics librarian (Co-PI) (start date: 2016 for one year).[7]

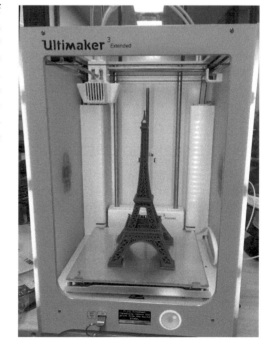

FIGURE 4.4
Eiffel Tower, modified and printed by the Marston
Science Library's 3D
Laboratory using an
Ultimaker 3 Extended
Bed 3D Printer

Photo by Jean Bossart, https://ufdc.ufl.edu/
IR00011033/00001

Epilogue

The project was fully funded. By the time the team was ready to purchase the multicolor paper 3D printer, the manufacturer of the printer was experiencing supply chain difficulties. The team requested and was approved for several no-cost extensions to complete the project, but in the end the manufacturer went bankrupt. With permission from the sponsor, funds that had not been expended for the paper 3D printer were used to purchase an Ultimaker 3 Extended Bed 3D Printer allowing for complex geometries and mixed materials (including dissolvable materials) to reduce printing restrictions.

Funding budgeted to purchase the twelve circulating 3D printers, on the other hand, was a successful venture. Patrons were loaned small 3D printers and given filament for their printing projects at no cost. The filament (1,000 kilograms) was funded by the award. Within six months, the service had been increased to include ten additional 3D printers, for a total of twenty-two circulating 3D printers. During the one-year period from May 15, 2017, through May 14, 2018, these circulating 3D printers were checked out 272 times, even though not all of the twenty-two portable printers were consistently available, with some needing repair at any given time, and others on loan to faculty members. These printers were, however, prone to breaking, even though the ones purchased were the most durable at the best price points. However, this vendor also went out of business, but the team was able to find a better-designed printer for $250 per unit. A 3D fund was created using the fees patrons paid for printing their models, and other internal library funding, to cover the costs of ongoing expenses related to circulating the small 3D printers. The two librarians leading the project attended the Construct 3D Conference in Atlanta, Georgia, in October 2018 to present "Teaching 3D: Developing Learning-by-Doing Experiences" and a poster session, "Lending 3D-Printers: The Nuts and Bolts of Circulating 3D Technology." A journal article authored by the team, "Retrospective Analysis of a Sustainable 3D Printing Service in an Academic Library," was published in *Library Hi Tech* 37, no. 4, in 2019.

HEALTH INFORMATION DISSEMINATION

National Library of Medicine / HIV/AIDS Community Information Outreach Project

Prologue

For a team of Health Science Center Library (HSCL) librarians, the motivation to create the proposal for the *HIV/AIDS Community Information Outreach Project* arrived with a call for proposals distributed by the sponsor, the National Library of Medicine (NLM), which receives funding from the National Institutes of Health to re-grant to libraries. HSCL had just hired a liaison librarian in consumer health. Her outreach skills matched up with the skills needed to create partnerships in the greater Alachua County communities, as well as in Jacksonville, a metropolitan city that has been significantly affected by new HIV/AIDS cases. Health librarians working at the University of Florida serve both Alachua County and Jacksonville. Regardless of the funding, the team had wanted to initiate partnerships with community organizations around topics of health information dissemination, although the topic of HIV/AIDS was not on their radar at that time. If successful, the proposal would support, for the first time, a health outreach project that would train the staff members of participating organizations outside of UF in how to find high-quality information on HIV/AIDS.

Having completed two consecutive NLM-funded grant projects focused on women's health issues, the team was confident in its ability to create a fundable proposal for the HIV/AIDS outreach project. They began by brainstorming the assets within reach that would add value to their proposal, including those with subject expertise. To acquire partners, the team first considered its existing relationships with organizations inside and outside of UF. For instance, the director of HSCL had previously met with the Alachua County Public Library director, who had voiced a desire to increase community outreach in the county. The public library director shared contact information for various public library system employees who could assist in connecting HSCL librarians with public libraries in the county. One public branch library in particular, the Library Partnership, agreed to participate in the project. This library serves as a branch within the county system, as well as a place for families to access neighborhood resources for health, prevention, and wellness information.[8]

UF campus groups agreed to participate as well, including HealthStreet. The medical humanities librarian had cofounded UF's Center for Arts in Medicine, which agreed to partner on the project. The director of the Borland Library (a part of HSCL) in Jacksonville was connected to UF CARES (Center for HIV/AIDS Education and Research), which joined the project. SHARC (Southern HIV and Alcohol Research Consortium), another UF-based organization, was recruited by an HSCL librarian through an existing connection and agreed as well. Finally, connections with the Jacksonville Public Library resulted in yet another partner.

In considering access to other existing assets, the team reviewed its recent success using the CoLAB Planning Series®—"Collaborating with Strangers Workshop" (see chapter 3) facilitated by the grants manager, to initiate collaborative relationships among graduate students and faculty at the UF on the topic of women's health. Its awarded grant projects from the National Network of Libraries of Medicine had supported the evaluation of two such workshops, with documented successful results. The team decided to include a CoLAB Workshop in its proposed project activities as a means of initiating collaborative relationships among nonprofit community organizations and UF entities to increase the dissemination of reliable health information about HIV/AIDS topics. Given that producing training videos on how to find high-quality health information is a strength of the Center for Arts in Medicine, the production of four training videos to benefit the participating organization staff also was proposed for the project.

Proposal Summary

Partnering to Provide HIV/AIDS Information Outreach ($50,000 cash request)

This project is a collaborative outreach initiative between numerous units at the University of Florida, led by its Health Science Center Libraries in Gainesville and Jacksonville, in partnership with local public libraries and with the support of the Alachua County Disease Control Unit. The goal is to increase and enhance access to HIV/AIDS information resources to vulnerable populations in these geographic areas, which have both a large and rapidly growing population of HIV-infected individuals. Florida has the highest number of newly diagnosed HIV infection cases in the United States, and the third-highest HIV infected population overall. The project team will (1) facilitate collaboration between health care providers and organizations focused on HIV/AIDS education, prevention, and treatment through the hosting of two Collaborating with Strangers Workshops (CoLABs); (2) develop and disseminate accessible and locally relevant HIV/AIDS educational materials designed for populations with limited literacy and limited access to health care; (3) train health care professionals, community service providers, and health consumers in the use of

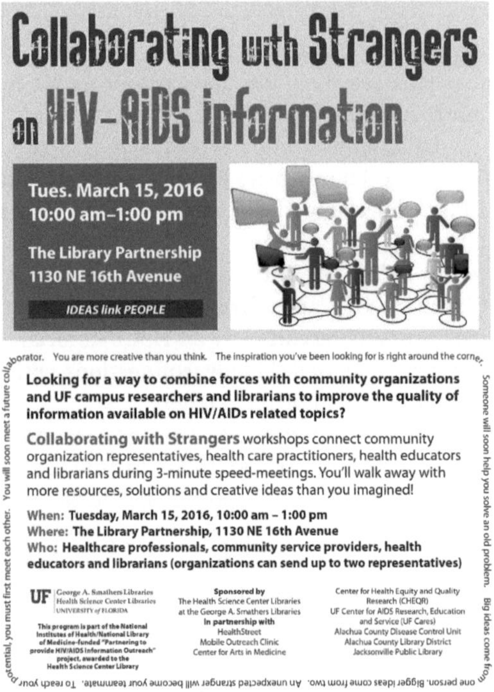

FIGURE 4.5

Electronic postcard promoting the CoLAB Workshop on HIV/AIDS Information

Image by Barbara Hood

Photo by Bess de Farber, https://ufdc.ufl.edu/IR00011033/00001

FIGURE 4.6
Participants in the Collaborating with
Strangers Workshop share information
about their work and converse during a
speed meeting.

authoritative HIV/AIDS information resources from the NLM
and other venues through a series
of workshops and presentations
aimed at increasing their HIV/
AIDS information-seeking skills;
and (4) raise public awareness of
HIV/AIDS's history and societal
impact through the NLM's "Sur-
viving and Thriving: AIDS, Politics,
and Culture" exhibit and an associated speaker. The partners include
HealthStreet, the Mobile Outreach
Clinic, Center for Arts in Medicine, Center for Health Equity and
Quality Research (CHEQR) and
the UF Center for AIDS Research,
Education and Service (UF Cares),
and has commitments for partnerships from the Alachua County Library Dis-
trict (Headquarters and the Library Partnership branch) and the Jacksonville
Public Library. Project team includes the HSCL associate director (PI), three
health science liaison librarians (Co-PI), with the health outreach librarian,
graphic designer and webmaster, director of medical humanities, Borland
Library director, and Borland Library medical information services librarian
(one year: 2015 to 2016).[9]

Epilogue

During the grant review process, an NLM staff member sought out more information from the team about its ability to harness participation by clinicians
who are often too busy with patients to commit to such partnerships. The
team replied that it was quite confident about its strong relationships with
identified clinical partners (more so than its nonprofit partners, but NLM was
only concerned about the clinicians). The proposal was fully funded, to the
team's surprise, given that awards to academic institutions for this type of
project are rare.

The project team successfully completed all of its proposed activities, serving twenty organizations and researchers during the CoLAB, producing four training videos, acquiring an NLM HIV/AIDS traveling exhibit, presenting a guest speaker at the public library, and providing eleven in-person training sessions for community organizations working on HIV/AIDS prevention and care in Alachua County and Jacksonville.[10] All of this, of course, brought the team new community organizations with which to engage (which was especially beneficial because some proposed partners had been unable to participate), and deeper relationships with those who agreed to participate.

The NLM award guidelines specify that NLM-specific information resources must be the source of the health information about HIV/AIDS that was disseminated. The NLM's portal of resources provides reputable information for general public consumption that social service, health care, and librarian professionals may not be aware of. In connecting to the nonprofits in person, and to broader communities through the videos, the project team was able to push out these valuable health resources. Two HSCL librarians providing outreach services continue to serve medical and social service practitioners, volunteers, and others through the relationships developed during the project.

DIGITIZATION/PRESERVATION

National Historical Publications and Records Commission / Digitizing Historical Records

Prologue

The curator of UF's P.K. Yonge Library of Florida History had been pondering for years about what to do with a large collection of manuscripts in the collection he managed. These included fourteen collections of family papers, 134 volumes of diaries and memoirs authored by forty different writers, and 240 folders of letters, reports, and sketches covering the period from 1784 to 1912. The "glue" that held these items together was their detailed accounts of life in tropical Florida during this formative time in Florida's history, and their common fragile condition—essentially limiting access to patrons in the Special Collections Reading Room during normal hours of operation. Much care was needed in handling these items.

Due to advances in the technology and availability of scanners that have reduced their impact on fragile materials, the curator began making inquiries about the possibility of digitizing these materials. Several problems needed to be solved. For instance, some of the diaries were tiny, and had been carried by soldiers during the Civil War and Seminole wars in a small pocket. Some were written in very light pencil, and mostly in meticulously beautiful handwriting that was difficult to read. These and other factors caused the curator to wonder whether or not these materials would survive digital processing, and what steps would be necessary in order to prevent damage to them. After testing these possibilities, the Digital Library Center staff, in partnership with the conservator, determined that a full-time technician exclusively dedicated to the project over two years would be necessary to conduct imaging and attach metadata records to each of the items. The test also revealed the speed at which pages could be digitized with accompanying metadata attachment, as a means of determining the anticipated length of time of the project, as well as the staffing needs and accompanying cost-per-page estimate.

There was much discussion about the estimated digitization cost-per-page average of $4.38. This average considerably exceeded the suggested highest cost-per-page estimate for proposals being submitted to the National Historical Publications and Records Commission (NHPRC)—a prospective funder. The $4.38 per page estimate included expenses related to the temporary full-time technician. Ultimately, the project team could not reduce the cost per page without removing the technician from the budget. It was decided that the project would have to move forward using the high cost per page average.

With this information in hand, the curator convened a project team and the grants manager to assess which sponsor to approach. Two sponsors, the NEH's Humanities Collections and Reference Resources Program (HCRR) and the NHPRC's Access to Historical Records: Archival Projects, were determined to be the most suitable ones. Due to previously committed plans to develop another project proposal for HCRR Program submission during this time frame, the team focused on assessing the feasibility of applying to the NHPRC; however, the project's cost per page (cash request), even though it was supported by contributed UF labor, appeared to eliminate this prospect. Nevertheless, the team went ahead and prepared a draft proposal for review by the NHPRC program officer while knowing that the per-page cost would be problematic. To mitigate this, the team emphasized the value of the collection to scholars who were aware of its existence, and added the creation of learning modules designed for K–12 schoolteachers to use in conjunction with the digital materials as a proposed output of the project.

For NHPRC proposals, there is a window of opportunity to submit pre-proposal drafts as a means of getting feedback from program officers. Obtaining this program officer's feedback was critical to understanding his concerns about aspects of the project narrative that needed further clarification. With the program officer's recommendations and encouragement, the application was finalized and submitted.

FIGURE 4.7
Example of a watercolor illustration from the Abraham Paul Leech Letters and Sketches (1873–1874), which contain twenty-one letters, totaling 121 pages, plus ten manuscript poems, totaling forty-three pages, all of which are illustrated with fifty-eight watercolors. The letters detail the travels of Abraham Paul Leech and his oldest son Abraham Duryea Leech in Jacksonville, Palatka, Green Cove Springs, and Mellonville, Florida; Savannah, Macon, and Atlanta, Georgia; and Knoxville, Tennessee. The letters are directed home to Leech's wife and younger son in New York.

Page 19, Watercolor illustration by Abraham Paul Leech, https://ufdc.ufl.edu/AA00028687/00002/

Proposal Summary

Pioneer Days in Florida: Diaries and Letters for the Settling of the Sunshine State, 1800–1900 ($79,950 cash request; $79,950 cost share contribution)

This two-year project proposes to digitize 36,530 pages of diaries and letters from the Florida Miscellaneous Manuscripts Collection at the P.K. Yonge Library of Florida History, describing frontier life in Florida from the end of the colonial period to the beginning of the modern state. A website and education module will be developed, and the project will be promoted widely through the Florida Historical Society, the Florida Humanities Council, teacher workshops, and website links, press releases, public presentations, and brochures. Project team includes the curator of P.K. Yonge Library of Florida History (PI), associate chair of collection services (Co-PI), director of digital library services (Co-PI), with the head of conservation, education librarian, metadata and quality control coordinator, digital assets coordinator, and digital scholarship librarian (two years: 2013 to 2015).[11]

Epilogue

The project was fully awarded. A project technician was hired and trained to complete the digitization. The main concerns of the project were twofold: (1) to prevent any damage to the items, and (2) to replicate the experience of turning the pages of diaries and journals as though the reader were experiencing the items in the Smathers Libraries reading room, but in an online environment. A patron perusing these materials in the reading room first would see the entire collection of say, diaries, and then select a particular diary to investigate further. Or, if the contents pertained to letters, the patron would first receive the entire folder of letters. Likewise, in the digital version, those searching the content will view a list of collection diaries, and then select a particular diary that includes the cover and presents a flip-book option where the pages are turned electronically by the user.[12]

Ultimately, the total project costs per page were far less than anticipated because of the efficiencies developed by the technician, who remained in the position for most of the grant period until being hired as an engineering librarian to lead the Made@ UF makerspace program at UF's Marston Science Library. Another full-time employee was hired and trained to complete the project within the original grant period. At the project's conclusion, a fund balance remained which allowed the team to request a no-cost extension to digitize more pages. This was approved. The final count of digitized items included 313 collections, diaries, and other papers comprising 52,459 pages of online material, or 15,929 pages (43 percent) more than the proposed goal.

DIGITIZATION/PRESERVATION

National Park Service / Save America's Treasures

Prologue

In 2010, the Libraries' Special Collections acquired a collection on deposit from Flagler College that consisted of historically significant architectural drawings for the Ponce de León Hotel, an important Gilded Age building in St. Augustine designed by the Carrère & Hastings firm—influential designers of the New York Public Library and other important landmarks. In 1888 Carrère & Hastings, then a fledgling architectural firm in New York City, completed its first successful commissioned project—and the first large building using cast-in-place concrete in the country—the Ponce de León Hotel, which ultimately became the home of Flagler College.[13]

These drawings had been presumed destroyed but were rediscovered in 2004 in a boiler room at Flagler College, where they had been unfortunately stored in terrible environmental conditions for decades. In some cases, the drawings could not be unrolled without disintegrating. Rodents, insects, and fluctuations in temperature and humidity had seriously damaged the drawings.

At the same time, the Libraries acquired drawings of the Flagler Memorial Presbyterian Church in St. Augustine, also designed by Carrère & Hastings and built in 1889. The Presbyterian Church drawings were in much better condition and had never been lost, but they were inaccessible to historians and architects. The project team sought to ensure the preservation of both of these collections of drawings by proposing to apply conservation treatments, and to digitize all of the drawings so that they could be made available to the world.

The team was excited about the opportunity to preserve and provide access to the drawings because they incorporated many unique design elements which would be of interest to broad audiences. For instance, the hotel drawings included the work of design collaborators Louis Comfort Tiffany and Thomas Edison. And both the hotel and the church used a relatively new method of poured concrete mixed with coquina shell stone; the hotel became the largest structure built using poured concrete at this time, adding to its intriguing characteristics.

The historic preservation faculty member at Flagler College, who was a UF alumnus, suggested that the Libraries join forces with the College to seek funding from the National Park Service's Save America's Treasures program—a sponsor that had awarded a previous historic preservation grant to the College. The curator of architecture collections at the Libraries brought the UF team together and facilitated communication between the grants manager, the faculty member at the College, and the Memorial Presbyterian Church staff who served as partners. Both drawing collections were on deposit at the Libraries because neither the College nor the church had the resources or expertise to preserve and provide access to the drawings. It is well known in Florida that the Libraries have excellent digitization and conservation personnel, equipment, and technologies (including UF Digital Collections), and these were necessary to establish credibility with the sponsor to achieve the project goals.

Proposal Summary

Saving St. Augustine's Architectural Treasures (cash request subaward for Libraries of $41,181; $41,232 cost share contribution)

In partnership with the applicant organization, Flagler College (applicant organization), and the Flagler Memorial Presbyterian Church, this Save America's Treasures project will conserve and digitally preserve an irreplaceable collection of the earliest architectural drawings of John Carrère (1858–1911) and Thomas Hastings (1860–1929). Created for Henry Flagler in St. Augustine, Florida, these drawings had been "lost" for decades. Project team at UF includes the curator of architecture archives, architecture librarian, head of conservation, digital audiovisual resources manager, and digital assets coordinator (two years: 2010 to 2012).[14]

FIGURE 4.8
Postcard front and back, with photograph of the Hotel Ponce de Leon,
St. Augustine, Florida

Source: https://ufdc.ufl.edu/USACH00408/00001

Epilogue

The project received full funding. The project team was able to achieve all of
its project goals as planned. Some of the drawings were in somewhat worse
condition than expected, and the conservator had a difficult time applying
conservation treatments to these items. Otherwise, the project was rather
straightforward, and the team completed exactly what it set out to do.

The 267 architecture drawings of the two structures dating from 1896
to 1957 include blueprints (55 percent), pencil drawings on various types of
paper (30 percent), and other types of prints such as Vandyke prints, diazo-
type, ink on linen, and a few printed materials (15 percent). Many of the
blueprints are working copies that contain notes, corrections, and changes
in pencil, pen, and red and blue grease pencil. A number of the drawings have
hand-applied color. The sizes range from 8" × 8" to over 4' × 8'. Since completion of the project, the digital items have attracted more than 325,000 views.[15]

TRAINING

National Endowment for the Humanities /
Preservation and Access Education and Training

Prologue

The chair of a steering committee for a grant-funded program called *Opening
Archives: Improving Access to Primary Sources in Florida* also served as assistant
chair for Special Collections and Area Studies at the Libraries. This committee
sought to increase access to archival materials in the state of Florida through
better online description, preservation, and digitization. It had identified a

significant roadblock to executing the Opening Archives program: many of the archivists and cultural heritage professionals in Florida lacked up-to-date knowledge of current access and preservation standards, and best practices. The committee learned, through informal survey data, that professionals serving in preservation roles lacked the funding (both institutional and/or personal) to seek up-to-date training in these professional activities. In an effort to mitigate this alarming gap in knowledge and expertise, committee members decided to seek grant funding to deliver a training program to the professionals and volunteers who were working throughout the state. In their analysis, the committee members determined that Florida (the third most populous state in the country) was woefully behind other states in receiving federal funding for projects relating to the support of primary sources, particularly regarding preservation and access.

The assistant chair of Special Collections and Area Studies was excited about the prospect of providing training to those who couldn't afford to remain current with professional standards and practices, and the opportunity to elevate the competencies of the professionals in Florida who were managing historically significant collections, which in turn would result in better preservation and access for archival materials. With this enthusiasm, a number of partners were recruited, including the Florida Center for Library Automation and multiple universities including the University of Central Florida, the University of Miami, Florida State University, and the University of South Florida. Members of the steering committee had experience in managing previous projects, including Library Services and Technology Act (LSTA) funded projects awarded through the State Library for providing training throughout Florida. The project team had an excellent relationship with the Society of American Archivists' education office staff who managed a program to produce and distribute training materials to archivists in the United States, and these materials were proposed to be used during the Florida trainings.

Proposal Summary

Advancing Access and Preservation Best Practices in Florida ($32,225 cash request; $10,141 cost share contribution)

The George A. Smathers Libraries at the University of Florida, in partnership with the Florida Center for Library Automation, Florida State University, the University of Central Florida, the University of Miami, and the University of South Florida, plans to provide training to archivists and others who care for historical records through a workshop series covering preservation and access standards and practices, including (1) the preservation and management of photographs, (2) minimal-level processing of multi-format archival collections, (3) descriptive standards, and (4) archival information systems used to document and access historical materials. NEH funding will support a regional education program, which will provide training at no cost to participants. A secondary goal is to establish a level of expertise among key Florida archivists and professionals so that they can implement and sustain an in-state education program. A third goal is to determine educational needs through surveys and evaluative tools. Project team includes the assistant chair of Special Collections and Area Studies (PI), Society of American Archivists staff and members and partner institutions (one year: 2010).[16]

Epilogue

The proposal was fully funded. The team conducted a survey to identify current education needs and future training priorities, and 148 individuals responded. One of the project's important results (though not a particularly surprising one) was that most professionals were seeking training related to digitization and digital materials.

The project team offered four workshops in Gainesville, two in Miami, and one in Tampa, at no cost to the 115 participants representing thirty-nine repositories from around the state. The participants comprised an appropriate mix of staff from a range of cultural institutions, large and small, public and private. Trainers changed the topic for one of the workshops because the expert presenter was unable to offer the workshop previously selected (managing archival photographs), and instead offered another workshop on archival arrangement and description. This change was well received by participants, since the replacement topic also met a need identified in the survey.

DIGITIZATION/PRESERVATION

Florida Department of State, Division of Library and Information Services / Library Services and Technology Act Grants

Prologue

The map librarian was relatively new to the Libraries when she learned about two previous grant awards to digitize historical aerial photographs of Florida produced by the U.S. Department of Agriculture. Library Services and Technology Act (LSTA) grant funding had supported both projects. This suggested an opportunity to submit a third proposal to the same sponsor to augment the collection and also enhance the online interface for users, making it easier for them to geographically search the photographic database. The librarian believed that adding online educational modules geared toward middle and high school students would enhance the usability of the collection. Most importantly, the librarian wanted all of the photographs to be downloadable without any mediation—at the time, this mediation was costing the Map and Imagery Library staff extensive effort to satisfy each patron request.

One of the most difficult aspects of preparing this LSTA grant application was defining the population that "needs" access to this type of collection. The first two phases of funding had produced 84,000 digitized aerial photographs of Florida. The team wondered how it could determine the types of people who were using the existing photograph collection, while also determining the ways they were using the photographs. To solve this mystery, the programmer on the team devised a survey with a pop-up link that asked collection users to complete the brief survey as a means of helping the Libraries staff apply for additional funding to add more aerial photographs to the collection. The survey successfully generated data to answer the two questions: many government- and private land-use planners rely on the collection, as well as hunters and environmentalists.

The team, with mentoring from the grants manager, moved forward to complete the application narrative and the outcomes chart, which required highlighting detailed descriptions of the resources needed, activities to be performed, outputs expected for expanding the collection, and anticipated outcomes that would result from completing the digitization, interface enhancement, and educational module.

Finally, it was determined that to make the project fundable, the team would need to include a plan to test the efficacy of the educational modules created during the grant period with students and teachers at a middle and a high school. Two Florida schools were selected: the P. K. Yonge Development Research School, which is affiliated with UF in Gainesville and serves K–12 students; and a middle school in West Palm Beach with a magnet program dedicated to environmental science and GIS that the grants manager was familiar with. Through multiple conversations, the map librarian was able to acquire commitments from teachers at both schools and they became project partners. The plan was to visit selected classes to assess improvements in students' ability to find and interpret the photographs they accessed online using the proposed new Google Maps interface, and to gather feedback about improvements that would enhance these users' experiences with the collection.

Proposal Summary

From the Air: The Photographic Record of Florida's Lands ($67,008 cash request; $23,994 cost share contribution)

This Phase III project proposes to provide (1) digitization of the historic Aerial Photography Florida Collection from 1971 to 1990; (2) a technology infrastructure upgrade for open access and retrieval, and database enhancement; and (3) broader public access through a user-friendly interface that will increase use by middle and high school students, and the general public. Project team includes the map librarian (PI), with GIS librarian, digital collections software developer, senior archivist for Map and Imagery Library, digital

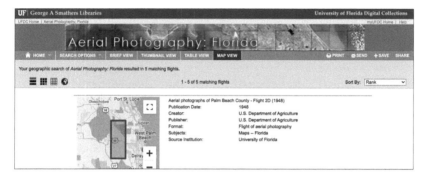

FIGURE 4.9
Screen capture of map interface to select region related to downloadable aerial photographs
Source: https://ufdc.ufl.edu/aerials/results/?coord=26.888535728819363,-80.6053466796875

assets coordinator, metadata and quality control coordinator, and education librarian (one year: 2009 to 2010).[17]

Epilogue

The proposal was fully awarded, and the project was carried out as it had been planned and described in the application. Because this particular sponsor requires extensive details of the project steps, results, and evaluation methods, the team simply followed their proposed plans. The aerial photographs collection is one of the most heavily used of the Libraries' digital collections (second only to the newspaper collections) and, with approximately 160,000 digital aerial photographs, is arguably the largest collection of this kind in the state.[18] It is thrilling (at least for the map librarian) to know that users can see, for example, how specific places in Florida looked before and after Disney World, and how the Ocklawaha River which borders the Ocala National Forest has changed in North Florida as a result of man-made canals. All of the photographs are now downloadable and use a Google Maps interface.

CHAPTER 4 TAKEAWAYS

- *To emphasize their needs, use actual quotes made by the population targeted to be served by the award.* For instance, grant review panels within academic institutions may include student peers as reviewers. Within the *Large Format Scanning* project, the proposal included direct statements from students articulating their needs. When student voices are represented this way, they likely resonate with student reviewers serving on the panel. This narrative can be difficult to ignore.

- *An invitation from a large foundation to apply for grant funding can create transformative partnership opportunities if the applicant directly responds to the exact interests of sponsor.* The Mellon Foundation senior program officer's invitation to apply to the Higher Education and Scholarship in the Humanities Program, along with his interest in supporting UF's undergraduate pipeline into the Humanities through faculty research and course development, created the impetus to develop a project that otherwise would not have materialized. As a result of the subsequent award (*Intersections*), six interdisciplinary faculty partnership groups were funded (four sponsored by the Mellon Foundation and two supported through UF internal funding) with librarians serving in all six of these groups. An incalculable number of new relationships, scholarship, and collaborative community engagement presentations emerged from this three-year project awarded to UF's Center for the Humanities and the Public Sphere.

- *The project team including its partners should determine the strongest candidate to serve as the applicant in order to create a feasible proposal and project.* This concept was illustrated in the *Books about Florida and the Caribbean* project where the owner of the out-of-print books (the University Press) did not have the staff capacity to manage the project as the applicant entity. Instead, the Libraries served as the applicant.

- *The project team's best estimates may be too high and may seem unreasonable, but it is better to ask for what you actually estimate even if in the end the awarded amount is more than the project requires to complete.* The NHPRC program officer who reviewed the project team's draft for *Pioneer Days* was concerned about the high cost per page to digitize a fragile collection of diaries, letters, and materials, as was the project team. His advice to provide sufficient justification and evidence of the team's methods to determine this cost was articulated thoroughly in the narrative. With full funding, the project team developed efficiencies during the process. With preapproval from the sponsor, it maximized the excess grant award funds to exceed the project's production expectations by 46 percent or over 15,000 digitized pages.

- *Finding out and sharing information about who uses a digital collection and why can inspire grant reviewers to support an expansion of those online resources.* A simple pop-up survey tool was used to define the future users of Florida statewide land-use photographs within the LSTA proposal, *From the Air*. Sharing evidence that the collection's users included a wide variety and large number of

Florida's citizens successfully supported the request to expand the collection, improved its service to those users, and went beyond to create an interface that would be accessible to students and teachers in middle and high school.

NOTES

1. Jessica Aberle, Ann Lindell, and Bess de Farber, "Large Format Scanning in the Libraries," George A. Smathers Libraries, University of Florida Digital Collections, https://ufdc.ufl.edu/IR00010418/00001.
2. The Andrew W. Mellon Foundation, "Mission," https://mellon.org/about/mission.
3. Bonnie Effros, Sophia Acord, and Bess de Farber, "Intersections: Animating Conversations with the Humanities," George A. Smathers Libraries, University of Florida Digital Collections, https://ufdc.ufl.edu/IR00010962/00001.
4. University of Florida, Center for the Humanities and the Public Sphere, "Intersections," https://intersections.humanities.ufl.edu.
5. Laurie Taylor, Bess de Farber, Meredith Morris Babb, et al., "Books about Florida and the Caribbean: From the University Press of Florida (UPF) to the World," George A. Smathers Libraries, University of Florida Digital Collections, https://ufdc.ufl.edu/AA00032435/00001.
6. University of Florida Digital Collections, George A. Smathers Libraries, "LibraryPress@UF," https://ufdc.ufl.edu/librarypress.
7. Jean Bossart, Sara Russell Gonzalez, and Bess de Farber, "New Functionality for UF Libraries' 3D Printing Services," George A. Smathers Libraries, University of Florida Digital Collections, https://ufdc.ufl.edu/IR00010965/00001.
8. State of Florida, "Library Partnership," April 26, 2012, hwww.flgov.com/wp-content/uploads/childadvocacy/communityhighlights4.26.12.pdf.
9. Michele Tennant, Hannah Norton, Gretchen Kuntz, et al., "Partnering to Provide HIV/Aids Information Outreach," George A. Smathers Libraries, University of Florida Digital Collections, https://ufdc.ufl.edu/IR00010980/00001.
10. UFHSCL, "HIV/AIDS Awareness" (playlist), YouTube, December 8, 2016, www.youtube.com/playlist?list=PLIgMqnaPv2swW1SCbH6CX2BICJ73aBcav.
11. James Cusick, John Nemmers, Bess de Farber, et al., "Pioneer Days in Florida: Diaries and Letters for the Settling of the Sunshine State 1800–1900," George A. Smathers Libraries, University of Florida Digital Collections, https://ufdc.ufl.edu/IR00001005/00001.
12. University of Florida Digital Collections, George A. Smathers Libraries, "Pioneer Days in Florida," https://ufdc.ufl.edu/PIONEERDAYS.
13. National Park Service, "Hotel Ponce de León," https://nps.gov/nr/travel/geo-flor/26.htm.
14. Leslee Keys, John Nemmers, Bess de Farber, et al., "Saving St. Augustine's Architectural Treasures," George A. Smathers Libraries, University of Florida Digital Collections, https://ufdc.ufl.edu/UF00094090/00001.

15. University of Florida Digital Collections, George A. Smathers Libraries, "Architectural Drawings of Hotel Ponce de León, St. Augustine, Florida," https://ufdc.ufl.edu/UF00089836/00006/allvolumes; University of Florida Digital Collections, George A. Smathers Libraries, "Miscellaneous Architectural Drawings from the Florida East Coast Hotel Co.," https://ufdc.ufl.edu/AA00009988/00001/allvolumes.

16. John Nemmers and Bess de Farber, "Advancing Access and Preservation Best Practices in Florida," George A. Smathers Libraries, University of Florida Digital Collections, https://ufdc.ufl.edu/UF00093942/00001.

17. Carol McAuliffe, Stephanie Haas, and Bess de Farber, "From the Air: The Photographic Record of Florida's Lands (Phase III)," George A. Smathers Libraries, University of Florida Digital Collections, https://ufdc.ufl.edu/UF90000014/00001.

18. University of Florida Digital Collections, George A. Smathers Libraries, "Aerial Photography: Florida," https://ufdc.ufl.edu/aerials.

5
Grant Partnership Proposals over $100,000

This chapter contains thirteen stories about funded grant projects with budgets ranging from $108,890 to $1.7 million awarded to the George A. Smathers Libraries staff and its partners from 2009 through 2021. These proposals share some common characteristics. All were awarded funding; all but one were projects with grant periods lasting for two to three years; and some of these required an extension of an additional year to complete the project. The project teams for these projects were generally larger than those described in previous chapters, and they included contributions by a variety of job positions due to the complexity of some of the projects.

The types of projects featured in this chapter include digitization, preservation, digital humanities scholarship training, research, professional development, collection development, fundraising through a capital campaign, museum and library collaboration, training and outreach, and collaboration network development. The stories are organized in reverse chronological order, from those most recently submitted to those submitted earlier.

Included in this chapter are awarded proposals submitted to the following sponsors and respective programs:

- Council on Library and Information Resources / Digitizing Hidden Collections and Resources

- Council on Library and Information Resources / Fellowship Program in Caribbean Studies Data Curation
- Institute of Museum and Library Services / National Leadership Grants / Library-Museum Collaboration
- National Endowment for the Humanities / Challenge Grants
- National Endowment for the Humanities / Institutes for Advanced Topics in the Digital Humanities
- National Endowment for the Humanities / National Digital Newspaper Program
- National Historical Publications and Records Commission / Access to Historical Records: Archival Projects
- National Institutes of Health / National Networking and Resource Discovery
- National Science Foundation / Ethics Education in Science Education
- University of Florida / Technology Fee
- U.S. Department of Education / Technological Innovation and Cooperation for Foreign Information Access

DIGITIZATION/PRESERVATION

Council on Library and Information Resources / Digitizing Hidden Collections and Resources

Prologue

In 2018, the Libraries' director of preservation concluded an assessment of the condition of the acetate microfilm holdings in UF's Special Collections and Area Studies. The findings indicated that a large percentage of the microfilm collections were experiencing a process known as "vinegar syndrome" which dissolves the film into a vinegar compound, creating a strong odor while destroying the film. The microfilms exhibiting the most deterioration were concentrated among those affectionately labeled "boat film." Boat film came about as the result of the federal government's Farmington Plan of 1949, when the University of Florida was assigned the job of preserving historically important primary materials in countries and territories of the Caribbean. Librarians traveled in boats throughout the Caribbean recording materials, mostly newspaper publications, on acetate microfilm for long-term preservation and use by future students and scholars. The collection of boat film represents the only known copies of these Caribbean historical newspapers.

With the findings in hand, which included a damaged microfilm inventory, the preservation librarian, the digital partnerships and strategies librarian, and the grants manager began strategizing ways to secure funding to digitize this content that was quickly disappearing. A nonprofit organization, the Council on Library and Information Resources (CLIR) offers a grant program called Digitizing Hidden Special Collections and Archives which supports large-scale digitization projects of threatened historical materials through funding provided by the Andrew W. Mellon Foundation. This program became the obvious choice as a sponsor, particularly in light of the impending threat of the permanent loss of many thousands of legacy newspaper pages. Although past awards for this program had not included historical newspapers, the team believed that by tapping into the Libraries' partnerships and past demonstrated successes in executing similar newspaper digitization projects, the new project's feasibility and fundability justified the time and effort to submit a round-one proposal.

The maximum funding available for collaborative Hidden Collection digitization projects is $500,000. To qualify, the team determined that its best partners were institution members of the Digital Library of the Caribbean (dLOC), an organization cofounded by the Libraries and Florida International University Libraries, with the Libraries serving as dLOC's technical lead organization. All of dLOC's 300 digital collections containing thirteen million pages of content are hosted by the Libraries in the University of Florida Digital Collections. Among dLOC's member institutions, the Libraries' strongest partner in digitizing historic newspapers had been the University of Puerto Rico–Rio Piedras Campus Libraries (UPR). Since 2012, these two libraries had secured $923,000 in NEH funding to digitize 300,000 pages of Florida and Puerto Rican newspapers for inclusion in the Library of Congress's Chronicling America: Historic American Newspapers program. (See later in this chapter.) UPR has plenty of newspaper microfilm that is available for digitization. However, UPR's historic master microfilm reels were pristine in comparison to UF's boat film. Could the team marry the two separate projects into one, or should it apply for two separate applications (which is permissible according to CLIR's guidelines)?

The team concluded that regardless of the differences in microfilm quality, both collections truly met the definition of "hidden," and both equally presented accessibility challenges for scholars, teachers, students, and the general public. In the case of UPR, the recent hurricanes Irma and Maria had left a trail of devastation on its campus and in its communities that had debilitated the day-to-day infrastructure. To access UPR's newspaper microfilm reels, one must request by e-mail that a copy be made and then mailed to the requester. This sounds simple, but each step of communicating with the requester, locating the film, verifying the content, making a duplicate, checking the duplicate for quality, and mailing the film requires infrastructure and personnel. Another factor that influenced the team's decision to submit a single application was that it could propose the digitization of a much larger volume of newspaper pages by including UPR's newspapers within the request, thus creating a proposal with considerable impact.

FIGURE 5.1
File drawer containing deteriorating film reels

Photo by Fletcher Durant, https://ufdc.ufl.edu/ IR00011033/00001

In terms of creating an impactful title, the team deliberated on whether *Film on a Boat* was a justifiable title. The goal was to ensure that the reviewers would retain the image of UF's proposal theme—microfilm reels that were actively deteriorating, even though Puerto Rico's film was not. The team ultimately embraced *Film on a Boat* as a title because it could be interpreted as a metaphor for the barriers that scholars face in accessing UPR's island newspaper microfilm holdings.

Project Summary

Film on a Boat: Digitizing Historical Newspapers of the Caribbean ($424,214 cash request; $28,448 cost share contribution)

This three-year project in partnership with the University of Puerto Rico–Rio Piedras (UPR) plans to digitize each institution's unique, hidden holdings of Caribbean newspapers on master microfilm. The team will digitize and make freely available 800,000 pages of pre-1923 Caribbean newspapers. The partners will produce new second-generation microfilm negatives; catalog individual titles; conduct issue-level collation; send to a vendor for the digitization, creation of derivative files, and OCR text files; perform quality control on deliverables; and ingest into the Digital Library of the Caribbean and Biblioteca Digital Puertorriqueña. Once available digitally, these resources will provide scholars with access to previously unavailable information on daily life in the Caribbean; this will enable new research and research questions from various fields and disciplines on cross-cutting issues such as migration, social movements, history, and literature. Selected materials were originally published in Antigua, the Bahamas, Barbados, Dominica, Guyana, Puerto Rico, St. Lucia, and Trinidad and Tobago. Project team includes the preservation and conservation librarian (PI), digital scholarship librarian (Co-PI), digital library coordinator (UPR) (Co-PI), curator of Caribbean Collections, senior associate dean for scholarship and services, and former journalism librarian; director of digital production services, chair of cataloguing and discovery services, journalism and communications librarian, European Studies librarian, African-American studies librarian, manager of digital production services, digitization workflow supervisor, digital assets coordinator, digital support metadata specialist, social media specialist, cataloger, technician for the Microfilm Center (UPR), and head librarian of the Puerto Rican Collection (UPR) (two years: 2019 to 2021).[1]

Epilogue

More than 100 round-one applications were received by CLIR in the spring of 2018. UF was invited to submit a full proposal in fall 2018 and was one of seventeen national awardees. The proposal received full funding. One unusual result of this grant project was the reinstatement of the management position in UPR's Microfilm Center. At the time the proposal was being prepared, that position had been occupied by a longtime UPR employee who was planning to retire at the end of 2018. Upon retirement, the UPR administration had planned to sunset the position. The prospects of this project opened a dialogue about the importance of the position as advocated by the UPR Libraries administrators. Were it not for the grant award, the position would have disappeared.

The stories of this project's impact cannot yet be written. However, its impacts will be far-reaching in that the project will produce such a critical mass of digital materials that those mining, interpreting, and creating new scholarship from the collections will forever change the landscape of future scholarship on and about the Caribbean.

DIGITAL HUMANITIES

National Endowment for the Humanities /
Institutes for Advanced Topics in the Digital Humanities

Prologue

In reviewing previous project awards made to applicants to the NEH's Institutes for Advanced Topics in the Digital Humanities, the digital scholarship librarian determined that a possibility existed for developing a fundable proposal for an intensive training series that would serve representative members of the Digital Library of the Caribbean (dLOC). dLOC is both a membership organization serving more than fifty national and international partner institutions, and a digital collection hosted in the University of Florida Digital Collections. The actual idea for the project arose during a discussion at the West Indian Literature Conference. Conference attendees who engaged in dLOC's initiatives posited that to grow the community of scholars working with dLOC materials, dLOC would need to convene and train new scholars and faculty who wanted to work with digital content in their research and geographical areas. They also identified a need to increase the capacity of scholars to experiment with digital tools.

Since its inception, dLOC's mission has been largely concerned with building community and capacity, especially technologically, among scholars, teachers, and students who may have varying levels of technological proficiency. Submitting an application to the Institutes for Advanced Topics in the Digital Humanities made natural sense when embarking on the next steps in the evolution of dLOC's many scholarly communities in the United States, its territories, and the Caribbean. Originally, dLOC leaders had planned to submit the institute proposal in 2017, with a plan to host it at the University of Puerto Rico's Rio-Piedras Campus. But after Puerto Rico was devastated by Hurricane Maria in 2017, followed by austerity measures imposed to deal with Puerto Rico's debt, this plan became infeasible based on the complexity of hosting and providing lodging for a large group there over several days.

As an affordable option, the digital scholarship librarian was able to determine methods for offering meal plans and dormitory lodging at the University of Florida during the summer, when the campus has the capacity to provide such housing. This strategy reduced the costs for presenting the institute (and accommodating its participants) to convene in Gainesville, Florida, making the project expenses reasonable for serving a large number of participants, especially those with limited access to travel funds. The entire project plan was developed with the Libraries, UF, and dLOC partners to ensure the distribution of technical assistance to all participants so they could work together in an environment empowered by their access to a variety of assets. Ultimately, the desire to increase the capacities of those wanting to grow dLOC through its scholars and digital scholarship output came together to support the librarian and grants manager in submitting a viable NEH proposal on behalf of dLOC's institutional members.

Project Summary

Migration, Mobility, and Sustainability: Caribbean Studies and Digital Humanities ($231,093 cash request; $6,639 cost share contribution)

This project team in partnership with the Digital Library of the Caribbean (dLOC) seeks to host a week-long, in-person workshop and five additional monthly virtual workshops on collaborative Digital Humanities (DH) and Caribbean Studies. The participants, especially from under-resourced institutions and those with preservation concerns, will gain DH teaching experience and in-depth knowledge of how to utilize digital collections in teaching. The Institute will provide training in tools, processes, and resources for developing lessons, modules, and/or courses. Twenty-six participants will achieve (1) the acquisition of concrete digital skills and DH approaches for teaching and research utilizing open-access digital collections, (2) participation in an enhanced community of practice for DH, and (3) creation of open-access course and teaching materials that blend DH and Caribbean Studies. Project team includes the director of digital partnerships and strategies, formerly the digital scholarship librarian (PI), European Studies librarian (Co-PI), director of UF's Samuel Procter Oral History Program (Co-PI), with UF architecture librarian, director of the Digital Library of the Caribbean (dLOC)/Florida International University, UF director of the African American Studies Program and associate professor of Political Science, dean of Academic Affairs at Dominica State College and director of the Create Caribbean Research Institute, director of the English Department and assistant dean for Student Affairs in the College of Humanities at the University of Puerto Rico, professor of History at the

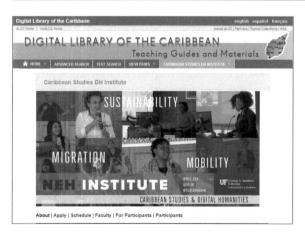

FIGURE 5.2
Home page for the Migration, Mobility, and Sustainability: Caribbean Studies and Digital Humanities Institute

Photographs and banner design by Tracy MacKay-Ratliff, https://www.dloc.com/teach/dhinstitute

University of Curacao, lecturer in the History Department at the University of the West Indies, St. Augustine, Trinidad and Tobago, associate professor of English at the University of Puerto Rico, UF grants manager, Caribbean Studies Data Curation postdoctoral fellow, UF National Digitization Newspaper Program coordinator, UF associate director of the Center for Latin American Studies and outreach and business programs project manager, UF professor of English with a focus on Caribbean literature, and the UF Latin American and Caribbean Studies Special Collections librarian (two years: 2018 to 2020).[2]

Epilogue

The project was awarded full funding. First, a web page was created on the Digital Library of the Caribbean's website to document all aspects of the Institute, including application information, with Institute faculty (and later participant) photos and bios.[3] The intention was to consolidate documentation about the Institute into a single online location. A major effort was made to widely distribute the call for applications to attract a sizable return from a diverse pool of applicants. Distribution of the call for applications included targeted e-mail lists such as the African American Intellectual History Society, Seminar on the Acquisition of Latin American Library Materials, Alliance of Digital Humanities Organizations / Digital Humanities Global Outlook Community, West Indian Literature Conference (attendees who participated in the pedagogy collaboration session), and the Repeating Islands (Caribbean Studies Digital Humanities blog). Ninety-three applications were received by the project team from prospective participants, including librarians, faculty, students, museum professionals, independent scholars, and teachers across the country and beyond. The team selected twenty-six participants based on criteria that prioritized historically black colleges and universities, Hispanic-serving institutions and those from Puerto Rico or the U.S. Virgin Islands, among other criteria. Coordinating the participants' accommodations in the UF dorms was one of the team's major challenges.

Prior to arriving, the participants received a reading list with links to complete in advance. The five-day in-person Institute included agenda content beginning with a Collaborating with Strangers Workshop (see chapter 3) to allow participants to immediately interact with each other while learning about each other's assets, interests, past projects, and future aspirations.[4] Participants were given the opportunity to revise the agenda after the first few days to ensure they had access to the program tours, group discussion, and training in specialized skills. They were organized into groups to ensure that UF expertise was distributed throughout each of the nine working groups. The only negative feedback had to do with the dorm accommodation arrangements for the participants. In the future accommodations will be made through Airbnb, which is now a viable option for securing accommodations near UF.

A few months after the in-person Institute, the team began presenting its virtual sessions—a mix of live sessions with Q&A, and flipped classrooms where recordings of content are produced in advance and sent to participants in preparation for live online discussions at a later time. The sessions' topics include how to conduct oral history projects, minimal computing, bilingual metadata in online exhibits, and collaborative grantseeking, among others related to engaging in the digital humanities for scholarship and teaching. These virtual sessions continued throughout the second year, and will culminate in each participant sharing their pedagogy materials openly online in dLOC for infusing the digital humanities into Caribbean Studies instruction. A no cost extension request, submitted in year two, was approved to extend the project until 2021 to make up for time lost during the COVID-19 quarantine.

DIGITIZATION/PRESERVATION

National Endowment for the Humanities / National Digital Newspaper Program

Prologue

In 2013, the Libraries' digital humanities librarian convinced the journalism and mass communications librarian to consider leading a project team to submit an application to NEH's National Digital Newspaper Program (NDNP) for digitizing Florida's newspapers. As the state's designated steward of Florida's master newspaper microfilm collection, the Libraries' project team determined this prospect to be promising. Collaborative projects fare better in the grant review process in general and specifically at NEH. The team began looking for a viable partner in geographic proximity to Florida—essentially, a partner would need to be an entire state that wasn't already contributing digital content to the NDNP. A review of past funded projects in this program revealed that the U.S. territory of Puerto Rico had never before participated.

After initial discussions with the staff of the University of Puerto Rico–Rio Piedras (UPR) Libraries, the team learned of UPR's longtime practice of creating master microfilm from printed pages of the island's daily newspapers through its Center for Microfilm. Essentially, this meant that Puerto Rico's historical master microfilm collection was in excellent condition; this was a bonus for a partnership with UF, whose microfilm quality across its newspaper collections did not consistently meet a high standard. Another asset brought to the table by the prospect of digitizing Puerto Rico newspapers was the inclusion of digitized Spanish-language newspapers into the Library of Congress *Chronicling America* collection. These factors raised the quality of the application. It should be noted that applicants to the NDNP enjoy a higher rate of success than those who apply to most other NEH funding programs. This is because the applications are usually submitted by the organization in the state that is charged with the centralized task of digitizing that state's newspapers. These guidelines inherently limit the number of applications.

Project Summary

Florida and Puerto Rico Digital Newspaper Project ($343,850 cash request; $106,984 combined cost share contribution from UF and UPR)

In partnership with the University of Puerto Rico (UPR), the Libraries will select, digitize, and make available to the Library of Congress 80,000 newspaper pages through the National Digital Newspaper Program (NDNP). Approximately half of the pages will come from historical Florida newspapers (1836–1922) and the remaining half from newspapers published in Puerto Rico (1836–1922). Project team from UF includes the chair for the Humanities and Social Sciences Library (PI), Caribbean Basin librarian (Co-PI), with digital humanities librarian, digital services manager, principal serials cataloger, quality control coordinator, microfilm specialist, archiving and preservation coordinator, digital newspaper projects coordinator, and assistant head librarian for the Education Library. Project team from UPR includes the digital library coordinator, Microfilm Center technician, head librarian of the Puerto Rican Collection, director of technical services and automation coordinator, head librarian of the Cataloging Section, and three undergraduate students (two years: 2013 to 2015).[5]

FIGURE 5.3
Promotional image for the Chronicling America website, featuring excerpts from historical newspapers from Florida and Puerto Rico

Design by Melissa Jerome, https://ufdc.ufl.edu/IR00011033/00001

Epilogue

The project was awarded $325,000 for Phase I in 2013. Two subsequent applications for this partnership project, one in 2015 and another in 2017, to expand these digital newspaper collections also were successful and resulted in awards of the three phases totaling $923,000. Because they were continuations of the original project, Phase II and Phase III required less information than the original Phase I application. According to the NDNP guidelines, three funding phases is NEH's maximum allowable for a single project. Over the three phases, the project team added more than 325,000 digitized newspaper pages of historical newspapers published in Florida and Puerto Rico to Chronicling America, a website managed by the Library of Congress.[6]

Encouraged by the success of six years of awarded newspaper digitization proposals and soon to be completed projects, the project team determined that submitting a new Phase I proposal in 2018 could be feasible and fundable if the project team (including the UPR-RP project director) agreed to add Virgin Islands newspapers to the next digitization project proposal, as this U.S. territory was not yet represented in Chronicling America. Calls to the library director at the University of the Virgin Islands (UVI) produced information about the existence of master microfilm reels owned by the Public Library System of the Virgin Islands, along with interest to participate in this new partnership. In the Virgin Islands, the Public Library System is a unit of local government, which shifts leadership depending on leadership changes following elections. In this case, the deadline posed another hurdle because of a recent change in government officials and the potential changes in management of the Public Library System. Through negotiations with the UVI's library director, a letter was secured which outlined the Public Library System's commitment to loan the microfilm to the project in collaboration with UVI.

Another issue that required planning of this new proposal was the need to include a new theme for prioritizing the Florida newspapers to be digitized that would align with the content of the other newspapers in some way. The team had to answer the question: What interesting set of Florida newspapers will be the most compelling for reviewers in this next round? The UF team settled on ethnic newspapers, including those published by labor unions in Florida such as the one in Tampa for cigar makers, which were heavily supported by immigrant labor representing a variety of ethnicities.

With these two new project elements—the inclusion of Virgin Islands newspapers and ethnic newspapers of Florida—the project team with a new partner member, the Library director of the University of the Virgin Islands, felt confident in moving forward to prepare the new phase proposal.

Project Summary

U.S. Caribbean and Ethnic Florida Newspaper Project ($324,967 cash request; $96,722 cost share contribution)

The University of Florida (UF) in partnership with the University of Puerto Rico (UPR) and the University of the Virgin Islands (UVI) seeks to select, digitize and make available to the Library of Congress 100,000 historical newspaper pages through the National Digital Newspaper Program (NDNP). Approximately one-third of the pages will come from Florida papers, one-third from newspapers published in Puerto Rico, and one-third from those published in the U.S. Virgin Islands. This project builds on three previous phases of NEH/NDNP newspaper digitization grant awards, since 2013, received by the George A. Smathers Libraries at UF in partnership with UPR. Project team includes the associate dean for scholarly resources and services, and former journalism librarian (PI), with director of digital partnerships and strategies, project coordinator, social media coordinator, digital projects manager, technologist, cataloguer, multilingual digital support metadata specialist, education librarian, along with library staff members of the UPR and the UVI (two years: 2019 to 2021).[7]

This proposal was partially awarded at $309,706, eliminating funding for an outreach education coordinate due to changes in the award guidelines. Since the time of application, the UPR project leader has retired and her replacement at the library has assumed responsibility for managing the project. Both UPR and UVI personnel are making progress on their subaward projects. As it turned out, the master microfilm reels maintained by the Public Library System in the Virgin Islands had been damaged and discarded. UVI personnel are moving forward to digitize its own collection of newspaper reels, which are the only existing copies that remain.

PROFESSIONAL DEVELOPMENT

Council on Library and Information Resources / Fellowship Program in Caribbean Studies Data Curation

Prologue

For years, the Libraries' digital scholarship librarian had been working with the grants manager to create a project suitable for funding from the Andrew W. Mellon Foundation because an award from this prestigious humanities sponsor brings with it the potential for future funding awards. The day finally arrived in 2017 when a call for proposals appeared on the Council on Library and Information Resources' (CLIR) website requesting applications for funding to hire a postdoctoral fellow in Caribbean Studies. The Mellon Foundation provides pass-through funding to CLIR to manage this grantmaking program for supporting postdoctoral employment. For the 2017–2019 grant period, CLIR's call for proposals focused on soliciting applications for hiring a post-doctoral fellow in Caribbean Studies Data Curation.

In this case, the feasibility of securing the award was high due to the Libraries' long-term technical leadership in cofounding and developing the Digital Library of the Caribbean (an international partnership with more than fifty member institutions and a digital collection). The list of assets that could be offered to the future fellow, if the proposal were awarded, included access to one of the largest collections of Caribbean primary materials in the country, and to a community with expertise in a range of diverse disciplines such as digital scholarship and collection development, teaching, online exhibition development, and collaborative grantseeking, among many other relevant options.

One of the most challenging aspects of grantseeking is obtaining the sponsor's blessing to include budget lines to hire new personnel who will execute or coordinate the proposed activities. Sponsors generally discourage the inclusion of new full-time personnel to be funded by the award. This is largely because sponsors seek to support projects that will be sustainable after the grant period has ended. Dependence on a sponsor for long-term funding of permanent salaries and fringe benefit costs should be averted if at all possible. In this case, however, 100 percent of the award would be used to provide salary, fringe benefits, and travel funding for a full-time postdoctoral (temporary) employee. This CLIR fellowship application was recognized as one of those rare opportunities to fulfill a much desired library aspiration—to hire an employee exclusively dedicated to advancing the mission and activities of the Digital Library of the Caribbean. Beyond this, the digital scholarship librarian has had a history of mentoring graduate and undergraduate interns to support their professional development, and these satisfying experiences had influenced her desire to mentor a postdoctoral student in a full-time Libraries position.

Project Summary

Postdoctoral Fellow in Caribbean Studies Data Curation ($164,970 cash request)

This project proposes to host a fellow within the Digital Library of the Caribbean program. If awarded, the CLIR fellow will become a team member with dLOC, the Latin American and Caribbean Collections, and the Center for Latin American Studies. Several projects for the fellow to lead include identifying new data sources, contacting known sources for data access and use, creating a listing or database for data sources, designing and delivering training in data access and use, and performing outreach on the newly accessible data. These may become a first-of-kind project series, where the fellow can utilize this as a model to meet additional data needs for Caribbean Studies. In addition to newly identified opportunities, UF and dLOC have active collaborations focused on digitizing legal materials for Haiti and Cuba, Anglophone literary journals, Caribbean newspapers, grey literature, government documents, and Caribbean-related theses and dissertations at UF. Project team includes the director of digital partnerships and strategies (PI), with the dean of University Libraries; data management librarian; director of digital support services; associate dean of discovery, digital services, and shared collections; and the chair and associate chair (digital projects) of Special Collections and Area Studies (two years: 2017 to 2019).[8]

Epilogue

The proposal was fully funded. Candidates for this new postdoctoral fellow in Caribbean Data Curation submitted their applications directly to CLIR. The Libraries selected a candidate who was just finishing up her doctoral degree program in cultural anthropology with a focus on disaster studies, specifically in Haiti. In spring 2018, the postdoc taught "Haitian Culture and Society" at the University of Florida. This course was structured as a digital humanities course; students learned to use digital tools to create a final project that centers on sociocultural life, human agency, and self-determination in Haiti. Five students from this course accompanied the postdoc to the Haitian Studies Association conference to share their projects. Upon completing the CLIR Fellow Program, the postdoc was hired by the Federal Emergency Management Administration as an emergency manager, fulfilling the goal of the program to further the careers of humanities scholars.

COLLECTION DISCOVERY

National Historical Publications and Records Commission / Preservation Program

Prologue

The Governor's House in St. Augustine, Florida, contains a treasure trove of legal documents, photographs, maps, surveys, meeting minutes of the Historical Society, and archeological records documenting St. Augustine's history from the time of Spanish rule. Unfortunately, a lack of funding for administrative support and the aging of Historical Society volunteers prevented ongoing maintenance of the collection to keep up with the growth of contributed materials and a growing interest in the city's history. Consequently, the archive was handed over to the University of Florida and the Libraries to maintain. Beginning in 2008 through the acquisition of grant funds, from small mini-grants to major awards, the Libraries' curators have been able to

FIGURE 5.4
Photo reproduction
of a 1764 watercolor
painting of
"View of the
Governor's House at
St. Augustine
in East Florida"

Source: https://ufdc.ufl.edu/
AA00005466/00001

organize the archive's content to assess its preservation needs and digitize important holdings.[9]

By 2017, the curators had completed processing and preserving large portions of the Governor's House Library's archival collections, but they could not complete the preservation and processing of its photographs, maps, and architectural drawings. The project team wanted to take advantage of the collections' digital assets which had been created during previously awarded grant periods. At the same time, the curators wanted to promote these digitized yet still hidden images and records more aggressively by posting them on social media and apps such as WhatWasThere and HistoryPin. Prioritized photographs, maps, and drawings are some of the archive materials most requested by patrons, but the project team needed to process other parts of the collection before tackling difficult assignments such as identifying and dating unidentified photos. Since these collections are focused on geography—the built environment of St. Augustine—the team was particularly excited to use the geographic-based apps WhatWasThere and HistoryPin to enable them to associate St. Augustine's photographs geographically and temporally.

To strengthen the proposal for an Access to Historical Records: Archival Projects grant opportunity (offered by the National Historical Publications and Records Commission), the project team sought support and assistance from members of the Historic St. Augustine Research Institute, which provided access to the considerable knowledge and experience of local historians, archaeologists, and architects. Finally, the team offered its own assets to the project in terms of its wide range of historical knowledge, preservation, and processing skills, much of which was the result of work previously performed in the Governor's House Library.[10]

Project Summary

Opening St. Augustine: Preserving and Providing Access to 450 Years of American History ($116,032 cash request; $144,986 cost share contribution)

This project seeks to identify, arrange, describe, preserve, and promote the availability of approximately 23,000 photographs, 2,400 maps, and 1,150 architectural drawings documenting the history of St. Augustine, Florida. Over the past almost sixty years, Government House (now known as the Governor's House Cultural Center and Museum) has been the home of efforts to preserve, restore, and reconstruct the important historic structures of St. Augustine. Primarily created by a now-defunct state agency, the Historic St. Augustine Preservation Board (HSAPB), the collections in the Government House Research Library document the city's built environment and also provide invaluable historical information about the city and its inhabitants through time. The unique and rare maps, architectural drawings, and photographic materials document the Spanish colonial periods (1565–1763 and 1784–1821), the British colonial period (1763–1784), the U.S. Territorial period and early statehood (1821–1860), the Civil War, the Gilded Age and the birth of tourism in Florida in the 1880s and 1890s, the Land Boom of the 1920s, and the Civil Rights movement in the 1960s. Not only do the collections document the city's built heritage, its inhabitants, its government, and the culture of its people over time, they also document the attitudes and values of the people from the 1950s to the 1990s who were engaged in historic preservation, education, and tourism. Project team includes the associate chair of Special Collections and Area Studies (PI), with architecture librarian, project archivist, director of preservation, preservation assistant, and two map cataloguers (two years: 2017 to 2019).[11]

Epilogue

The proposal received full funding. The project team achieved or exceeded all of the goals as planned in the original proposal (with the assistance of a three-month, no-cost extension), even though it experienced considerable staff turnover because several people left their positions at UF. However, those positions were filled promptly with extremely qualified professionals who capably caught up to meet the project's production requirements. A new employee for the position of project archivist completed the arrangement, description, and preservation activities for the maps, architectural drawings, and photographs. Now, for the first time in decades, these collections are fully processed and accessible. At project completion, the Map Collection includes 882 items stored in nineteen flat file drawers. Dozens of duplicate maps were discovered and deaccessioned with approved appropriate permissions, and transferred to the Map and Imagery Library at UF. The Architecture Collection includes over 1,000 sets of drawings, and after processing, the Photograph Collection contains approximately 6,000 negatives, 16,000 slides, and 7,000 prints. Three new finding aids for each of these collections are available online. In terms of community engagement, the team completed the Governor's House Library website and blog, exceeded the number of projected posts to apps (WhatWasThere and HistoryPin), articles in professional newsletters, discussion list announcements, postings to Facebook and Instagram, and created or edited fifty-two *Wikipedia* pages.[12]

TECHNOLOGY

University of Florida / Technology Fee

Prologue

The head of the Architecture and Fine Arts Library had seen high-speed scanners promoted at various library conferences and had met a few academic library staff members from around the country who had purchased these scanners for use by patrons. The benefit of these scanners, as she came to understand, was that they eliminated the stress put on books that are scanned on flatbed scanners. She assessed this benefit to be a priority for the Libraries. During her sabbatical, which she spent researching ways to create a materials collection for exposing students to a variety of building materials for both arts and architecture students, the librarian visited the University of Texas in 2014, and the fine arts librarian there shared that the KIC Bookeye Scanner was the most popular thing for students and faculty, for a variety of reasons. It is super fast, offers ADA-accessible features, has an option for optical character recognition, contains an 18" × 24" cradle to avoid impact on the spines of books, and the document feeder can scan large amounts of single pages easily and quickly, converting pages at a rate of twenty-two pages per minute into a single PDF. After speaking with the associate chair of the Social Sciences Library at UF, the two formed a team to request funding for the purchase of six scanners that would be placed in the Social Sciences Library (i.e., Library West), Marston Science Library, Architecture and Fine Arts Library, the Map and Imagery Library, the Special and Area Studies Collections, and the Education Library.

FIGURE 5.5
A student learns how to use the KIC Bookeye high speed scanner.

Photo by Barbara Hood, https://ufdc.ufl.edu/IR00011033/00001

Project Summary

Self-Service, Express Digital Scanning: KIC Bookeye High Speed Scanners ($131,364 cash)

The team plans to purchase six KIC Bookeye 4 Scanners which will provide easy access to quality high-speed digital scanning options for students and faculty in the Social Sciences Library, Architecture and Fine Arts Library, Marston Science Library, Education Library, Map and Imagery Library, and the Special Collections and Area Studies Library. This equipment has an intuitive interface with embedded universal accessibility features. Project team includes the associate chair of the Social Sciences Library (PI) and head of the Architecture and Fine Arts Library (Co-PI) (one year: 2016 to 2017).[13]

Epilogue

The six high-speed scanners were installed in 2017. Over the next year, the scanners recorded the following usage statistics, totaling 17,710 sessions with 399,418 images scanned:

- Social Sciences Library: 7,369 sessions with 188,991 images scanned
- Marston Science Library: 5,241 sessions with 74,406 images scanned

- Architecture and Fine Arts Library: 2,949 sessions with 80,584 images scanned
- Education Library: 1,512 sessions with 32,499 images scanned
- Special and Area Studies Collections: 639 sessions with 22,938 images scanned

With these high usage results confirming the popularity of KIC scanners in the Libraries, a new team of librarians was formed to explore the submission of a subsequent Technology Fee program proposal to request five additional high-speed scanners. By this time, the cost of the scanners had diminished slightly, creating another incentive to move forward. The team felt confident that they should request funding for scanners in libraries that had not been part of the original project, as well as the placement of a scanner in the Disability Resource Center. The usage data also supported the need to add a second high-speed scanner to those libraries experiencing the highest usage.

The team was unsure if reviewers would seriously consider funding their proposal for five additional scanners, with two going to the same libraries which had installed them in the previous year. Because these Technology Fee proposals require two rounds—an initial, cursory application to determine the interest from reviewers to consider a full application, and a second, more detailed submission of the full proposal for final determination—the team felt it best to include all five scanners in the initial round, giving reviewers the option to request that the team reduce the number of scanners in the full proposal. Taking higher risks in proposals that provide reviewer feedback prior to a final proposal submission can often pay off in the long run.

Project Summary

Self-Service, Express Digital Scanning ($108,890 cash request)

This project team seeks to purchase five KIC Bookeye 4 Scanners and five Dell OptiPlex 7050 computers to be located in the Disability Resource Center, Health Science Center Library, Latin American and Caribbean Collection, Library West, and Marston Science Library. This equipment possesses an intuitive interface with embedded universal accessibility features to provide easy access to quality high-speed digital scanning options for students and faculty. Previous funding awarded in 2016 allowed the Smathers Libraries to purchase six KIC Bookeye 4 Scanners for Library West, Marston Science Library, Education Library, Architecture and Fine Arts Library, Map and Imagery Library, and Special and Area Studies Collections. Project team includes the associate chair of the Health Science Center Library, with staff members representing each of the four other proposed scanner library locations and the Disability Resource Center (one year: 2018 to 2019).[14]

Epilogue

The proposal was fully awarded, and all of the new scanners were installed as proposed. At the time of this writing, the total number of scanned pages for all nine scanners exceeds 1.3 million.

RESEARCH

Institute of Museum and Library Services / National Leadership Grant

Prologue

In 2012, two librarians at UF's Marston Science Library attended a conference presentation comparing two e-book usage surveys that represented data from 2008 and 2011, respectively. The presenters expressed bafflement that students in 2011 reported they were using e-books less frequently than in 2008, even though the presenters had data to show that e-books were growing in popularity. One of the science librarians immediately surmised that this was most likely due to the surveyed students having no idea that they were actually using an "e-book." When discussing this hypothesis with the engineering librarian, who studied information-seeking behavior, they decided it was sufficiently interesting to see if other researchers were studying this "container confusion" issue. No researchers on this topic could be found, but "container confusion" behavior had been noted in the literature, encouraging a call for further study. The two librarians were unaware at the time, but it dawned on them after reflecting more on the issue that misidentification might be the problem. The conference presenters later sent out an addendum to the original student survey respondents asking, "When you are using electronic resources at your library, how often do you know what type of document you are using (e.g., a journal vs. a book vs. a report, etc.)?" Only 47.4 percent of the students said "always."

This led the duo to initiate a pilot study, with funding from a UF Faculty Enhancement Opportunity, to determine whether students could identify different types of online information.[15] That same year, the science librarian was accepted to present the project at the National Academies Keck Futures Initiative (NAKFIO conference, "The Informed Brain in a Digital World").[16] Attendees at this conference were subsequently eligible to apply for seed grants. In 2013 the duo applied for NAKFI funding to support container confusion research activities but were declined.

After a library-wide brainstorming session to get feedback and recommendations from Libraries faculty and staff, one recommendation suggested reaching out to the Online Computer Library Center (OCLC) researchers who also may have been considering the issue. This connection expanded the project team and created a new collaboration with OCLC that resulted in the submission of a one-year IMLS Research Planning Grant application for $50,000. The 2014 round-one planning proposal received feedback from the reviewers declining the application but encouraging the submission of a new proposal to fully execute the research project. Evidently, the review panelists felt the project was sufficiently developed to warrant a National Leadership Program implementation grant application in the Research category. In 2015, the collaborative team submitted a round-one summary proposal, and were invited to submit a full proposal with a recommendation to add a K–12 media-specialist researcher to the team. An ideal candidate was found at Rutgers University, and she joined the team.

Project Summary

Researching Students' Information Choices: Determining Identity and Judging Credibility in Digital Spaces ($491,822 cash request; $232,289 cost share contribution)

This three-year partnership with researchers at OCLC and Rutgers University will draw from prior research. The team posits that students operating in digital spaces (e.g., the open web) are "format agnostic." Usage studies have shown that students cannot or do not identify the document type (i.e., the "container") when viewing digital information resources. Targeting 200 students, this project will investigate: (1) How do students (grades 4–12,

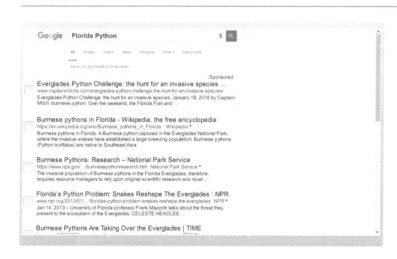

FIGURE 5.6
Simulated Google search results page for students engaged in the IMLS research grant project

Figure created by Amy Buhler, Tara Cataldo, Randy Graff, https://ufdc.ufl.edu/IR00011058/00001

community college, and university) working in science, technology, engineering, and mathematics (STEM) disciplines identify types of digital resources? (2) How do students determine the credibility of digital resources? Project team includes the engineering librarian (PI), biology librarian (Co-PI), with education librarian, engineering librarian for Made@UF, and director of educational technology in UF Health Sciences Educational Technology; OCLC director of library trends and user research groups and OCLC senior research scientist; and Rutgers University assistant professor of teaching (three years: 2015 to 2018).[17]

Epilogue

This proposal was awarded full funding for a three-year grant period. A major part of the project was to develop a simulated Google search for students in Gainesville, Florida, who were recruited for the study, to use when selecting sources for a fictitious class project. These simulated searches and selections were recorded by the software and also by video during the talk-aloud user experience. Because of the large amount of data collected by investigators resulting from the 180 student participants, the team requested a no-cost extension that was approved by the IMLS to add one more year to the project, with a new end date of fall 2019. Annually, all of the team members, including temporary employees and graduate student employees on the project, convened at the Marston Science Library for an intensive week-long meeting. The team gathered initial findings during the qualitative coding of participant data. A sample of these findings were presented at the 2019 Charleston Conference during the team's presentation of "Snake News or Fake News? The Game Show." For instance:

- Only 32 percent of students found an Associated Press story on YouTube to be helpful, while 59 percent found a National Public Radio interview to be helpful and citable.
- The *New York Times* received a credibility score of 3.6 out of a five-point Likert scale.
- 48 percent indicated that a SpringerLink e-book was a book.
- 82 percent gave a JSTOR magazine article a credibility score of 4 or 5 using a five-point Likert scale.
- Only 12 percent recognized that a JSTOR magazine article was contained in a magazine.
- 78 percent recognized a *New York Times* blog post as a blog.
- 13 percent of students found a *Wikipedia* article helpful and also citable.[18]

Members of the team have presented at conferences nationally and internationally to raise awareness of the project and its theme, container collapse.[19]

COLLECTION DEVELOPMENT

National Endowment for the Humanities / Challenge Grant Program

Prologue

The story of this project began with an inspiring speech given by the curator of the Isser and Rae Price Library of Judaica during the celebration to officially open the new Judaica Suite at the Libraries in 2013, to showcase books from the Judaica collection—the most significant Judaica collection in the southeastern United States. UF's president, Bernie Machen, was in attendance and was impressed by the beauty of the space renovation project (from a former staff processing area), as well as with the importance of UF's Judaica collection, and he suggested that the Libraries' dean let him know how he could help to raise awareness of the Judaica Library to a national level—a level of preeminence on which UF had recently embarked. The Judaica Library's curator prepared a report on the collection's outstanding holdings and included recommendations for ways to bring attention to the collection in comparison to other national peers. The result was an offer by President Machen to provide $300,000 in UF funding that could be used to purchase extraordinary items for the collection, which in turn would inspire new donor gifts.

The curator was now motivated to investigate a way to build a permanent endowment whose earned interest revenue would support future acquisitions of rare materials, and digitization efforts of materials that could be shared in the open domain. At the same time, the grants manager was seeking a suitable project to develop in response to a call for proposals from the NEH's Challenge Grant Program. This program is the only federal program intended to incentivize the raising of new funds specifically for the humanities, including funds for capital projects, to establish new personnel positions, and other long-term initiatives such as endowments. The maximum grant funding that could be requested in this program was $500,000, with five years for the grantee to raise an additional $1.5 million to reach the goal of $2 million. In other words, for every $3 the Libraries' project team raised in new funds, up to a maximum of $1.5 million, the NEH would provide $1 in matching funds up to $500,000. In 2013, the NEH's Challenge Grant Program was similar to that of the Kresge Foundation, which seeks to stimulate philanthropic giving to a worthy cause through the acquisition of large numbers of small donors.

Although they lacked a large and diverse pool of donors to the Judaica Library, the curator and the grants manager set out to create a fundable project theme and rationale for supporting the creation of a new endowment. The questions they pondered included: What assets do the Judaica Library, the Smathers Libraries as a whole, and UF have that are unique and that when combined could produce a powerful impact? What other academic libraries in the world are collecting, preserving, and digitizing Caribbean and Latin

American primary materials about the stories of Jewish immigrants? How much would an endowment of $2 million generate in earned interest, and how would the curator plan to expend those interest funds in order to achieve the most impactful results for building this humanities area? What partnerships could be identified to support a fundraising effort, especially in the state of Florida? The answers to these questions led the duo to propose a new focus and direction for collecting and fundraising that would leverage the existing Judaica assets at UF while at the same time distinguishing the project from other Judaica libraries, collections, and programs across the country and around the world.

Project Summary

Repositioning Florida's Judaica Library: Increasing Access to Humanities Resources from Florida, Latin America, and the Caribbean Communities ($500,000 cash request to match $1.5 million in new funds raised by the Libraries)

The project team plans to raise $1.5 million in the next four years to endow acquisitions, public and scholarly outreach activities, and collaborative digitization projects related to the Jewish experience in Florida, Latin America, and the Caribbean. With the Price Library of Judaica and the Digital Library of the Caribbean partnerships as the project's underpinnings, UF is uniquely prepared to lead a national and international effort to inspire greater study of the Jewish diaspora. The expanded and enhanced Judaica collections and services will be the foundation for the American digital portal of Florida, Latin American, and Caribbean Jewry (now known as the Jewish Diaspora Collection), and will emphasize the importance of scholarship, preservation, and access to exceptional primary resources that have previously been inaccessible.[20] Project team includes the curator of the Judaica Library (PI), dean of University Libraries (Co-PI), with the development director, development assistant, curator of the P.K. Yonge Library of Florida History, director of digital support services, grants manager, director of communications, chair of special collections and area studies, associate dean of administrative services and faculty affairs, interim chair of the Latin American Collection, associate chair of special collections and area studies, exhibits coordinator, and the Caribbean studies librarian (five years: 2013 to 2018).[21]

Epilogue

The proposal was fully awarded by NEH, and was one of only sixteen awards made by that body in 2013.[22] It happens that this was the last funding cycle in which the NEH Challenge Grant Program offered this particular design of a capital fundraising grants program. The Libraries staff were successful in raising eligible new donor gifts each year for four years, and received appropriate

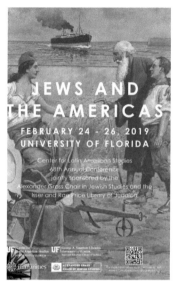

FIGURE 5.7
Artwork by Fransico Fortuny (1865 to 1942) contained in an album made by Jewish immigrants to Argentina, dedicated to the director of immigration to thank him for his liberal policies. The rest of the album contains the emigres' signatures. This album was purchased using interest funds generated by the endowment created by the NEH Challenge Grant award.

Source: http://ufdc.ufl.edu/AA00046752/00001

FIGURE 5.8
Poster containing Fransico Fortuny's artwork, promoting the UF Center for Latin American Studies Annual Conference.

Source: http://ufdc.ufl.edu/AA00046752/00001

matching funds from NEH. Changes in the Libraries' development directors over these years made the fundraising efforts inconsistent, but the dean of the Libraries' commitment to raising the required match persisted throughout. A change in personnel in the NEH's Challenge Grant Program in 2018 led to an invitation to extend the project timeline in an effort to allow the Libraries additional time to complete its fundraising goals. In 2020, just as the program was about to complete its final year, the NEH approved another extension (because of impediments posed by the COVID-19 quarantine) with a new end date of July 2021 to complete the Libraries' remaining fundraising goals.

In general, fundraising with annual goals imposed by a sponsor can be difficult, especially when donors are most interested in meeting with curators (instead of development professionals) who serve large numbers of patrons. Further complicating these efforts was the entrenchment of available Jewish donors who showed more interest in supporting their own projects and ideas. The concept of trying to preserve and digitize historical documents in the Caribbean and Latin America was almost too far-reaching, impersonal, and visionary a goal for many prospective donors. To mitigate this resistance, the curator became adept at customizing the fundraising story of the project to meet the existing interests of each prospective donor and family.

Overall, the amount received from NEH to create this new endowment at this writing totals $433,789, which has matched the new funds raised by the Libraries for an endowment total of $1,727,548. Funding from private family foundations, including the Shorstein Foundation, the Fanny Landwirth Foundation, and the Jack Chester Foundation, supplemented individual donor contributions. However, these are not the only grant project outcomes that should be valued. Awareness of UF's Library of Judaica has spread throughout Florida and beyond. One result was the use of a 200-year-old Bible held by the Judaica Libraries—the first Hebrew Bible printed in America—during the 2019 swearing-in of the first Jewish woman to serve in a statewide elected Florida post, as secretary of agriculture.

Other results of the project include the purchase of more than 10,000 rare publications; the creation of sixteen community and personal archives through purchases or material donations; and the completion of 800,000 pages of primary materials digitized through partnerships with libraries, archives and organizations in Argentina, Mexico, Jamaica, Barbados, and Cuba to form a new digital collection, the Jewish Diaspora Collection.[23] The success of the project influenced the theme of UF's Center for Latin American Studies' 68th Annual Conference: "Jews and the Americas," and inspired an accompanying visiting research fellowship program at UF.

COLLABORATION DEVELOPMENT

Institute of Museum and Library Services / National Leadership Grants

Prologue

In 2011, the administrators of the Libraries convened a meeting with members of the board of the Panama Canal Museum (PCM), a small nonprofit organization located in Seminole, Florida. The museum's board members had initiated discussions with the University of Florida Foundation's development director, who was positioned in the College of Liberal Arts and Sciences, to explore a possible partnership with UF. At the meeting, board members described their vision of a grand capital campaign project to expand the museum's Seminole facility and exhibitions to provide a more complete history of the Panama

Canal's construction and mechanical functions, and to more fully describe the culture of those who had lived in the Canal Zone, a former territory of the United States. Without the necessary funding, however, the aging board members concluded that the museum's collection should be moved to the stewardship of the Smathers Libraries at UF. Coincidentally, the members of the board and its sister organization, the Panama Canal Society (PCS), wished to continue fundraising, providing artifacts and information, contributing to the available history of the Canal and Canal Zone residents, and promoting the upcoming 2014 Centennial of the Canal's opening.

To support these efforts, the Libraries' grants manager explored funding opportunities and, through discussions with a program officer at the Institute of Museum and Library Services (IMLS), determined the feasibility of moving forward to apply for a National Leadership Grant (NLG) for a Library-Museum Collaboration Program; offered by IMLS. The difficulty in crafting a fundable proposal emanated from the NLG guidelines, which prohibit the use of awarded funds for new acquisitions. Instead, a case was made for funding aspects of the project that were unique to this library-museum merger, namely the continued stewardship of the community and individuals who had lived in the historically significant Canal Zone, and who wanted to continue contributing to the future Panama Canal collection work in partnership with the Libraries' faculty, staff and administrators.

Finding and documenting evidence about the need for activities to support mergers between libraries and museums presented another challenge. It was discovered that neither the American Association of Museums nor its program, the Future of Museums, maintained complete data on museums that had closed their doors at the time the application was being prepared. Proving that these instances were occurring more frequently around the country since the start of the Great Recession in 2008 did not come easily. Museums in general try not to publicize their financial suffering. On the other hand, the project offered the prospect of enlightening other administrators in museums and libraries about the many benefits of finding new homes for threatened collections, and their former stewards.

To ensure that the project's activities and results were well documented and assessed, the project team enlisted the assistant director (and social and behavioral sciences professor) of the Center for the Humanities and the Public Sphere (CHPS) to create and implement a project assessment plan, should the project receive grant funding. This added another partnership that brought credibility to the project as an authentic contribution to the field of museum and academic library administration.

In addition to the PCM, PCS, and CHPS partners, other partners were needed to fill various roles, most importantly to ensure there were sufficient venues in which to present exhibits related to the Panama Canal's Centennial Celebration which would unveil the recently acquired museum objects (from among the more than 12,000 collection items), and promote the merger of

PCM's board members with the Libraries. Other UF partners recruited to participate in the project included the Harn Museum of Art, Florida Museum of Natural History, Samuel Proctor Oral History Program, Center for Latin American Studies, College of Business, College of the Arts, College of Engineering, Health Science Center, and the Legal Information Center. Partners external to UF included the Museum of Science and Industry (Tampa, FL), Flagler Museum (Palm Beach, FL), Nationaal Baggermuseum (Sliedrecht, Netherlands), National History Museum of San Diego, Museo del Canal Interoceánico de Panamá, the National Archives and Records Administration, and the Association of Southeast Research Libraries. The ultimate goal of this partnership was to document, interpret, and articulate the role played by the United States in the history of Panama, focusing on the construction, operation, maintenance, and defense of the Panama Canal and the contributions to its success by people of many nationalities.

To emphasize the importance of stewarding the integration of a museum into an academic library system, the project team recruited an international consultant who was proposed to serve as an advisor to the program. His extensive knowledge of both museums and libraries, and his service as a council member of the Center for the Future of Museums, offered leadership planning expertise. If the project were to be awarded, he agreed to serve as its consultant during the three-year grant period.

Project Summary

The Panama Canal—Preserving a Legacy, Celebrating a Centennial, Leveraging an Extraordinary Human Achievement ($485,000 cash request; $541,976 cost share contribution)

This project proposes to: (1) actualize, integrate, evaluate, and disseminate museum materials from the Panama Canal Museum; (2) lead a multi-institutional centennial celebration of the opening of the Panama Canal in 2014–2015 to promote public understanding of the achievement, and of the heritage resources available for scholarly, educational, and civic purposes; and (3) initiate a national dialogue about the potential for best practices in library-museum collaborations, strategic alliances, and partnerships. Libraries project team includes the dean of the UF Libraries (PI), associate dean of technology and support services (Co-PI), grants manager and facilitator, book and paper conservator, international documents librarian, associate dean of advancement, exhibit coordinator, subject specialist for the Latin American and Caribbean Collection, digital projects manager, international government documents librarian, digital humanities librarian, director of Digital Library Center, and the Health Science Center Library archivist and historian (three years: 2012 to 2015).[24]

FIGURE 5.9
Construction crews in a lock chamber of the Panama Canal, Panama Canal Museum
Collection, 1913
Source: https://ufdc.ufl.edu/UF00093708/00001

Epilogue

The project was awarded at a reduced amount. The actual award to the Libraries totaled $477,312 cash, with $541,976 contributed cost-share commitments. The Panama Canal Museum closed on July 31, 2012. And surprisingly, the NLG grant cycle for the Library-Museum Collaboration Program was eliminated after the 2012 deadline, proving that grantseekers should never assume that funding opportunities will carry onward indefinitely. Midway through the grant period, the departure of the project co-leader from UF led the dean of the Libraries to appoint the Libraries' exhibits coordinator (who has a master's degree in Museum Studies) to serve in this role; this ultimately supported the project well in terms of her knowledge of the eleven exhibits to promote the integration of the two entities. The project could not be completed in the three years of the grant period and was extended by one year until 2016.

The funding and contributed cost share of this project ultimately led to the forging of a unique partnership with the Panama Canal Museum, the only museum in the world solely dedicated to preserving the history of the American Era of the Panama Canal (1904–1999). What was noteworthy about this project was the inordinate investment of resources, beyond grant funds, that were made by Libraries, UF, PCM, and the other partner personnel who numbered forty on the proposal, including Panama Canal Museum and Panama Canal Society board members and volunteers, without whom the project would have been impossible. During the grant period, fifty-two volunteers contributed over 3,400 hours of service, many of which were performed by students who accessioned, researched, or rehoused the collection items. Former residents of the Canal Zone volunteered virtually along with members of the general public, contributing to the PCM Collection blog by identifying collection items, adding missing metadata, and sharing personal stories.[25] As of the end of the project, seventy-nine oral history interviews with former Canal Zone residents had been recorded and are currently available for free access online.[26] The Friends of the Panama Canal Museum Collection was formed; their efforts raised over $100,000 to provide support for the library-museum partnership, and they continued to raise funds after the project's end.

The digital PCM Collection featuring 1,300 titles and 7,000 items is freely available online.[27] It contains a wide range of historically significant research materials, including government publications and photographs, as well as personal letters, albums, and artifacts. From January through September 2016, the digital collection received over 3.3 million views.

In terms of publications, an online exhibit incorporating highlights from the eleven exhibits was released shortly after the Centennial weekend.[28] Through September 2016, this exhibit received 11,651 page views, or approximately 16 percent of the Libraries' online exhibit traffic at the time. In July 2015, team members published *SPEC Kit 347: Community-Based Collections* through the Association of Research Libraries (ARL).[29] This publication reports the survey results of ARL member institutions on their holdings which may be similar to those of the Panama Canal Museum Collection. The findings revealed an increase in academic libraries collecting or seeing a need to collect these types of items. The survey gathered information regarding stewardship practices and governing documents. The *Spec Kit* includes examples of collection descriptions, finding aids, community stewardship support structures, donor support opportunities, and job descriptions for supporting similar community-based collections in libraries.

The Panama Canal Museum Collection at UF provides online access to the results of those partnerships which have continued after the project's end.[30] A membership group to support the Panama Canal Museum Collection was formalized within the Libraries' donor development program. The Albert H. Nahmad Panama Canal Gallery, located in the Smathers Library (formerly Library East), now shares artifacts, information, and stories through rotating exhibits about the daily lives of the Zonians.[31] The Executive Council of the Friends of the Panama Canal Museum Collection continues to work together as part of the Libraries to promote this history, ensuring it will never be lost.

Since this project's completion, the Libraries' staff members have steered away from applying for grant projects that involve large numbers of internal and external partners. The IMLS-funded project ultimately involved the

contributions of more than thirty staff members and countless other participants. Its complexity tested the limits of the Libraries' staff to complete project activities while performing their regular duties. The project itself took its
toll on those who labored for its completion.

TRAINING

National Science Foundation /
Ethics Education in Science Education

Prologue

Plagiarism is a ubiquitous problem among students on college campuses
throughout the United States. Each campus supports its own policies and
protocols for dealing with students who plagiarize. Librarians at UF's Marston Science Library had been offering remedial training for students who
were found to be plagiarizing, either intentionally or inadvertently, to help
them avoid committing these offenses in the future. It happens that many
foreign students find themselves unknowingly violating plagiaristic policies.
UF attracts a large number of international students who arrive with a mix
of scholarship practices, many of which do not conform to U.S. standards for
avoiding plagiarism. These Marston Science librarians were also engaged in
developing new methods for raising awareness of the different types of plagiarism and ways to avoid them.

In 2010, during a training session for Libraries staff members who were
interested in learning how to search for funding opportunities online, the
grants manager instructed participants to consider the interests of those
working in the Libraries as a means of searching for grant opportunities that
would match up with extant Libraries initiatives. A couple of participants in
the Cataloging Department who were sharing one computer decided to search
for opportunities that might support those working on anti-plagiarism strategies at the Marston Science Library. They came across the National Science
Foundation's Social and Behavioral Sciences Directorate guidelines describing
funding for new projects focused on improving ethics in STEM educational
disciplines. With this information in hand, the grants manager set up a planning meeting with five Marston Science librarians to determine if they were
interested in exploring the ethics grant opportunity with regard to plagiarism.

First, the team led by the grants manager reviewed all of the previously
funded awards and then dissected the guidelines to determine what it would
take to propose a fundable project. Next, the team members distributed
tasks, the results of which would help to determine whether or not the project
idea would be feasible and reasonably fundable. Some benchmarking activities included learning about the ways in which plagiarism instruction was
already being delivered. An analysis of search results using an assessment grid

differentiated each training methodology's strengths and weaknesses. Then one of the team members floated the idea of creating an electronic game that could be played to teach players the different types of plagiaristic actions that could potentially land a student in trouble. In fact, none of the instruction methods found during the search included using gaming technology to deliver plagiarism instruction. Still in the determining-feasibility mode, the team completed two literature reviews—one on plagiarism in STEM higher education and another on the benefits for students of receiving remedial instruction through electronic games. Finally, the team reviewed previously funded projects to determine if any included gaming technology—none did.

Next, the team began searching for faculty at UF who had sufficient programming expertise to create electronic games for educating STEM students and faculty on the types of plagiaristic activities often found at the university. The answer was revealed during conversations with staff members at UF's Digital Worlds Institute. Its director had recently hired a highly respected faculty member with expertise in gaming design and programming. A partnership was formed and combined with the information the team had already gathered during its feasibility phase, the expanded team began putting the pieces of the project together. Two consultants from outside UF were identified and recruited to play roles in advising and assessment—one with expertise in evaluating the efficacy of educational electronic games, and the other, a recognized scholar in ethics and integrity in higher education.

Project Summary

Gaming Against Plagiarism (GAP) ($298,660 cash request)

This two-year project plans to create, test, and refine an online game that will help graduate science and engineering students learn to recognize and avoid plagiarism, in partnership with UF's Digital Worlds Institute, UF's NSF-funded I[3] Program, and seven university partners: Purdue University, Virginia Commonwealth University, University of Houston, Loyola Marymount, Oakland University, Rowan University, and the University of Central Florida. The two consultants on the project will be Donald McCabe, PhD (Rutgers University - expert in college cheating) and Rick Ferdig, PhD (Kent State University - expert in game pedagogy). Project team includes the wildlife science librarian (PI), engineering librarian (Co-PI), science outreach librarian (Co-PI), agriculture librarian, director of the Digital Worlds Institute, professor of gaming in the Digital Worlds Institute, and professor of Ornithology representing the NSF-funded I[3] Program (two years: 2010 to 2012).[32]

FIGURE 5.10
Homepage of Gaming Against
Plagiarism (GAP) Project website
Source: https://cms.uflib.ufl.edu/games/
gap/gameoverview

Epilogue

The proposal was fully funded. Monthly project team meetings, facilitated by the grants manager, served to reduce miscommunication and overcome glitches as they arose. The librarians focused on major phases, including content and game development, beginning with the creation of storyboards for three mini-games highlighting various forms of academic plagiarism; user testing not just by the librarians, but also by students at the seven partnering institutions after obtaining IRB (Institutional Review Board) approval with required consent documentation for participating students; and external evaluation review of the extent to which the games met the goals of the project. The game developers at the Digital Worlds Institute determined how to proceed given the parameters of the storyboards, which were based on self-paced, role-adapting play. Developers for each of the three mini-games processed feedback to produce periodic iterations of the games.

The resulting mini-games are (1) Cheats & Geeks, which focuses on data falsification, data fabrication, and plagiarism; (2) Frenetic Filing, a fast-paced game in which the player organizes ethics violations into various categories using an arcade-style format; and (3) Murky Misconduct, in which the player assumes the role of a detective in building a case against potential violators.[33] As a whole, the mini-games present issues related to misconduct, including stealing, misquoting, patchwriting, fabrication, falsification, insufficient paraphrasing, and self-plagiarism.[34]

Since project completion, the GAP mini-games have been played by thousands of users, with over 3,300 registered participants and countless guest players (registration is not required). The team has learned that professors, teachers, and students use the games worldwide as a means of providing plagiarism avoidance training, in-class assignments, and extra credit in coursework. Members of the team have presented extensively on the games at conferences, including three American Library Association national conferences. In 2013, the team authored a *SPEC Kit* (monograph series) published by the Association of Research Libraries on the topic of responsible conduct in research. It should be noted that Digital Worlds Institute staff continue to maintain the games on a Linux server.[35]

COLLABORATION DEVELOPMENT

National Institutes of Health / National Networking and Resource Discovery

Prologue

This project was the brainchild of two science librarians in the areas of agriculture and physics. While attending a conference in Ithaca, New York, hosted by Cornell University, they learned of VIVO, a search engine developed by librarians and programmers at the Cornell University Library to reveal information about scholars and their respective research who were working at Cornell's Weil Medical College. The physics librarian had been creating lists of publications authored by UF faculty in the Astronomy, Physics, and Geology departments. A short time after the conference, the agriculture librarian was given the opportunity to present information about the VIVO model to faculty at UF's Institute of Food and Agricultural Sciences (IFAS). It was here that the VIVO model received its original endorsement. The librarians co-developed the idea to collaborate with VIVO's creators at Cornell and IFAS faculty to replicate the system at UF in 2007. The first UF VIVO proof of concept proposal was submitted to the Libraries' Grants Management Committee for a Mini-Grant.

Project Summary

GatorScholar: Developing a Database to Foster Interdisciplinary Communication and Collaboration ($5,000 cash request)

This proposal requests funding to implement VIVO, a tool with the ability to improve access to faculty publications and to strengthen communication channels between departments, colleges, and the library. VIVO is a search engine created by Cornell University Libraries that displays faculty and department information harvested from a variety of sources. The seed funds from the Mini-Grant will be used to hire one student assistant to input data for a select number of departments. Once populated, GatorScholar will serve as a promotional tool to recruit campus support, as well as allow the Libraries to explore the dynamic harvesting of data.

During the grant period from 2007 through 2008, the VIVO project team received training from Cornell librarians, set up the system, and implemented it, thus cumulating and loading faculty information to GatorScholar—UF's version of VIVO. The information focused on agricultural faculty researchers and their respective areas of expertise, publications, and grant proposals as a starting point. The associate director and chief operating officer of UF's Clinical and Translational Science Institute (CTSI) became interested in the potential for GatorScholar as the tool he had been seeking to expose the CTSI's faculty assets. He later wondered whether VIVO could be a possible platform for building collaborative relationships within and across disciplines in response to the National Institutes of Health's call for applications to design a national collaborative system for biomedical researchers. The NIH's call for proposals was the result of the American Recovery and Reinvestment Act, which was passed to counteract the effects of the Great Recession.

A project team was quickly recruited to respond to the NIH's request for proposals. It included the agriculture librarian, the Libraries grants manager, and the CTSI associate director, along with teams at Cornell University Library and five other academic libraries (Washington University, Scripps Research Institute–La Jolla, Indiana University, Ponce School of Medicine–Puerto Rico, and Weill Medical College of Cornell University–New York). The proposal was developed and submitted to NIH in 2009.[36]

Project Summary

VIVO Enabling National Network of Scientists ($12 million total cash request; $1,729,030 subaward cash request for the Libraries)

UF's partnership with the Cornell University Library and six academic medical research institutions plans to create an integrated national information network for biomedical researchers. This network will serve not just researchers but also students, administrative and service officials, prospective faculty and students, donors and funding agencies, and the public. This proposal will fully implement "GatorScholar" (under a new name, possibly "VIVO @ UF") at UF and replicate this system with UF's partners. The proposed work will establish a national network of scientists by providing a new software system (VIVO) and support for scientists using VIVO. Scientists using VIVO will be able to find other scientists and their work. Conversely, scientists using VIVO will be found by other scientists doing similar or complementary work. VIVO leverages work done over the past five years by Cornell University to support researchers and the finding of researchers by representing data about them and their publications, awards, presentations, and partners. VIVO is

FIGURE 5.11

Slide presentation; "Implementation of a new research discovery tool by the university libraries at Cornell University and the University of Florida" at Special Libraries Association Conference in 2009

Slide created by Valrie Minson, Sara Russell Gonzalez, and Michele Tennant, https://ufdc.ufl.edu/IR00000110/00001

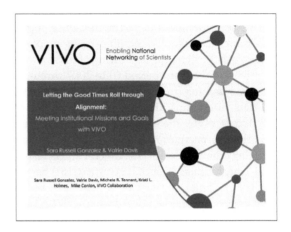

fully extensible and is based on Semantic Web concepts ensuring sound data representation, vastly improved search functions over existing text-based methods, and the integration of data with other applications. Support for researchers using VIVO will be provided by librarians of the research institutions—they will offer an existing and fully integrated resource that will enable both individual researchers and the national network. Libraries project team includes the agriculture librarian, physics librarian, several health science librarians, and the science and engineering outreach librarian (two years: 2009 to 2011).[37]

Epilogue

NIH reviewers awarded only one national project, which was awarded to the University of Florida. A distinguishing element of the proposal, which may have influenced the NIH reviewers, was the intent to center the project in academic libraries at each of the six partnering institutions rather than awarding applications that proposed hosting the project in campus information technology units. Based on the previous VIVO systems at Cornell and UF, this model offered a unique, feasible, and competitive operating structure. Project team members at UF and its partner institutions believed in the project's potential to leverage the many inherent assets found in academic libraries: outreach expertise, extant relationships with faculty, and established trust in the areas of the organization and dissemination of information. These combined assets, which every participating academic partner's library had available, could help develop a community of contributors to and users of a national version of VIVO, and this made a strong case for selecting UF. The NIH award to UF totaled over $12 million, of which $1.7 million was awarded to the Libraries in the form of a subaward for outreach and implementation services.

As this example illustrates, a very small proof-of-concept project can take on grander forms when shared with others. Cornell University librarians and programmers wanted VIVO to be replicated at other sites; and UF's unique combination of enthusiasm for VIVO and leadership experience in acquiring NIH grant awards became the catalyst that unlocked the project's national potential. No one could have predicted the ultimate impact of a $5,000 investment in a library idea. VIVO is now hosted by over fifty VIVO implementation sites in the United States, and VIVO projects are now underway in more than twenty-five countries.

DIGITIZATION/PRESERVATION

U.S. Department of Education / Technological Innovation and Cooperation for Foreign Information Access

Prologue

By 2008, the Digital Library of the Caribbean (dLOC) had existed for two years. Its members had voiced interest in creating a subcollection of digitized Caribbean newspapers—the historian's most valued sources of information on daily life. The Libraries' collections of microfilm reels of historic newspapers published in the Caribbean are vast in number. The director of UF's Digital Library Center (now known as Digital Support Services) and the grants manager determined that the best funding source for this project would be the U.S. Department of Education's TICFIA grant program. The Libraries had previously secured grant funding from this source which supported the initial digitization of various primary resources about the Caribbean that became the foundation for dLOC. Because Florida International University (FIU) served as the administrative leader for dLOC operations, its director agreed to serve as the applicant organization.

Project Summary

Caribbean Newspaper Digital Library: Disseminating and Preserving Records of Daily Life ($440,000 total cash request; $123,702 cash request subaward for the Libraries; $41,224 cost share contribution)

This four-year subaward for the Libraries, negotiated annually, will digitize newspaper runs from various countries in the Caribbean. The leaders are FIU's Latin American and Caribbean Center and UF's Center for Latin American

FIGURE 5.12
Homepage of the
Caribbean
Newspaper Digital
Library website

Source: https://ufdc.ufl
.edu/cndl

Studies, with partnering libraries at FIU, the University of Central Florida, University of South Florida, and University of the Virgin Islands. UF Project team includes the director of the Digital Library Center, with UF Digital Collections programmer and other Digital Library Center staff (four years: 2009 to 2013).[38]

Epilogue

Less than one year after receiving the award notification for full funding, the Department of Education eliminated funding for the TICFIA program, causing the project to end abruptly. However, many subsequent grant awards to digitize Caribbean newspapers came to fruition and are described in stories in this chapter and in other chapters.

CHAPTER 5 TAKEAWAYS

- *Assessing the benefits and detriments of increasing the scope of a project can lead a project team to add a partner that broadens the project scope (which may be a detriment) but, at the same time, augments the project's assets deemed important by the sponsor. This was the case with* Film on a Boat *and the* Florida and Puerto Rico Digital Newspaper Project. *Adding the University of Puerto Rico (UPR) as a sub-awardee to the* Film on a Boat *proposal, offered the sponsor (CLIR) the opportunity to support this academic institution representing a U.S. Territory for the first time in* the sponsor's history. Adding UPR to NEH's National Digital Newspaper Project proposal provided the first opportunity for NEH to include this U.S. Territories' newspapers to the Library of Congress' Chronicling America program.

- *Community demand can be a powerful driver of fundable partnership proposals.* The NEH Institutes for Advanced Topics in the Digital Humanities proposal *(Migration, Mobility, and Sustainability)* offered members of the Digital Library of the Caribbean the opportunity they were seeking: a way to increase digital humanities scholarship using its dLOC collection (hosted at UF) by providing necessary professional training and ongoing technical and curriculum development support.
- *Requesting grant funding to complete the digitization of a major historically significant archive can be a strong incentive for a sponsor to invest its funds.* This was the case with *Opening St. Augustine.* After several awards from various sponsors, NHPRC reviewers could see the value in finally completing this massive project by funding UF's proposal to digitize its remaining collections of maps, photographs, and architectural drawings.
- *Timing is everything.* Is there an impending and important historical anniversary that creates a now or never funding opportunity for a particular sponsor? Or, is this the first year a sponsor is offering a particular funding opportunity that aligns with the applicant organization's past experiences and current readiness to apply? In either of these cases, if the answer is yes, then the applicant should take advantage of this timing. The benefits of timely application submissions were realized in the proposal to IMLS for *The Panama Canal* project which was propelled by the centennial celebration of its opening, August 15, 2014; and in the *VIVO* project where the project team was able to construct a proposal with six academic library partners for submission to the first and only NIH request for proposals in response to lack of scientific collaborative platforms for connecting researchers in the time of the Great Recession. In this last case, UF's *VIVO* proposal received the only national grant award.

NOTES

1. Fletcher Durant, Laurie Taylor, Bess de Farber, et al., "Film on a Boat: Digitizing Historical Newspapers of the Caribbean," George A. Smathers Libraries, University of Florida Digital Collections, https://ufdc.ufl.edu/AA00064298/00001.
2. Laurie Taylor, Bess de Farber, Hélène Huet, et al., "Migration, Mobility, and Sustainability: Caribbean Studies and Digital Humanities," George A. Smathers

Libraries, University of Florida Digital Collections, https://ufdc.ufl.edu/IR00010262/00001.

3. Laurie Taylor, "Migration, Mobility, and Sustainability: Caribbean Studies and Digital Humanities Institute," Digital Library of the Caribbean, September 2018, https://dloc.com/teach/dhinstitute.

4. Laurie Taylor and Hélène Huet, "Course Outline and Institute Schedule," Digital Library of the Caribbean, https://dloc.com/AA00067359/00001.

5. Patrick Reakes, Margarita Vargas-Betancourt, Bess de Farber, et al., "Florida and Puerto Rico Digital Newspaper Project," George A. Smathers Libraries, University of Florida Digital Collections, http://ufdc.ufl.edu/AA00019344/00001.

6. Library of Congress, "Chronicling America: Historic American Newspapers," https://chroniclingamerica.loc.gov.

7. Patrick Reakes, Margarita Vargas-Betancourt, Bess de Farber, et al., "U.S. Caribbean and Ethnic Florida Newspaper Project," George A. Smathers Libraries, University of Florida Digital Collections, https://ufdc.ufl.edu/AA00019344/00001.

8. Laurie Taylor, Bess de Farber, Judith Russell, et al., "Postdoctoral Fellow in Caribbean Studies Data Curation," George A. Smathers Libraries, University of Florida Digital Collections, https://ufdc.ufl.edu/AA00048442/00001.

9. Thomas Caswell, "Historic St. Augustine Block and Lot Files Digitization Project," George A. Smathers Libraries, University of Florida Digital Collections, https://ufdc.ufl.edu/UF00091743/00001; Thomas Caswell, James Cusick, and Bess de Farber, "Unearthing St. Augustine's Colonial Heritage: An Interactive Digital Collection for the Nation's Oldest City," George A. Smathers Libraries, University of Florida Digital Collections, http://ufdc.ufl.edu/AA00004298/00001; Thomas Caswell, "Bringing Order to Chaos: Government House's Archives Processing," George A. Smathers Libraries, University of Florida Digital Collections, https://ufdc.ufl.edu/IR00003572/00001.

10. Matt Armstrong, "A Guide to the Governor's House Library Research Collection," George A. Smathers Libraries, University of Florida, http://www.library.ufl.edu/spec/manuscript/guides/ufgh0001.htm.

11. John Nemmers and Bess de Farber, "Opening St. Augustine: Preserving & Providing Access to 450 Years of American History," George A. Smathers Libraries, University of Florida Digital Collections, https://ufdc.ufl.edu/IR00009161/00001.

12. Lauria D. Marion, "A Guide to the Governor's House Library Map Collection," May 2018, George A. Smathers Libraries, University of Florida, http://www.library.ufl.edu/spec/manuscript/guides/ufgh0002.htm.

13. Stacey Ewing and Ann Lindell, "Self-Service, Express Digital Scanning: KIC Bookeye High Speed Scanners," George A. Smathers Libraries, University of Florida Digital Collections, https://ufdc.ufl.edu/IR00008783/00001.

14. Hannah Norton, "Self-Service, Express Digital Scanning," George A. Smathers Libraries, University of Florida Digital Collections, https://ufdc.ufl.edu/IR00010420/00001.

15. Amy Buhler and Tara Cataldo, "Identifying E-Resources: An Exploratory Study of University Students," *Library Resources & Technical Services* 60, no. 1 (2016), https://journals.ala.org/index.php/lrts/article/view/5899.

16. The National Academies Keck Futures Initiative, "The Informed Brain in a Digital World (2012)," www.keckfutures.org/conferences/informed-brain.html.

17. Amy Buhler, Tara Tobin Cataldo, Randy Graff, et al., "Researching Students' Information Choices: Determining Identity and Judging Credibility in Digital Spaces," George A. Smathers Libraries, University of Florida Digital Collections, https://ufdc.ufl.edu/AA00028722/00001.

18. Amy Buhler, Tara Cataldo, Samuel Putnam, et al., "Snake News or Fake News? The Game Show," presentation at the Charleston Conference, Charleston, NC, November 2019.

19. George A. Smathers Libraries, University of Florida, "Researching Students' Information Choices: Presentations and Papers," http://guides.uflib.ufl.edu/RSIC/presentationsandpapers.

20. "Jewish Diaspora Collection," George A. Smathers Libraries, University of Florida Digital Collections, https://ufdc.ufl.edu/judaica.

21. Rebecca Jefferson, Judith Russell, Bess de Farber, et al., "Repositioning Florida's Judaica Library: Increasing Access to Humanities Resources from Florida, Latin America, and the Caribbean Communities," George A. Smathers Libraries, University of Florida Digital Collections, https://ufdc.ufl.edu/AA00022790/00001.

22. Isser and Rae Price Library of Judaica, George A. Smathers Libraries, "The University of Florida's National Endowment for the Humanities (NEH) Challenge Grant," https://cms.uflib.ufl.edu/Judaica/NEH.

23. University of Florida Digital Collections, George A. Smathers Libraries, "The Jewish Diaspora Collection," https://ufdc.ufl.edu/judaica.

24. Judith Russell, Rachel Schipper, Bess de Farber, et al., "The Panama Canal: Preserving a Legacy, Celebrating a Centennial, Leveraging an Extraordinary Human Achievement," George A. Smathers Libraries, University of Florida Digital Collections, https://ufdc.ufl.edu/AA00009715/00001.

25. Lourdes Santamaria-Wheeler, "The Panama Canal Museum Collection at UF," WordPress, George A. Smathers Libraries, University of Florida, http://ufpcmcollection.wordpress.com.

26. University of Florida Digital Collections, George A. Smathers Libraries, "Panama and the Canal Oral History Project," http://ufdc.ufl.edu/ohpcm.

27. University of Florida Digital Collections, George A. Smathers Libraries, "Panama and the Canal," http://ufdc.ufl.edu/pcm.

28. University of Florida, George A. Smathers Libraries, "Panama Canal Centennial Online Exhibit," http://exhibits.uflib.ufl.edu/canal100.

29. Lourdes Santamaria-Wheeler, Jessica Belcoure Marcetti, Rebecca Fitzsimmons, et al., *SPEC Kit 347: Community-Based Collections* (Washington, DC: Association of Research Libraries, 2015), http://publications.arl.org/Community-based-Collections-SPEC-Kit-347.

30. University of Florida, George A. Smathers Libraries, "The Panama Canal Museum Collection," https://cms.uflib.ufl.edu/pcmc/index.aspx.

31. University of Florida, George A. Smathers Libraries, "Albert H. Nahmad Panama Canal Gallery," https://cms.uflib.ufl.edu/pcmc/gallery.

32. Michelle Leonard, Amy Buhler, Bess de Farber, et al., "Gaming Against Plagiarism," George A. Smathers Libraries, University of Florida Digital Collections, https://ufdc.ufl.edu/UF00098766/00001.

33. University of Florida, George A. Smathers Libraries, "Game Overview: Gaming Against Plagiarism," https://cms.uflib.ufl.edu/games/gap/gameoverview.

34. Rami J. Haddad and Youakim Kalaani, "Gaming Against Plagiarism (GAP): A Game-Based Approach to Illustrate Research Misconduct to Undergraduate Engineering Students," paper presented at the American Society for Engineering Education, Southeast Section Conference, 2014, Macon, GA, https://digitalcommons.georgiasouthern.edu/electrical-eng-facpubs/42.

35. University of Florida, Digital Worlds Institute, "Gaming Against Plagiarism Project," https://digitalworlds.ufl.edu/research-production/projects/gaming-against-plagiarism-gap.

36. Valrie Davis and Sara Russell Gonzalez, "GatorScholar: Developing a Database to Foster Interdisciplinary Communication and Collaboration," George A. Smathers Libraries, University of Florida Digital Collections, https://ufdc.ufl.edu/UF00091758/00001.

37. Michael Conlon, "VIVO Enabling National Network of Scientists," George A. Smathers Libraries, University of Florida Digital Collections, https://ufdc.ufl.edu/UF00094181/00001.

38. Brooke Wooldridge, Laurie Taylor, and Bess de Farber, "Caribbean Newspaper Digital Library: Disseminating and Preserving Records of Daily Life," George A. Smathers Libraries, University of Florida Digital Collections, https://ufdc.ufl.edu/UF00091464/00001.

6
Ten Steps for Successful Grantseeking with Partners

This chapter outlines the basic steps for submitting collaborative grant proposals and managing awarded projects. In general, most people have little or no training or experience in developing grant proposals. And to make things even more complicated, imagine doing this work with little or no familiarity with the partners themselves. This chapter seeks to demystify the grantseeking process, while including time-tested strategies employed at the George A. Smathers Libraries for creating a culture of grantsmanship.

The first thing to understand is that increasingly, most sponsors expect to fund proposals that support multiple organizations or investigators. The days when sponsors routinely awarded funds to just a single investigator (unless for an individual fellowship award) are mostly gone. This means that becoming adept at gaining commitments from reliable partners is now a virtually indispensable part of the grantseeking process. For both seasoned and novice grantseekers, and for applicants and their partners, the following steps demystify the partnership grantseeking processes.

I. Create a workflow for securing buy-in and approvals for grant applications.

II. Continuously search for and disseminate information about appropriate funding opportunities, and share these discoveries.

III. Present trainings to introduce potential grantseekers and possible collaborators to appropriate funding opportunities and deadlines that may offer benefits to their organizations and communities.

IV. Create a checklist to interpret the requirements of an identified grant proposal opportunity based on the sponsor's guidelines.

V. Find partners, develop an idea, and determine the feasibility of submitting a fundable proposal.

VI. Create a draft timeline, draft budget, draft project summary, and a list of possible partners; and complete a project feasibility meeting (in this order, if possible).

VII. Prepare, package, and submit the proposal elements to the sponsor.

VIII. Communicate with partners while the proposal is being reviewed by the sponsor.

IX. Receive notification of award or declination, and if awarded set up financial management, communication lines, and workflow processes; if declined, seek reviewer comments.

X. Complete and celebrate the successful conclusion of the grant project.

Each of these steps will be treated in detail in the sections below.

STEP I

CREATE A WORKFLOW FOR SECURING BUY-IN AND APPROVALS FOR GRANT APPLICATIONS

When the team wants to submit a proposal to a sponsor based on the sponsor's published deadline, it should first ask this question: Do we know all of the review, approval steps, and authorities within our organization that are required to approve the proposal prior to submission? If the answer is "no," then ascertaining this information will be the first step.

A problem with grantseeking for those who plan to do this for the first time in their organization is that it appears to be a deceptively easy process if the sponsor's guidelines are clear, correct, and complete. But if one simply followed the guidelines in a step-by-step process as offered by the sponsor, to provide a final version ready for submission twenty-four hours prior to the deadline, then there would probably be insufficient time to share the proposal with the necessary approvers within the organization, given the time required to read and fully understand the proposal—and especially its budget—with opportunities for providing feedback, and making corrections if necessary. To be sure, at a minimum, the organization's accountants must be engaged at the outset of the proposal development phase to ensure that all requested budget items have been correctly calculated, while determining whether funds can easily be expended for these types of budget items.

For instance, at the University of Florida, the Division of Sponsored Programs (DSP) uses an electronic submission and grants management process known as UFIRST. Once the proposal's budget and narrative are loaded into the system, it is routed to approvers within the Libraries, and then it is reviewed by staff members at DSP for compliance with both the sponsor's guidelines and UF's funding policies. If a Libraries project team plans to serve as a partner with an external applicant (this is one of the least risky ways to start grantseeking), the Libraries' grants management team must submit a description of the portion of the project to be undertaken by its team, along with a budget reflecting the cash request for the Libraries' subaward, and any cost share the team plans to contribute to the project as a percentage of effort. This subaward document must be approved internally by the Libraries administrators as well as by DSP reviewers. Once all the documentation has been approved, the Libraries staff are free to submit a letter of commitment to the external partner. (See Step VII below.)

Making sure that the organization's administrators have endorsed the feasibility of a project and project budget prior to circulating electronic approvals is a key step to submitting any grant application. Administrators and others in an organization who are impacted with extra work that results from "surprise" grant projects can possibly sabotage a grantseeking culture. Accordingly, organizations should try to maximize transparency about grant projects that are in development well in advance of the approval process.

STEP II

CONTINUOUSLY SEARCH FOR AND SHARE DISCOVERED INFORMATION ABOUT APPROPRIATE FUNDING OPPORTUNITIES

All organizations with personnel who are interested in grantseeking should be provided with a periodic list of grant deadlines for impending and appropriate funding opportunities that will support the type of work pertinent to an organization's mission and strategic goals. At the Smathers Libraries, the grants assistant weekly searches for new funding opportunities geared toward supporting the Libraries' ongoing initiatives and goals. Other organizations that lack a dedicated employee for this can recruit employees with excellent searching skills to combine their efforts in searching for grant opportunities online. For instance, if a group of three librarians searched for one hour biweekly, this would uncover a treasure trove of opportunities that, over time, would become an important resource for those interested in grantseeking.

To do this effectively, those doing the searching must be aware of the organization's inherent assets, the interests of its employees, and past project themes on which to build. Creating an asset map of resources, projects, past sponsors of funded proposals, and past published articles is a way to build continuous knowledge of what is happening in an organization that may inspire new proposals for funding, whether internal or external to the organization.

At the Smathers Libraries, the grants management program circulates a monthly Funding Alert. The Alert includes funding opportunities divided into two categories: those awarding $5,000 or less; and those awarding more than $5,000. This annotated list includes the deadline, the sponsor and sponsor's program name, eligibility requirements, range of award amounts, and a description of the types of projects or programs that are appropriate for submission. Finally, a link is included that takes the reader to the sponsor's online guidelines. Links to a list of previously awarded grants, and to past awarded proposals to this funding program, are also added, when available. This time-saving device is well appreciated by those in the Libraries who, at any given moment, have time to peruse the list at their leisure without pressure to pursue any of these grant opportunities.[1]

STEP III

PRESENT TRAININGS TO INTRODUCE POTENTIAL GRANT-SEEKERS AND POSSIBLE COLLABORATORS TO APPROPRIATE FUNDING OPPORTUNITIES AND DEADLINES THAT MAY OFFER BENEFITS TO THEIR ORGANIZATIONS AND COMMUNITIES

To create a continuous learning community, consider presenting workshops that help others learn about specific sponsors and their funding programs. Choose a sponsor and program to highlight from your funding alert list of upcoming deadlines in the next three to six months. Federal grant programs such as those offered by the Institute of Museum and Library Services or the National Endowment for the Humanities, or state libraries' annual Library Services Technology Act grant programs, will be good examples to highlight, for a few reasons. First, their guidelines are fairly stable year after year, and the programs often announce the list of grant awardees during each funding cycle in a news release, along with abstracts that describe the projects being awarded. Potential applicant organizations can subscribe to newsfeeds produced by these sponsors to routinely receive award announcements, and any number of other interesting news items.

Analyzing these award lists, during a training session using small groups, can help contextualize the types of awarded projects that these sponsors have chosen to invest in. Groups of workshop participants can be instructed to determine which projects could be replicated in their own organizations. Or groups can be asked to try to think up new projects that might have more benefits and impacts because of an innovative element coming from within their organization. Groups can categorize the number of proposals that feature various types of projects, such as research, outreach, literacy, technology, and so on. The result of this analysis will further participants' understanding of the priority interests of a particular sponsor, in any given year. The whole process offers a window into the funding trends of a sponsor that can be applied to next year's grant application planning efforts.

Going a bit further, the workshop agenda can include small-group analyses of funded applications that are available online in the IR@UF open repository (including the links to funded proposals featured in chapters 2 through 5) at sponsors' websites under the program names. The sponsor's goal in sharing awarded applications is to inspire replication of the high quality of these applications. Reading awarded applications and discussing the meritorious components of awarded project ideas is one of the best ways to learn grantseeking strategies. It is not just the quality of the writing, but rather (1) the strategies being employed that leverage extant organizational and partner assets to meet a defined need or gap, (2) the evidence of innovation and knowledge of similar work occurring in the field, and (3) how the idea is different from, yet builds on what has already been successfully executed.

STEP IV

CREATE A CHECKLIST TO INTERPRET THE REQUIREMENTS OF AN IDENTIFIED GRANT PROPOSAL OPPORTUNITY BASED ON THE SPONSOR'S GUIDELINES

All sponsor guidelines, including the application content, are not uniformly equal in quality. There are many authors of sponsor guidelines who have never planned, prepared, or written a grant proposal. This means that the quality of the proposal can be compromised by the quality of the guidelines, since the guidelines essentially serve as the applicant's "container." If the container is flawed in some small way, then so goes the application. Unless, that is, the applicant creates their own container. This can be achieved by translating the application guidelines into a checklist of questions and ensuring that the criteria for evaluation of the proposal are embedded in the checklist, as additional questions to be answered by the project team.

Starting with the narrative components of the application as listed in the guidelines, an applicant will create two columns to make their own checklist: one for the questions to be addressed; and another to identify the person who is responsible to author or lead the production of draft responses for each specific question or narrative section. Most guidelines, except (notably) the Institute of Museum and Library Services, typically ask the applicant to "describe the project's significance," or "describe the project's outcomes and impacts." The applicant's checklist should convert all of these statements into questions. Completing this activity will be likely to generate an excellent container for the grant application's narrative sections.[2]

Most importantly, the project team should locate the criteria for proposal evaluation in the guidelines. This section is not always easy to find. Often it is available at the end of the guidelines or on a separate web page, detached from the section in the guidelines that describes the required narrative components and attachments for completing a full application. Applicants should always seek out the criteria for how proposals will be evaluated. Otherwise, the project team is merely guessing that their proposal will align with the sponsor's funding review matrix for scoring the quality of applications.

Take the list of criteria for evaluation and convert it into a list of questions. Then take the criteria questions and embed them into the appropriate narrative sections to make sure the team is addressing each criterion. Another important step is to find the award amounts and awardees the sponsor has granted during its most recent round of awards. This will help the team to formulate its proposed project and budget request when it comes time to do this.

FIND PARTNERS, DEVELOP AN IDEA, AND DETERMINE THE FEASIBILITY OF SUBMITTING A FUNDABLE PROPOSAL

This can be tricky for those with limited experience. Let's say your team has found a funding opportunity that appears promising. It has secured the list of previously awarded projects and award amounts, has completed its checklist, and is ready to define what the project will be. At this point the team should ask itself: What assets are readily available within the organization or in close proximity (geographically or through an existing relationship) to enhance and improve the quality of the project (or expand the project team membership and the types of project beneficiaries)? Once this list has been generated, the team should ask: What assets are potentially available in external organizations, with which the team has positive relationships, that may enhance and improve the quality of the project? Finally, the team should consider: What asset contributors are potentially available in external organizations that are unknown to the project team, but could enhance and improve the quality of the project? (See chapter 1, figures 1.2 and 1.3.) Obviously, the more access the team has to potential asset contributors, the less resistance the team will encounter to quickly onboard these new prospective partners. As some of the grant stories in this book convey, the more interest and excitement the project idea generates, the more others will want to get on board, even if they are "strangers."

The team may not have the answers to these questions, which is why it is best at this stage of project development to convene a brainstorming session. The team can invite everyone in its organization and others whom they believe would have good insights into possible partnerships, invisible assets, or solutions to gaps in the project's concepts. Essentially, the team is asking others to provide free advice during a twenty-minute brainstorming session.

Using large easel pad sheets affixed to the meeting room walls, write one question at the top of each sheet. For instance:

- Who else should be on the team?
- Who should the team consider partnering with?
- What are the benefits of this project?
- Which types of populations or audiences would benefit from the project, and how?
- What risks should the team be aware of? Or, what could go wrong?
- Why is this project significant to the organization, or to the field being targeted?
- What else should the team consider?

Provide a sign-in sheet for the brainstorming session so that the team will know who participated. The team presents no more than a five-minute overview of its idea and then answers any questions participants may have. Then Post-it notes are distributed to each participant who wants to give responses to the questions that interest them. As participants write their answers (one answer per Post-it note), the room becomes quiet, naturally. People can generally brainstorm for no more than ten minutes at a time. When it looks like participants have shared most of their answers, the team can ask for closing comments. The results of the brainstorming session are then transcribed and distributed to everyone who participated. This exercise accomplishes a few important objectives:

1. It opens the door to external ideas that would likely never make it to the team.
2. It allows others to feel they are involved, even in a small way, generating a sense that this is "owned" by the organization, not just the project team.
3. People who don't like to participate orally can share freely without feeling self-conscious.
4. It helps the team feel as though they are not alone in their journey to create a fundable proposal.
5. It contributes to a culture of mutual assistance in a safe environment.
6. It decreases the sense of competition among an organization's employees and volunteers.
7. And finally, it doesn't take up much time!

Another aspect to consider when project teams are identifying, negotiating, and onboarding partners is to determine whether they plan to engage a partner in activities of a cooperative, coordinative, collaborative, or mentoring nature. The first three aspects of these grant partnership working relationships demonstrate a gradient of progressively higher risks. Cooperating is much less risky than coordinating, which requires more communication and may require sharing some assets. Collaborating, on the other hand, may be the first time two people or organizations are sharing their assets freely; engaging in work that is new to both entities as they combine forces; and sharing the risks equally, which can be much greater at this level of engagement, but also can mean more equal sharing of the credit for project results. Then there is mentoring where one organization's assets lead the other organization's personnel in learning and executing new skills—creating future sustainability of these skills for the mentee organization.

These ways of working with partners can inspire a sponsor to invest in a partnership to a lesser degree or more substantially depending on the level of partnership engagement. When applicants use the word *collaboration* but the proposal activities indicate that partners are more likely to be *cooperating*, this may cause the sponsor to be careful in its assessment of the true level of engagement planned for the future partnership, should it be awarded. On the other hand, when a sponsor can see true mentorship between a large, well-funded organization and a smaller organization, the sponsor may take notice and be inspired to invest in these activities that build capacity in communities.

CREATE A DRAFT TIMELINE, DRAFT BUDGET, DRAFT PROJECT SUMMARY, AND A LIST OF POSSIBLE PARTNERS; AND COMPLETE A PROJECT FEASIBILITY MEETING (IN THIS ORDER, IF POSSIBLE)

The project team must be able to visualize all of the individual steps and activities required to execute their project. The draft timeline is continuously fine-tuned throughout the project planning process—whether using time increments of semesters, annual quarters, months, or weeks. The timeline is the glue that holds the project together. The more detail that is available to describe each activity, including identification of the proposed responsible parties to carry out the stated activity, the more easily prospective partners will be able to visualize and understand the project as a whole, and their prospective roles in its execution.

Ideating the various expenses associated with each of the outlined activities operationalizes the draft timeline. Building the draft budget will determine the grant amount to be requested. The total amount of contributed effort (cost share or in-kind contributions) can be quantified by those involved in executing the timeline (whether required by the sponsor or not). The estimate should include lump sums to cover pending expenses that partners may need in order to participate. With this general sense of the budgeted funds necessary to complete the project as envisioned, in comparison to previously awarded grant amounts for this specific sponsor, the team can decide whether or not it is reasonable to proceed to invite partners to consider performing a role in the project.

If the team plans to proceed, it will prepare a draft paragraph or two describing the project's overall goal, specific objectives to be achieved by the project, and how the grant funds would be used. A working title will help to communicate the project's essence. Next, the team is ready to approach possible partners to ascertain their interest in participating in the project; this is done by creating an e-mail message exploring the opportunity, providing the project summary and possibly a description of the role the partner might play, and providing the draft timeline. The team should also attach the checklist to complete the proposal—asking the recipient to indicate their interest in a face-to-face or virtual meeting by a certain date. If they aren't interested, the team can move on to the next prospect as soon as the team is able.

During the meeting with prospective partners, after describing the project and partnering opportunity, each partner is asked: Why might you be interested in possibly participating? What do you think you might gain from your participation? What do you foresee would be your involvement in the various activities outlined in the timeline (and beyond)? Going further, the team can ask: What previous experiences does your organization have, or what resources (internally or externally available) would you be able to contribute to the proposed project? If this conversation is fruitful and the parties feel energized by the opportunity, then the team can ask: Would your (organization's) participation require a portion of the funds requested or can participation be contributed as cost share, or a combination of both? Once you have this information, you can request specific budget amounts for estimating a subaward budget for the partner and can determine the value of cost share contributions during the budget development phase. After receiving answers to these questions from each partner, the team can theoretically determine the total amount of grant funds they plan to request. The costs for each partner's participation in the project are added to the draft budget to decide whether or not the project remains feasible. There probably will be some back-and-forth negotiating with some or all of the partners to reach a budget that presents a reasonable request for grant funds, along with the estimated cost sharing value to be contributed by the applicant and its partners.

There are times when partners don't require any budgeted expenses to participate in the project. They may be happy simply to contribute to a worthwhile project that aligns with their organization's or department's mission. This infusion of contributed effort by other entities, without budgeting any grant funds for them, has the power to persuade the reviewers of the significance of the project through the altruistic in-kind contributions committed by its partners. It demonstrates that the project is of such importance that others are willing to contribute their own resources to see it come to fruition.

These types of project investments are powerful statements that augment the value of the project in the eyes of grant reviewers.

When at least a core group of partners has been identified, and before proceeding to flesh out the narrative elements of the grant proposal, the team should send a request for a brief phone meeting to the sponsor's program officer, including the working title, a summary of the project, and the list of prospective partners. The conversation with the program officer should elicit any weaknesses in the project's purpose, design, or budget. The team should seek to determine whether or not the program officer believes the project's purpose aligns with the funding program's goals. The team is not necessarily looking for praise, but rather is seeking input about its project's weaknesses, and any reason why the project team should not move forward to submit a grant proposal. The program officer's suggestions for improving the project strategies should be taken seriously and addressed by the team in its planning.

Writing the narrative sections is the most time-consuming part of preparing the application. If there is any chance that the project lacks enthusiasm or at least a consensus to move forward, then the team should seriously reconsider preparing the narrative. The team should convene (together in one meeting, if possible) with its respective supervisors and all of those who may be involved in the project. This meeting allows for a full review of the project. The remarks made by the program officer, and inquiries to clarify the project, the roles of each partner, and the planned activities should all be addressed. If all of these components receive positive reviews across all meeting participants, then follow-up e-mail messages to, or phone calls or Zoom meetings with partners, can then confirm that the proposal has been deemed by the applicant organization to be feasible. The team and its partners can now move forward to prepare the narrative (using the application checklist for guidance), finalize the timeline and budget, and gather the remaining application materials.

STEP VII

PREPARE, PACKAGE, AND SUBMIT THE PROPOSAL ELEMENTS TO THE SPONSOR

It may take months or even a year to get to this point, or it can happen quickly if all of the assets, application information, and documentation already exist and just need to be combined into a single proposal. Using the checklist prepared in Step IV, the team and its partners are ready to tackle each of the elements needed to complete the proposal package. First, seek out the elements that are dependent on other partners to complete and are therefore largely beyond the control of the team, such as letters of commitment, letters of support (if these are allowable by the sponsor), and two-page key personnel resumes, or short biographies; these are all typical requirements for most proposals. There might be some risk that the team will be unable to secure these documents in time to meet the submission deadline. At the Libraries, teams have experienced delays in acquiring the required documentation due to sabbaticals, vacations, illnesses, hurricanes, unforeseen holidays for U.S. territories, and more.

Letters of commitment from each of the partners can be addressed to the principal investigator. Each partner's representative will receive a request to answer these questions in their own words, by a certain deadline:

- What will be the partner's role in the project?
- Why is the project important to the partner, and why does the partner believe it is important to the field?
- What benefits will be derived from participating in the project?
- Who will be the project's beneficiaries?

Acquiring external letters of partnership commitment, and biographical material for key personnel participating in the project, should not be left to the last minute. They require at least four to six weeks of lead time to ensure receipt. Ask partner representatives to send the principal investigator any required two-page resumes, or biographical sketches, and a one-paragraph biography. Some partnering participants will not have a two-page resume on hand and may not be familiar with the process of preparing this required document. Suggest that they include their education history, most recent employment, publications, presentations, and grants received. In each subheading, they can include "most recent examples" to distinguish the abbreviated content. For biographies, they should share their current position title, and a synopsis of their responsibilities and their identified role in the project.

Ask partners to make sure that they have written permission from their respective institutions to (1) move forward with the requested budget to cover their expenses, (2) contribute the estimated cost-share effort toward the project, and (3) provide a budget narrative justifying the need for these expenses to carry out the project (this can be included in their letter of commitment or in a separate document). The principal investigator should receive these budget items at least two weeks before the submission for internal institutional proposal review and approval processes is scheduled to take place.

Some sponsors encourage the submission of no more than three letters of support (as compared to letters of commitment, which are never limited in number by the sponsor). A letter of support only—not one combined with a commitment to contribute to the project—ideally should be authored by a professional in the field related to the proposal's theme; this letter can attest to the project's value, both to the targeted beneficiaries, and to the field as represented by the author's knowledge and experience. Whenever possible, these letters should not be authored by employees from the applicant's organization or from the project's partners, since this may create the perception of a self-serving conflict of interest. In these cases, the author might not be seen as a neutral commentator about the project's quality or its strategies.

Quite similar to letters of commitment, the letters of support should provide answers to these questions:

- Why is the project important to the author, and why is it important to the field?
- What benefits will be derived from the project, and who will be its beneficiaries?
- Why should the project be awarded?

The authors of both letters of commitment and letters of support should answer the questions posed by the team in their own words. This creates authentic letters that are intended to educate the reviewers about the project from the perspective of a third-party expert. Choosing the most appropriate people to write letters of support is important—they should offer a variety of positive viewpoints that ideally represent diverse institutions, disciplines, and ethnicities. This strategy adds value to the proposal by making it a more interesting and enlightening read.

Other sections of the proposal that can pose writing challenges for the project team are the statement of significance and the statement of innovation, if these are required elements of the application narrative. Writing these sections successfully invariably entails providing evidence from the field that confirms the authors' awareness of what has come before, chronologically, in terms of advances and/or setbacks in the field or topic addressed by the proposal. These sections educate reviewers about the project theme and the problem(s) being addressed, and they present evidence of how others have contributed to implementing previous projects. The statement of significance essentially answers the question: So what? Why should the reviewers care about the proposed plan and objectives outlined in the application package? How does the proposed project compare to other, similar efforts? What are the project's distinguishing attributes? The reviewers will not be impressed by reading self-interested statements about why the team "believes" this proposal is a good idea. They want evidence which proves that the idea is one worth investing in.

The team can proceed to complete all of the other required narrative sections and components of the proposal as annotated in the customized checklist described in Step IV. One team member should be designated as the editor, to (1) ensure consistent language use, 2) reduce the use of jargon and superlatives throughout, (3) avoid the use of pronouns and generalizations whenever possible, (4) use active rather than passive or conditional verbs, (5) ensure that the activities scheduled for the grant period are described in the future tense, and those activities that have been completed or are about to be completed are described accordingly, and (6) make sure that the project is described so that anyone can understand it. After all of the edits have been made, the team members should read the narrative out loud to validate that no other errors can be found in it.

One last point about conforming to specific sponsor guidelines. The editor should try to avoid including any "creative" elements that are not standard to preparing grant proposals. Examples include: using colored text; underlining, bolding, or italicizing individual words or phrases to emphasize content for the reader; changing the order of the required narrative sections; adding section titles that cannot be found in the guidelines; adding too many appendix items; including appendix items for narrative content that could not be accommodated within the page (or character) limit specified in the guidelines; adding too much historical background information of activities that have occurred in previous years to build up to the current project idea; and submitting narratives that exceed the page limit allowable, or do not conform to the font size, margins, or font type if specified in the guidelines.

Packaging the proposal should begin at least forty-eight hours prior to the internal deadline for institutional authorized review and approval before submission. This should provide sufficient time to catch mistakes or missing documents. Check to make sure that the written confirmations from partners approving their grant budget allocations and commitments to execute specific scopes of work have been received by the applicant organization's project team. For federal government grants, the current negotiated F&A (Facilities & Administration) Rate Agreement outlining the IDC (Indirect Cost) rates of partner institutions, including IDC percentages for overhead in requested budgets, must be included in the application package. You should request that partners provide this document in advance of the institutional review deadline.

To package the partnership proposal, the narrative pages should include a header with the title of the proposed project, and the name of the applicant organization (nine- or ten-point font). The footer should include the page numbers. Appendix content should all be labeled with headers such as: "Key Personnel Resume," "Letter of Commitment," "Letter of Support," "Appendix A—Photograph of Collection in Storage," and so on. This helps the reviewers to successfully complete their reading, comprehension, and evaluation of multiple applications. (Most reviewers are volunteers and should be supported in their reviewer role as much as possible by the applicants.) Finally, it is best to print out the entire proposal package and view all of its elements in hard-copy format prior to submitting it for review. Reading the entire proposal out loud is one of the best ways to find mistakes or sections that are missing information. Seeing it in a printed format can expose all kinds of hidden errors.

COMMUNICATE WITH PARTNERS WHILE THE
PROPOSAL IS BEING REVIEWED BY THE SPONSOR

The project team should communicate with its partners while the proposal is being reviewed. Some review processes can take up to nine months. During that period, a lot can happen in an applicant organization or with its partners. People identified as key personnel in proposals can change jobs within the organization, or retire, or leave for positions elsewhere. Family or medical situations can arise that prevent partner representatives from participating in the project. The applicant team members must be made aware of such situations when they occur so that contingency planning can be made to accommodate the changes in advance.

During this dormant time, there are other reasons why the team may want to connect with its partners periodically and keep in touch with them. The team and its partners can collectively strategize about other possible funding sources, share plans for attending conferences where long-distance partners can meet up in person; or share information about other funding awards received for complementary aspects of the project, the progress made on project activities to prepare for possible funding, or the addition of new personnel who plan to contribute to the project if it is awarded.

RECEIVE NOTIFICATION OF AWARD OR DECLINATION,
AND IF AWARDED SET UP FINANCIAL MANAGEMENT,
COMMUNICATION LINES, AND WORKFLOW PROCESSES;
IF DECLINED, SEEK REVIEWER COMMENTS

Once the principal investigator is notified of the award or declination, this notification should be circulated among all members and supervisors of the project team, financial management administrators, the institution's central grants administrators, and the partners. If the proposal has been declined, then the team should request the grant reviewer's comments, which should be readily available for all government grant programs. Private foundations traditionally do not share reviewer comments. Another option is to request a phone meeting with the program officer to get feedback about the weaknesses in the proposal. The comments and oral feedback should be shared with all team members and partners.

In general, there are two types of awards: the full grant award or a partial grant award. For partial awards, the project team and partners must work diligently to determine (1) whether they can complete the project with a smaller award amount, or whether the shortfall can be made up by some other source; (2) what budget items can be reduced so as not to compromise the quality of the project; and (3) whether the sponsor has determined which budget items it expects to be reduced or eliminated. Regardless, during this award setup period there is little time to ruminate on how best to proceed. Revising the budget by removing or reducing expenses should be finalized quickly, approved by team members and partners, and submitted to the sponsor without delay. For grant applications receiving either full or partial funding, there likely will be other documents requiring the signatures of the organization's authorized signatory and the project leader (principal investigator), in order to formally commit to accepting the funds and executing the project under the terms and conditions offered by the sponsor. Likewise, if there have been changes to key personnel, the project leader should determine whether the sponsor is required to be notified of the changes, and whether the resumes for new personnel need to be sent to the sponsor.

The team and its partners should note in their calendars the dates when interim reports and final reports will be due. They will want to convene a kick-off meeting at which each participant shares the role they plan to play during the project, and the project leader reviews the project plan to make sure that everyone is on the same page. During the grant review process, personnel and other changes may have occurred, so it is beneficial to discuss all of the changes and new plans that have emerged during this dormant period. Also, it is important to review the timeline of activities with everyone at the start to determine if any dates need adjustment. Printing out a timeline (or Gantt chart) at the start of the grant period as a place to note scheduling changes, and posting these on walls and bulletin boards where team members work, will provide a visual reminder of the project plan to view often.

Next, the team and its partners should determine whether or not to inform the media about the award. There are a few options: (1) make the award announcement at the start of the project; (2) make the award announcement along with shared information about the results of the project at the end of the project, as a means of highlighting new products, services, or resources; or (3) make two award announcements, the first at the start of the project, and the second at the end to publicize the project's results. News releases should give the names of partner institutions, and possibly the names of partnering representatives. Once the news release has been drafted by the project team's applicant personnel, this can be circulated to offer a template news release for partners who also may want to distribute their own releases.

Scheduling regular grant project meetings with all participants and adopting a communication plan to keep everyone informed should be determined in the first month. The most common problem that partnership teams experience is a change in personnel or technology during the project. Adequate workflow and communication lines must support rapid responses, revised planning, and decision-making to account for any such changes.

STEP X

COMPLETE AND CELEBRATE THE SUCCESSFUL CONCLUSION OF THE GRANT PROJECT

The team and its partners may need additional time to complete any given grant project. Usually a sponsor will provide provisions for how to request a no-cost extension. Normally the team will need to prepare a narrative that includes:

1. The current status of the grant project;
2. The situation that has caused the team to request a grant period extension to complete the project; and
3. A new definitive end date by which the project will be completed.

Keeping tabs on all of the team's and partners' activities and progress will help to anticipate those situations that may require a grant period extension. Assessing these situations ninety to forty-five days prior to the end of the grant period is essential. Most extensions cover an additional year to complete the project, so as to avoid having to request multiple extensions. There will be situations in which the team must request more than one extension, but this is highly unusual. Sponsors usually are amenable to extensions to support the satisfactory completion of the project. It should be noted that some government sponsors are unable to offer extensions, and the team must be aware, at the start of the grant period, that this is not an option.

Monitoring the budget expenses throughout the project becomes even more important as the project winds down. The project leader will need to touch base with partners to confirm that all funds will be spent down as planned. Some situations, such as those in which equipment purchases were less than projected, or delays occurred in hiring time-limited personnel to execute grant-funded activities, can result in grant funds remaining at the end of the project. By anticipating these occurrences, if sufficient time exists prior to the end of the grant period, a request can be made to the sponsor to extend the grant period so that the funds can be expended and, if required by the sponsor, a budget revision request to use the remaining funds in a way that supports the overall purpose of the project, can be submitted. Some options include buying additional equipment to expand user access, increasing the amount of content to be digitized, or traveling to a conference to disseminate information about the project's results.

Finally, there should be some form of celebration to acknowledge the work of the team and its partners in completing the project. This is an important step. It can boost a sense of community and encourage those involved in the project to consider participating in other grant projects that arise. To support a culture of grantsmanship, consider having the project team present a show-case of their grant-funded work during a stand-alone presentation for staff members in the organization. Or, you can bring all of the grant project teams together to showcase their grant projects once a year, possibly using lightning-round presentations, to share stories about the projects with those who may be interested in learning about the organization's grantseeking activities. This presentation can be inspirational and uplifting—sharing stories about what is possible when assets are combined in new ways, when participants offer mutual assistance to activate these assets, and where there is a genuine sense of appreciation for those who have contributed to these efforts.[3]

NOTES

1. Bess de Farber and Danielle Sessions, "Funding Alert as of January 16, 2020," George A. Smathers Libraries, University of Florida Digital Collections, https://ufdc.ufl.edu//IR00011091/00001.
2. Bess de Farber, "National Endowment for the Humanities – Institutes for Advanced Topics in the Digital Humanities Checklist," George A. Smathers Libraries, University of Florida Digital Collections, https://ufdc.ufl.edu/IR00011092/00001.
3. Content in this chapter builds on the author's previously authored book: Bess G de Farber, *Collaborative Grant-Seeking: A Practical Guide for Librarians* (Lankham, MD: Rowman and Littlefiield, 2016).

Index

A. Quinn Jones Museum & Cultural
  Center, 29*fig*
ABC for Baby Patriots, An, 25*fig*
Abraham Paul Leech Letters and
  Sketches, 136*fig*
Access to Historical Records: Archival
  Project, 135, 161
*Advancing Access and Preservation Best
  Practices in Florida*, 139–141
Advancing Accessibility, 36–39, 70
Aerial Photography Florida Collection,
  141–143, 143*fig*
African American studies, 26–30
AFRO Publishing Without Walls, 26–30
Albert H. Nahmad Panama Canal
  Gallery, 176
American Association of Museums, 173
American Library Association, 34–36,
  45–48, 67–69, 70
American Museum of the Cuban
  Diaspora, 34

American Opera Company, 2
Ames, Craig, 59–61
*Analyzing Librarian-Mediated Literature
  Searches in the Health Sciences*,
  55
And the Band Played On (Shilts), 40
Andrew W. Mellon Foundation. *See*
  Mellon Foundation, Andrew W.
appreciative inquiry (AI), 4–5, 7–8, 7*fig*
Architecture and Fine Arts Library,
  120–122, 163–166
ARL: Position Description Bank, Phase I,
  107–108, 107*fig*
Arts and Humanities Research Council,
  UK, 23–26
asset-based community development
  (ABCD), 4–6, 5*fig*
assets, community, 7–8, 7*fig*
Association of Research Libraries (ARL),
  105, 176, 180
award, notification of, 202–203

Baldwin Library of Historical Children's Literature, 23–26, 34, 45–48, 56–58, 70

Bell Library, 44–45

Biblioteca Digital Puertorriqueña, 151

Blanding, Michael, 43

boat film, 148–151

Books about Florida and the Caribbean, 125–128, 144

Borland Library, 131

brainstorming, 194–195

budget, draft, 195–196

budget revision requests, 204

Building Makers, 34–36, 70

Buried Treasure, 43–45, 70

Burleigh, Harry T., 1–4, 6

Campbell, Bob, 55*fig*, 56

Caribbean Digital Newspaper Library, 10

Caribbean Newspaper Digitization Library, 183–184, 184*fig*

Carnegie-Whitney Grant, 34–36, 45–48, 70

Carrère, John, 138

Carrère & Hastings, 137–139

Carroll Preston Baber Research Grant, 67–69

Catalyst Fund, 80, 103

celebrating completion of project, 204–205

Center for Arts in Medicine, 131–133

Center for Health Equity and Quality Research (CHEQR), 133

Center for Latin American Studies, 159, 171*fig*, 172, 183–184

Center for the Arts and Public Policy (CAPP), 60–61

Center for the Humanities and the Public Sphere (CHPS), 13, 26–34, 60–61, 122–125, 173

Center for Research Libraries, 86, 88, 94, 97

Challenge Grant Program, 61, 169–172, 171*fig*

Chronicling America: Historic American Newspapers program, 149, 156*fig*, 157, 184

Clinical and Translational Science Institute (CTSI), 181

Collaborating with Strangers (CoLAB) Workshop, 29–30, 111–113, 111*fig*, 126, 131–134, 132*fig*, 133*fig*, 154

collaboration development, 122–125, 172–177, 180–183

collaborative grant partnerships, 1–18

collection development, 20–22, 30–36, 59–61, 125–128, 169–172

collection discovery, 43–50, 53–56, 160–163

commitment, letters of, 198–200

communication, 202

community assets, 7–8, 7*fig*

Composing a Heart, 59–61

Composing a Heart and Other Jewish Immigrant Stories, 61

Construct 3D Conference, 130

copyright, 26

Coral Way Bilingual Experiment Digital Collection (1961 to 1968), The, 30–34

Coral Way Bilingual Program, The, 32*fig*, 33–34

Coral Way Elementary, 32*fig*, 70

Cornell University, 180–183, 182*fig*

Council on Library and Information Resources (CLIR), 148–151

Council on Library and Information Services, 158–160

"Cradle and Grave" (course), 58, 58*fig*

Creative Campaigns to Promote HIV/ AIDS Awareness among UF Students, 39–43

Creative Campus Committee, 13, 80, 103

creativity, as motivation, 16–17

criteria for evaluation, 194

Cuba maps, 43–45, 44*fig*

Cuba Railroad, The, 44*fig*

Daly, Megan M., 21*fig*

de Bry, Theodor, 62–64

declination, notification of, 202

Decolonising Digital Childhoods, 26, 70

Dian Fossey: Secrets in the Mist, 56
digital annotated bibliographies, 34–36,
    45–48, 47*fig*, 70
*Digital Collaborations on Black History in
    Florida*, 70
Digital Collections in Children's Literature,
    23–26, 70
digital humanities, 61–64, 152–155
*Digital Humanities Collaboration
    Bootcamp*, 104–105
Digital Library Center, 183–184
Digital Library of the Caribbean (dLOC),
    149–155, 159–160, 170, 183–184,
    185
*Digital Publishing on Black Life and History
    Collaborative Workshop*, 26–30
Digital Support Services, 183–184
Digital Worlds Institute (DWI), 62–64,
    178–180
digitization, 48–53, 134–139, 141–143,
    148–151, 155–158, 183–184
*Digitization of a UNESCO World Memory
    Collection*, 90–91
Digitizing Hidden Collections and
    Resources, 148–151
Digitizing Historical Records, 134–137
Disability Resource Center, 165
Division of Sponsored Programs (DSP),
    191
drafts, 196–198
Dvorak, Antonin, 1–4, 6

e-book usage, 166–168
Edelmann, Jonathan, 21*fig*
Edison, Thomas, 138
editing proposals, 200–201
Education Library, 163–166
*Education Library Student Ambassador
    Program*, 64–67, 66*fig*
Elephant Data Sheets, 53–56, 54*fig*
Emerging Technologies grants program,
    8, 12*t*, 13, 92, 100
Ethics Education in Science Education,
    177–180
evaluation, criteria for, 194
*Expanding Undergraduate Research in the
    Baldwin*, 58

Facilitating Learning through Smart Pens,
    77–78
Fanny Landwirth Foundation, 172
Farmington Plan (1949), 148
feasibility, determining, 194–198
Federal Emergency Management
    Administration (FEMA), 160
Fellowship Program in Caribbean
    Studies Data Curation, 158–160
Ferdig, Rick, 178
*Film on a Boat: Digitizing Historical
    Newspapers of the Caribbean*,
    148–151, 184
*Finding a Sustainable Solution for 3D
    Printing Waste*, 80
Fisher, William Arms, 3
Flagler, Henry, 138
Flagler College, 137–139
Flagler Memorial Presbyterian Church,
    137–139
Florida African American Heritage
    Preservation Network, 27, 30
*Florida and Puerto Rico Digital Newspaper
    Project*, 155–158, 184
Florida Center for Library Automation,
    140
Florida Department of State, Division of
    Library and Information Services,
    141–143
Florida Digital Newspaper Collection, The,
    109–110, 109*fig*
Florida International University, 149,
    183–184
Florida Miscellaneous Manuscripts
    Collection, 134–137
Florida State University, 140
*Forging a Collaborative Structure for
    Sustaining Scholarly Access to
    the Baldwin Library of Historical
    Children's Literature*, 56–58
Fortuny, Fransico, 171*fig*
Fossey, Dian, 56, 70
France Florida Foundation for the Arts,
    61–64
France-Florida Research Institute, 62
French in Florida Online Video, 61–64, 63*fig*
Friends of the Panama Canal Museum
    Collection, 176

From Godzilla to Someone with a Stigmatized Illness to a Serial Killer, 81–83

From the Air: The Photographic Record of Florida's Lands, 141–143, 143*fig,* 144–145

Funding Alert, 192

Future of Museums, 173

Galdikas, Birute, 56

Gaming Against Plagiarism, 177–180, 179*fig*

Gannon, Michael, 63

Gator Tales, 61, 70

GatorScholar, 180–183

George A. Smathers Libraries, 8–16, 36–45, 48–6792, 100

Georgia Tech, 48

"Goin' Home" (Fisher), 3

Goodall, Jane, 56

Governor's House, St. Augustine, 160–163, 161*fig*

Graham, Alistair, 56

Grants Activities Update, 10

Grants Management Program, 1, 8–16

grantsmanship, history of, 8–16, 9*fig,* 11*fig,* 12*t,* 13*t,* 14*t*

graphic novel contest, 41–42, 41*fig*

Haitian Studies Association, 160

Handful of Leaves, A, 61

Hastings, Thomas, 138

health information dissemination, 39–43, 130–134

Health Science Center Library (HSCL), 53–55, 130–134

HealthStreet, 131, 133

Higher Education and Scholarship in the Humanities Program, 122–125, 144

Hindu Studies collection development, 20–22

"Hiring Non-MLS Librarians," 69, 69*fig*

Historic St. Augustine Preservation Board (HSAPB), 162

Historic St. Augustine Research Institute, 161

HistoryPin, 161

HIV/AIDS Community Information Outreach Project, 130–134

HIV/AIDS information, 39–43, 130–134, 132*fig*

Homerton Library, University of Cambridge, 23–26

Humanities Collections and Reference Resources Program (HCRR), 135

Huneker, James Gibbons, 3

Ian Parker Collections of East African Wildlife Conservation, 53–56, 54*fig,* 70

idea development, 194–196

Increasing Accessibility to Rare Florida Agricultural Publications, 98–100, 99*fig*

innovation, statement of, 200

Institute of Food and Agricultural Sciences (IFAS), 180

Institute of Museum and Library Services (IMLS), 51, 166–168, 172–177, 185, 192, 193

Institutes for Advanced Topic in the Digital Humanities, 152–155, 184–185

Intersections: Animating Conversations with the Humanities, 122–125, 124*fig,* 144

invitation-only applications, 122–125, 144

Isser and Rae Price Library of Judaica, 59–61, 60*fig,* 169–172

Jack Chester Foundation, 172

Jewish Diaspora Collection, 170–172

Johnson, Stephen, 6

Jones, A. Quinn, Sr., 29*fig*

Kennedy, William Stetson, 48–50, 49*fig*

KIC Bookeye Scanners, 163–166

Klan Unmasked, The (Kennedy), 48, 49*fig*

Kresge Foundation, 169
Kretzmann, John P., 4

Large Format Scanning in the Libraries, 120–122, 143–144
Latin American and Caribbean Center (FIU), 183–184
Latin American and Caribbean Collections, 159
Latin Americanist Research Resources Project, 88–89, 94
Le Moyne de Morgues, Jacques, 62–64
Leech, Abraham Duryea, 136fig
Leech, Abraham Paul, 136fig
Legacy of Stetson Kennedy, The, 48–50, 70
Librarian-Mediated Literature Searches project, 54–55
Library Enhancement Grants, 20–22
Library Leadership & Management Association's Human Resources Section, 69
Library Services and Technology Act Grants, 140–143, 108, 192
Library West One Button Studio, 101–103, 102fig
Library-Museum Collaboration Program, 173, 175
Lincoln High School (LHS) homecoming parade, 29fig
"Listín Diario": Preserving and Digitizing an At-Risk Dominican Republic Newspaper, 95–97, 96fig

Machen, Bernie, 169
makerspaces, 34–36
Map and Imagery Library, 120–122, 141–143, 163–166
Map Thief, The (Blanding), 43
Marston Science Library, 35, 128–130, 129fig, 163–166, 168, 177–180
McCabe, Donald, 178
McKnight, John L., 4
media notification, 203
Mellon Foundation, Andrew W., 122–128, 144, 148, 158–159

Merdinger, Emanuel, 61
microfilm collections, 148–151, 150fig, 155
Migration, Mobility, and Sustainability, 152–155, 153fig, 185
Mini Grants Program, 8, 19
Mobile Outreach Clinic, 133
motivations for grantseeking, 16–17
mutual assistance, 6–8, 7fig

Narayanan, Vasudha, 21fig
National Academies Keck Futures Initiative (NAKFI) conference, 166
National Conservatory of Music, 1–2
National Digital Newspaper Program (NDNP), 155–158, 184
National Endowment for the Humanities (NEH), 10, 57–58, 125–128, 139–141, 149, 152–158, 169–172, 184–185, 192
National Geographic, 56, 70
National Historical Publications and Records Commission (NHPRC), 134–137, 144, 160–163, 185
National Institutes of Health (NIH), 130, 180–183
National Leadership Grant (NLG), 166–168, 172–177
National Libraries of Medicine (NLM), 39, 130–134
National Networking and Resource Discovery, 180–183
National Park Service, 137–139
National Science Foundation, 177–180
needs assessment, 4, 5fig
NEH Challenge Grant. See Challenge Grant Program
New Functionality for UF Libraries' 3D Printing Services, 128–130
New World Symphony (Dvorak), 3, 5
New York Public Library, 51
news releases, 203
newspapers, digitization of, 149–151, 155–158, 156fig, 183–184, 184fig
non-MLS-degreed library faculty, 67–69, 69fig

Northeast Florida Library Information
Network, 78, 98
notification of award or declination,
202–203

Online Computer Library Center
(OCLC), 166–168
Open Book Program, 125–128, 127fig
Opening Archives: Improving Access to
Primary Sources in Florida, 139–141
Opening St. Augustine, 160–163, 185
out-of-print books, 125–128
outreach, 36–39, 59–61, 64–67

P. K. Yonge Development Research
School, 142
P. K. Yonge Library of Florida History,
48–50, 134–137, 170
packaging proposals, 201
Palmetto Country (Kennedy), 48
Panama Canal Museum Collection, 50–53,
52fig, 70, 175fig
Panama Canal Museum (PCM),
172–177
Panama Canal Society (PCS), 173, 176
Panama Canal—Preserving a Legacy,
Celebrating a Centennial, Leveraging
an Extraordinary Human
Achievement, The, 172–177, 185
Pantour, 38
Parker Elephant Data Sheets, The, 53–56,
70
partial awards, 202–203
Partnering to Provide HIV/AIDS
Information Outreach, 130–134
partnerships
building blocks of successful, 3–7
communication and, 202
creating collaborative grant, 1–18
finding, 194–196
for proposals up to $5,000,
19–71
for proposals from $5,001 to
$25,000, 75–115
for proposals from $25,001 to
$100,000, 119–145

for proposals over $100,000,
147–185
resources accessed through, 6fig
steps for successful grantseeking in,
189–205
Performing Arts Approach to Collection
Development, A, 59–61, 70
Pioneer Days in Florida, 134–137, 144
plagiarism, 177–180
planning, 23–26, 56–58
Ponce de León Hotel, 137–139, 139fig
Postdoctoral Fellow in Caribbean Studies
Data Curation, 158–160
preservation, 48–53, 134–139, 141–
143, 148–151, 155–158, 183–184
Preservation and Access Education and
Training, 139–141
Preservation and Access project, NEH,
44–45
Preservation Program, 160–163
Preserving Florida's Agricultural History,
87–88
Price Library of Judaica. See Isser and
Rae Price Library of Judaica
Procter & Gamble, 110, 112
professional development, 26–30,
158–160
Programs in the Public Humanities,
26–34
Project Ceres, 86–88, 97
project planning and management,
gaining experience with, 17
project summary, draft, 196
proposal elements, completing,
198–201
Prototype for the Digitization of Latin
American Jewish Newspapers, A, 89
Public Library System of the Virgin
Islands, 157–158

Rauch, Alan, 46
reciprocity, 7
REDCap database management system,
53–55
Repositioning Florida's Judaica Library,
61, 169–172
requirements checklist, 193–194

research, 67–69, 166–168
Research Networking in UK-US in
    Digital Scholarship in Cultural
    Institutions, 23–26
*Researching Students' Information
    Choices*, 70, 166–168
Ribault, Jean, 62
Ruiz, Richard, 30–31
Rutgers University, 167–168

Samuel Proctor Oral History Program
    (SPOHP), 30, 48–50, 61
Save America's Treasures, 137–139
*Saving St. Augustine's Architectural
    Treasures*, 137–139
scanners, 120–122, 121*fig*, 163–166,
    164*fig*
searching and sharing information,
    continuous, 191–192
Self-Service, Express Digital Scanning,
    163–166
Semantic Web, 182
Sequential Artists Workshop (SAW),
    39–40, 41–42
Shifting Patterns, 67–69
Shilts, Randy, 40
Shorstein Foundation, 172
significance, statement of, 200
Smathers Libraries, George A. *See*
    George A. Smathers Libraries
Social and Behavioral Sciences
    Directorate guidelines, 177
social media outreach, 41, 42–43
Social Sciences Library, 163–166
Sounds of the Panama Canal, 92–94
Southern HIV and Alcohol Research
    Consortium (SHARC), 131
*SPEC Kit 347: Community-Based
    Collections*, 176, 180
Special Collections and Area Studies,
    139–141, 148–151, 163–166
statement of innovation, 200
statement of significance, 200
stereograph collection, 50–53, 52*fig*
Strategic Opportunities Program (SOP),
    8, 12*t*, 13, 19, 26–34, 36–45,
    48–67

student ambassador program, 64–67,
    66*fig*
Students Lead the Library, 67
Stupniker, Leah, 61
support, letters of, 198–200

Technological Innovation and
    Cooperation for Foreign
    Information Access program, 10,
    183–184
technology, 120–122, 128–130,
    163–166
Technology Fee program, 13, 76–78, 83,
    120–122, 128–130, 163–166
tenure and promotion process, 16
3D printing, 128–130, 129*fig*
3D Printing (book), 40
Thurber, Jeanette, 2
Tiffany, Louis Comfort, 138
timeline, draft, 195
training, 139–141, 177–180, 192–193
transparency, 191

UF Center for HIV/AIDS Research,
    Education and Service (CARES),
    131, 133
UF Center for the Humanities and the
    Public Sphere, 20–22
UF Clinical and Translational Science
    Institute, 13
UFIRST, 15, 191
University of Central Florida, 140,
    183–184
University of Florida, 120–122,
    128–130, 163–166. *See also
    individual university libraries*
University of Miami, 140
University of Puerto Rico–Rio Piedras
    Campus Libraries (UPR), 149–152,
    155–158, 184
University of South Florida, 140,
    183–184
University of the Virgin Islands (UVI),
    157–158, 183–184
University Press of Florida (UPF),
    125–128, 144

U.S. *Caribbean and Ethnic Florida Newspaper Project*, 155–158
U.S. Department of Education, 10, 183–184
U.S. Higher Education Grant Program, 110–112
Useful Knowledge, 45–46

vinegar syndrome, 148–151
virtual tours, 36–39
VIVA Florida campaign, 61–64
VIVO Enabling National Network of Scientists, 180–183, 182*fig*, 185
VR/AR Development for Student Learning at MADE@UF, 84–86, 85*fig*

Walker, Desmon, 29*fig*
Waters, Hamilton, 2
WhatWasThere, 161
Where Good Ideas Come From, 6
Women-Authored Science Books for Children 1790-1890, 45–48, 47*fig*, 70
workflow for securing buy-in and approvals, 190–191

Yonge Library of Florida History, P. K. *See* P. K. Yonge Library of Florida History

Sponsor / Program Index

American Library Association
    Carnegie-Whitney Grant, 34–36, 45–48
    Carroll Preston Baber Research Grant, 67–69
Andrew W. Mellon Foundation, The
    Higher Education and Scholarship in the Humanities, 122–125
Arts and Humanities Research Council (UK)
    Research Networking in UK–US in Digital Scholarship in Cultural Institutions,
      23–26
Association of Research Libraries, 105–108

Center for Research Libraries
    Latin American Materials Project, 94–97
    Latin Americanist Research Resources Project, 88–91
    Project Ceres, 86–88, 97–100
Council on Library and Information Resources
    Digitizing Hidden Collections and Resources, 148–151
    Fellowship Program in Caribbean Studies Data Curation, 158–160

Florida Department of State, Division of Library and Information Services
    Library Services and Technology Act, 108–110, 141–143

Institute of Museum and Library Services
　　National Leadership Grants / Library-Museum Collaboration, 166–168, 172–177

National Endowment for the Humanities
　　Andrew W. Mellon Foundation, The / Open Book Program, 125–128
　　Challenge Grants, 169–172
　　Institutes for Advanced Topics in the Digital Humanities, 152–155
　　National Digital Newspaper Program, 155–158
　　Preservation and Access Education and Training, 139–141
National Historical Publications and Records Commission
　　Digitizing Historical Records, 134–137
　　Preservation Program, 160–163
　　National Networking and Resource Discovery, 180–183
National Library of Medicine
　　HIV/AIDS Community Information Outreach Project, 130–133
National Park Service
　　Saving America's Treasures, 137–139
National Science Foundation
　　Ethics Education in Science Education, 177–180
Northeast Florida Library Information Network
　　Innovation Project, 78–80

Procter & Gamble
　　U.S. Higher Education Grant Program, 110–114

UF, Academic Technology
　　Technology Fee, 76–78, 83–86, 120–122, 128–130, 163–166
UF, Center for the Humanities and the Public Sphere
　　Library Enhancement Grant, 20–22,
　　Programs in the Public Humanities, 26–30, 30–34
UF, Creative Campus Committee
　　Catalyst Fund, 80–83, 103–105
UF, George A. Smathers Libraries
　　Emerging Technologies, 92–94, 100–103
　　Strategic Opportunities Program, 26–30, 30–34, 36–39, 39–43, 43–45, 48–50,
　　　　50–53, 53–56, 56–59, 59–61, 61–64, 64–67
U.S. Department of Education
　　Technological Innovation and Cooperation for Foreign Information Access,
　　　　183–184

Project Type Index

Collaboration Development

GatorScholar, 180–183

Intersections: Animating Conversations with the Humanities, 122–125

Panama Canal—Preserving a Legacy, Celebrating a Centennial, Leveraging an Extraordinary Human Achievement, The, 172–177

VIVO Enabling National Network of Scientists, 180–183

Collection Development

Books about Florida and the Caribbean, 125–128

Building Makers, 34–36

Coral Way Bilingual Experiment Digital Collection (1961 to 1968), The, 30–34

Coral Way Bilingual Program, The, 32fig, 33–34

Library Enhancement Grant for Hindu Studies, 20–22

Collection Discovery

Buried Treasure, 43–45

Opening St. Augustine, 160–163

Parker Elephant Data Sheets, The, 53–56

Repositioning Florida's Judaica Library, 169–172

Women-Authored Science Books for Children 1790-1890, 45–48

Digital Humanities
ARL: Position Description Bank, Phase I, 107–108
French in Florida Online Video, 61–64
Migration, Mobility, and Sustainability, 152–155

Digitization/Preservation
Caribbean Newspaper Digitization Library, 183–184
Digitization of a UNESCO World Memory Collection, 90–91
Film on a Boat: Digitizing Historical Newspapers of the Caribbean, 148–151
Florida and Puerto Rico Digital Newspaper Project, 155–158
From the Air: The Photographic Record of Florida's Lands, 141–143
Increasing Accessibility to Rare Florida Agricultural Publications, 98–100
"Listín Diario": Preserving and Digitizing an At-Risk Dominican Republic
    Newspaper, 95–97
Panama Canal Museum Collection, 50–53
Pioneer Days in Florida, 134–137
Preserving Florida's Agricultural History, 87–88
Prototype for the Digitization of Latin American Jewish Newspapers, A, 89
Saving St. Augustine's Architectural Treasures, 137–139
U.S. Caribbean and Ethnic Florida Newspaper Project, 155–158

Digitization/Preservation/Collection Discovery
Legacy of Stetson Kennedy, The, 48–50

Health Information Dissemination
Creative Campaigns to Promote HIV/AIDS Awareness among UF Students, 39–43
Partnering to Provide HIV/AIDS Information Outreach, 130–134

Outreach
Advancing Accessibility, 36–39
Education Library Student Ambassador Program, 64–67
From Godzilla to Someone with a Stigmatized Illness to a Serial Killer, 81–83

Outreach/Collection Development
Performing Arts Approach to Collection Development, A, 59–61

Outreach/Training
Florida Digital Newspaper Collection, The, 109–110

Planning
Digital Collections in Children's Literature, 23–26
Forging a Collaborative Structure for Sustaining Scholarly Access to the Baldwin
    Library of Historical Children's Literature, 56–58

Professional Development
Digital Humanities Collaboration Bootcamp, 104–105
Digital Publishing on Black Life and History Collaborative Workshop, 26–30
Postdoctoral Fellow in Caribbean Studies Data Curation, 158–160

Research
Finding a Sustainable Solution for 3D Printing Waste, 80
Researching Students' Information Choices, 166–168
Shifting Patterns, 67–69
Sounds of the Panama Canal, 92–94

Technology
Facilitating Learning through Smart Pens, 77–78
Large Format Scanning in the Libraries, 120–122
Library West One Button Studio, 101–103
New Functionality for UF Libraries' 3D Printing Services, 128–130
Self-Service, Express Digital Scanning, 163–166
VR/AR Development for Student Learning at MADE@UF, 84–86

Training
Advancing Access and Preservation Best Practices in Florida, 139–141
Collaborating with Strangers Workshops, 111–115
Gaming Against Plagiarism, 177–180